ALSO BY DEBORAH MADISON

In My Kitchen

The New Vegetarian Cooking for Everyone

Vegetable Literacy

Seasonal Fruit Desserts

What We Eat When We Eat Alone

Vegetable Soups

Vegetarian Suppers

Local Flavors

This Can't Be Tofu!

Williams-Sonoma Vegetables

Vegetarian Cooking for Everyone

The Vegetarian Table: America

The Savory Way

The Greens Cookbook

An Onion in My Pocket

An Onion *in* My Pocket

—— MY LIFE WITH VEGETABLES ——

Deborah Madison

Alfred A. Knopf

NEW YORK

2020

THIS IS A BORZOI BOOK
PUBLISHED BY ALFRED A. KNOPF

www.aaknopf.com

Knopf, Borzoi Books, and the colophon are registered
trademarks of Penguin Random House LLC.

Grateful acknowledgment is made to New Directions
Publishing Corp. for permission to reprint "This Is Just to Say"
by William Carlos Williams, from *The Collected Poems: Volume I,
1909–1939*, copyright © 1938 by New Directions Publishing Corp.
Reprinted by permission of New Directions Publishing Corp.

Library of Congress Cataloging-in-Publication Data
Names: Madision, Deborah, author.
Title: An onion in my pocket : my life with vegetables / Deborah Madison.
Description: First edition. | New York : Alfred A. Knopf, 2020. |
Identifiers: LCCN 2019039918 (print) | LCCN 2019039919 (ebook) |
   ISBN 9780525656012 (hardback) | ISBN 9780525656029 (ebook)
Subjects: LCSH: Madison, Deborah. | Cooks—United States—
   Biography. | Food writers—United States—Biography. |
   Vegetarianism—United States. | Cooking (Vegetables) |
   Greens (Restaurant : San Francisco, Calif.)
Classification: LCC TX649.M326 A3 2020 (print) |
   LCC TX649.M326 (ebook) | DDC 641.5092 [B]—dc23
LC record available at https://lccn.loc.gov/2019039918
LC ebook record available at https://lccn.loc.gov/2019039919

Jacket photograph by Patrick McFarlin
Jacket design by John Gall

Manufactured in the United States of America
First Edition

To the memory of my very different parents,
each of whom made their best effort,
and to my very much alive and equally different siblings

Contents

Introduction

Onions, Snakes, and What Matters

If there are not onions in my pockets or my purse, maybe there are shallots, or some amaranth leaves, or seeds collected from the garden, or something else food related. Once there was a four-foot-long gopher snake in my purse—safekeeping for the walk home. These snakes do lower the numbers of those garden pests. But there was a day when there actually was an onion in my pocket because I had been cooking with my pal Dan, and I had brought the onions that we needed for a pizza. There was one left over. In Spanish class I pulled out the extra onion and put it on the desk so I could find my notes and pens—also crammed into my pockets that day. People started to laugh. To me it was utterly normal.

That's partially what it means to be a food person—that it is normal to find an onion in your pocket. Or that you fly home with quarts of fragrant berries on your lap, or you stuff a bag of superlong stalks of late-summer rhubarb into the overhead. It's likely that when a friend visits you in your new desert home she arrives with egg cartons in her suitcase—a ripe fig nestled into each little depression—or that another friend arrives with an extra suitcase filled with quince. Food swirls around us. We reach out for some of it; other times we toss something good into the swirl for others to enjoy. It's the forever potlatch of gift and exchange.

I didn't always know I'd be so involved with food and I've long tried to piece together when it first happened, when food became something good and compelling. I think it was when I was sixteen. My parents had gone to Europe for a sabbatical and farmed each of their four kids out to another family. I got to live with a couple who did not have children, who had lived many times in France, who loved food and knew how to cook. Living with them I discovered that food could be good every night of the week. Given my parents' uneven temperaments and my mother's frugality I had no idea that this could be so. But it was and it was miraculous. Cheese soufflés, chicken poached in wine with mushrooms and cream, salads from the garden—it was all so delicious and it was all new to me. When my parents returned from their trip, they remarked on my new round face, evidence that butter and cream, predinner gin and tonics, and the much better wines we drank—the plenty of very good food and drink, in short—had had an effect. When people ask me when I became interested in food, I tell them it was when I discovered that food could taste good. Every night of the week. These meals did change my life.

The man in my temporary household was, like my father, a botanist; only his specialty was alliums, not grass. Like all botanists and food people I have known, his eyes were open to all kinds of possibilities, especially culinary ones. Over a long weekend we took a trip to Mount Lassen. Once there and settled into our motel, we set out on a hike with the intention of spending the day on the trail. Shortly into our walk, I noticed some funny-looking things poking out of the ground. I asked what they were and the botanist and his wife both responded with ecstatic shouts: "Morels! They're morels!" We immediately filled our hats with them, abandoned the walk, and drove into town in search of butter and cream.

We simmered the morels in cream and piled them on buttered toast for lunch. They were magnificent and they taught me my first food rule: Break your plans in the face of something wonderful and utterly unexpected, like morels. Let them take over and push you here and there as they will. You will at least come away with a memory. This event is decades old, but it remains a vivid memory.

Despite this introduction to the pleasures of the table and my excitement about food tasting good, I didn't act right away. The thought "I want to be a chef" never occurred to me. Instead, I finished high school, went to college, dropped out, got back in, changed universities, graduated, got a job, went to Japan, then became a practicing, even ordained, Buddhist for about twenty years. It wasn't until I became a Zen student that I became interested in cooking and started to cook in earnest. It's supposed to be so austere, that Zen life, but people still have to eat and someone has to cook. That person became me in 1970.

I've cooked for a long time: in the San Francisco Zen Center; at our monastery at Tassajara; at our farm, Green Gulch; at Alice Waters's restaurant in Berkeley, Chez Panisse; at Greens, the vegetarian restaurant I opened in San Francisco; at the American Academy in Rome; at Café Escalera in Santa Fe; and at home—when I finally got one. (I lived in community until I was forty.) At some point I decided to look back to find out what matters when it comes to food, and that's what this book is about.

An Onion in My Pocket

1. Twenty Missing Years

I was twenty-one when I carried out a study for a professor at UC Berkeley interviewing people who had gone from rat-infested dark old dangerous Victorian buildings to what was considered to be a more enlightened concept of public housing than the monolithic high-rise apartment buildings that public housing programs usually produced. It was fascinating to go into the homes of people who were unlike anyone I knew and listen to them talk about their lives. But it was also discouraging. Despite their clean, safe, attractive new homes with nearby laundry rooms and grassy lawns for their children to play on, they were filled with complaints. They wanted bigger apartments; the laundry rooms were too far away; they wanted different playground equipment. I began to question human nature itself. And I had to ask myself if I really wanted to be a city planner. Did it make sense to work to satisfy people's wants if they'd never really be, for once and for all, satisfied? This was my big question, not what to eat. It's what ultimately drove me to the Zen Center, but so did other things.

After a Japanese class, a trip to Japan, and some other events I found the Zen Center in San Francisco. I spent nearly two decades there studying Zen Buddhism, but until recently I ignored that stretch of time, allowing those years, which for most people are important start-up career and family years, to remain blank in my personal history. There they are, unaccounted-for decades, an awkward pause that I haven't known what to do about. Should I admit to those years? Ignore them? Try to explain them?

Mostly I've been silent. I haven't talked about them. When I think of that stretch of time, I feel distanced from it, partly because it was a long time ago, but also because I used to find myself regretting that I didn't go to graduate school, where I felt I could be more effective at righting the wrongs of the world. Today there are students at the Zen Center who have gone to graduate school, gotten PhDs, and worked at interesting jobs before becoming involved with practice, but that wasn't the case when I was twenty-one. Almost none of us had much experience in life before sitting down and crossing our legs on the round black cushion. We had been to college, maybe worked some, and that was about it. I had more experience than most, and that wasn't a lot.

Still, those years were exciting ones in the culture at large, as well as a deeply vital time in my own life. It was a time of enormous upheaval and hope with the hippies, the Fillmore, Janis and Jimi and Bob Marley, the Black Panthers. Not that I really was a part of that, except as a Zen student. I only went to the Fillmore once, when I heard Cream. Still, one could have done worse. At a certain point, I probably should have left the formal Zen life of robes, ordinations, and positions, but I didn't know that so I stayed. When I did leave I was in my late thirties. I first lived in Berkeley, then in Rome. After a year I returned to Berkeley, wrote my first book, then moved to San Francisco, followed by a few years in Flagstaff, and finally, when I realized I'd never fit into life in northern Arizona, I moved to Santa Fe, New Mexico, mainly because there was a farmers' market there. I've been in the Southwest for almost thirty years. I do sit occasionally, sometimes even quite regularly for periods of time. But I don't belong to any Buddhist group. I tend to consider myself a recovering Buddhist.

In the early years of Zen Center most of us were in our twenties or maybe, in a few cases, thirties. Early thirties. It was an unlikely bunch composed largely of young men that were actually putting together Buddhist practice in America. They had been doing it for a few years before I arrived on the tail end of what was then an exciting experiment. It was a challenging time, a crazy time. We didn't know what we were doing exactly, but we were feeling our way into a practice life. Once Zen Center began to import Japanese teachers and with them all the rules and traditions of Japanese monastic life, many of these founding students peeled off and headed elsewhere. I saw Zen Center go from a group of young, eccentric, and enthusiastic individuals who were willing to do whatever had to be done to a center for Zen practice with an abbot who was a near miss for a CEO. This drift from the heart to the wallet corresponded to my time there—the end of the sixties, the seventies, and into the eighties. How did I even get there?

I blame it on a radio station.

I pretty much grew up with KPFA, Berkeley's then truly radical listener-supported radio station, and the only station on in our house. Each day began at seven sharp with the shimmering duet from Bach's Coffee Cantata, which for years served as my wake-up call. On Wednesday evenings I always listened to Pauline Kael's movie reviews. My fifteen-year-old friends and I daringly referred to her at that time as "Miss Bitch." But when she came to Davis and was on a panel with four men to discuss Vittorio De Sica's *Umberto D.*, I saw that she was warm and compassionate and very, very smart. I wrote her a fan letter and she answered me with an invitation to visit her at her home in Berkeley. I went, and eventually I got to know her and spend a brief time as a "Paulette," as her hang-about fans were called. Film was foremost on my list of interests for a long time.

Also on KPFA was Kenneth Rexroth, that important connector in the sixties, mumbling his poems on Sunday mornings. Phil Elwood played jazz later in the day. William Mandel spoke each week on contemporary Soviet politics, and then there was Alan Watts's program, *Philosophy: East and West*. These were the voices that came to feel intimate to me in my teenage years.

In his refined, elegant voice Watts talked about Eastern thought and religion, Buddhism in particular. My father always listened to his program very carefully, to both weekly broadcasts. One day Watts was describing the life of Buddhist monks. As he talked about their quest for enlightenment, the practices of sitting meditation, chanting, and begging for food, I could see lines of monks in their black robes as clearly as if they were bowing before me with their bowls uplifted. It was an odd and powerful moment, a tap on the shoulder, a gentle push toward what did become my life for a period of time. Although this was an unforgettable moment, when I was a young teenager devoting myself to the big questions in life via Zen study was a frightening prospect. I was just becoming interested in boys, clothes, and what I hoped would be my wonderful but unknown future. The path of the seeker hadn't figured in my life scheme at all and its first fit was an awkward one. "Later," I told myself, keeping the possibility of such a radical change safely at bay while not discarding it altogether.

When that "later" moment finally came, an impulse to go to Japan wasn't as out of the blue as I first thought. Japan meant Buddhism for me. I didn't know what I'd do once I got there but it was definitely a spiritual destination. I thought, vaguely, that I might end up studying Zen, but I didn't have a clue as to how that might happen. Nor did I know anyone who practiced Zen meditation, or know how to go about finding a teacher in Japan in 1969. But I did think it would be useful to learn something of the language. The Free University in Berkeley was offering a Japanese class.

I showed up one late afternoon at a house on Dwight Way and sat down at a wooden kitchen table with a handful of other students. I looked around. There was something very pleasing about this space. It was light, unlike my dark apartment on Shattuck Avenue. It was calm. Clean. Ordered. The kitchen shelves were lined with jars of beans and grains. Food was cooking on the stove and it smelled good. Tea was brewed and served in small Japanese cups. We had left our shoes at the door, which seemed a bit odd, but now I could see that the sanded floors were free of dirt and they gleamed. Dust motes freed themselves from our clothes and glimmered in the golden afternoon light. Things were in their places. I liked it. We sat at a large wooden table and

practiced writing and reading katakana characters until the calm
was broken by the sound of a bell, which caused most of the
students at the table to suddenly put their papers together, then
head for a room upstairs.

"What's going on?" I asked the student next to me. He
turned out to be Paul Discoe, the man who had organized the
class because he was going to Japan to study carpentry. For five
years.

"*Zazen,*" he said. It told me nothing. "Sitting meditation," he
added, as if that were an explanation.

I was, it turned out, in the Berkeley Zen Center. All at once
those disparate elements from my past collided, bringing me to
a place where Zen meditation was practiced—and just eighty
miles from where I grew up. Unable to ignore the coincidences,
I asked if I could sit, too. Mel Weitsman, the resident monk, gave
me some hasty instruction. *Keep your back straight, eyes lowered
but open, count your breaths from one to ten, and don't move even if
your legs hurt!* My Zen practice began the same day my Japanese
lessons did.

I did go to Japan a few months later, with my brother Mike.
We boarded the *Golden Bear,* a merchant marine ship, and at
the end of an ordinary weekday we pulled away from the pier
in San Francisco and sailed under the Golden Gate Bridge as
the afternoon fog poured in over the hills. There was the small
crew and eight passengers. It was heaven to be on the ocean.
My brother and I crouched on the deck and watched the waves
break over the bow during stormy weather. We saw large birds.
We ate well and often. We read and studied Japanese and all
was well.

Two weeks later four smiling people who had taken time off

work to greet us, bobbed and bowed as our ship docked in Yoko-hama. We had been invited to stay with a family whose daughter I had become friends with in San Francisco. Having heard that fruit was expensive in Japan, I had arrived with a gift of forty pounds of oranges. It was a strange, humorous, bewildering visit in which both my brother and I failed at our missions, his to remain for a year and mine to undertake a study of Zen. While I very much liked being in a Buddhist culture, I couldn't figure out how to begin a Buddhist practice. Visiting temples was a touristy must, but becoming a nun was not really conceivable.

Mike could actually speak Japanese because he had just com-pleted a year of intensive study of the language at Harvard, but the lessons at the Free University hadn't given me much fluency, which I needed just to be able to go forward with something as simple as taking the bus. Being in a place where I could neither speak nor read was bewildering and challenging. I found my way to and from Sendagi, the Tokyo neighborhood where our host family lived, by memorizing the sequences of neon signs—their colors, shapes, and sizes, and whether or not they flashed. When I offered to buy the vegetables for dinner at the neigh-borhood market, I glimpsed various family members following discreetly, ducking behind buildings to keep from being noticed, but managing to keep an eye out for me in case I got lost, which was easier than you or I could imagine. I appreciated that they were watching my progress from one vendor to another, then my return to their house. But it was embarrassing, too. I felt so incompetent.

My adventures were limited. I went to Kyoto. I visited gar-dens and temples. I sought out a *shakuhachi*, a bamboo flute, for Mel Weitsman and sipped green tea with its maker. In Kamakura

I stood in line for a charcoal-grilled sweet potato. A Japanese man turned and spat on me. It was the war and the bomb, I was pretty sure, and I didn't know what to say. For most of my teenage years I woke up in the night paralyzed in fear of the bomb. That day my heart felt broken. It wasn't until I was sixty that I was able to meet a survivor of the first bomb and bow deeply to him at a Zen temple in New Mexico.

I spent part of the summer in Japan, then returned to Davis, my hometown, giving up for the moment on the study-Buddhism-in-Japan program. My parents had gone to Europe, leaving behind an empty house. Mike, who had had an even more difficult time making sense of Japan and who was unable to free himself from the suffocating kindness of our hosts when he just wanted to be on his own, had preceded me home. I found him happily camped on the back porch with an electric coffeepot, some zucchini, and a stack of books. He didn't have a key to the house and it didn't occur to him to ask a neighbor for one. He told me about his arrival in Davis. It was the day we landed on the moon and he walked to my parents' house on empty streets as everyone was inside watching the landing on television. He didn't know this at the time so it just felt extremely strange, especially after the crowded streets of Tokyo. That same day I was in a Tokyo department store where Japanese people bowed to me and said, "Congratulations." I looked at a giant screen and thought I was seeing a sci-fi movie, then I remembered. My friend and I celebrated by eating little cakes made in the shape of fish, filled with red adzuki beans, in the basement of the Mitsukoshi department store.

As both Mike and I had returned so much earlier than we'd told people we would, no one expected to see us and we enjoyed the delicious sense of being invisible. It really felt as if no one could see us as we bicycled around town doing this and that. But this happy limbo state ended for me when a postcard arrived announcing a weeklong meditation intensive to be held in San Francisco. It was called a *sesshin*. I read and reread the card, turned it over, thumbed the edges until they had softened. I considered the larger picture: I had gone to Japan to find Buddhism and I had come home because I couldn't figure out how to get started, and here was an opportunity to take part in a major Zen event, a seven-day sitting, with an English-speaking (sort of, it turned out) Japanese teacher in San Francisco. Obviously I should go. But I had read that sesshins required superhuman effort. Could I even get through one? And what if I couldn't?

Of course, I went. The sesshin was hard, but not nearly as difficult as others I would sit in the future.

2. Sesshin

Think of it as a session, a very long session with you and your cushion, your aching knees, and your chattering monkey mind as the major participants. Then call it sesshin. It looks close to "session" but it's pronounced "sesheen." A sesshin is a traditional opportunity for focused meditation, or *zazen*. Sesshins usually last for a week and they consist of early morning risings, hours and hours of zazen interrupted by ten-minute periods of walking meditation (*kinhin*), a talk once a day, tea, formal meals, and of course, no talking at all or moving during zazen. Sesshins are hard, but they are also wonderful opportunities to focus and just sit.

This sesshin took place in a former Orthodox Jewish temple, so old that at this moment in 1969 it had already been owned for some years by the Japanese Buddhist community in San Francisco. Now with a Japanese name, Sokoji was drafty, dark, and decrepit.

Throughout the day we heard pigeons cooing and ambling around the rafters on their clawed feet. Suzuki-roshi, the Japanese Zen master I had heard about, led the sesshin and gave us encouragement. Sitting one forty-minute period after another was arduous and painful for a rank beginner. Meals came as a relief since they made it possible to stand for a while and loosen the kinks in my legs before returning to my cushion.

We got in a line, picked up a tray, then passed in front of the cook, a Chinese American monk named Bill Kwong, who was for a long time a Zen teacher in Sonoma County. Bill had this willowy look and gentle disposition that made him seem special to me, even spiritual, which is sort of a vague word, like "natural." But then I was grasping at straws for something that would set this group of people apart from other groups I had visited—Rabbi Shlomo Carlebach and his Hasidic followers, various yogic ashrams, the Gurdjieff people—something that made sense and, most important, was accepting. Spiritual would do. As we passed in front of Bill, he carefully set our meals on our trays—a heavy Japanese bowl full of white rice with a few sesame seeds sprinkled over the top, a smaller bowl of thin soup, and a third dish containing the same daikon pickles I had been eating in Japan just a week before. Chanting ensued, then we ate in silence.

I was always famished, but that wasn't the only reason this food tasted as good as it did. Eating in a formal posture without talking but accompanying the meal with a long chanted grace conspired to bring unexpected flavor to what was usually regarded as fairly bland food. It turned out that there was much to be savored in the sweet starchy goodness of the rice and the occasional toasty flavor of a sesame seed, followed by sips of the hot, thin, salty soup, then another crunchy bite of a pickle, this time a cool one. How wonderful it all tasted. The meal itself passed swiftly by the clock, but it seemed to last forever, time passing slowly as it does in extreme moments.

I was fairly neurotic about food at that time and I pursued with diligence those tastes of comfort, mostly in the form of pastry. So the goodness of plain rice, miso soup, and daikon pickle was truly startling. It seemed to me that this goodness resided in my mouth and my attention as much as it resided in the food itself. It was my mouth that was the cook, my tongue the seasoning, and eating this way transcended food as usual, even an exceptional cheese Danish or a fresh warm donut. Hunger, simplicity, and attention, not special ingredients, were all one needed to put aside obsessions and anxieties concerning food and to experience it in a more deeply nurturing way.

Years later another student, David Chadwick, told me that Suzuki-roshi found Bill's food too austere. When David drove him to lecture in Mill Valley, after another one of Bill's meals of rice, pickles, and miso soup, they'd go out for a real breakfast of eggs, hash browns, and toast. Maybe even bacon. But for me at that time, the austerity was a revelation; it was so plain and so good.

Many things happen during a sesshin, but this experience struck me deeply. Although I went on to sit many more sesshins with far more rigorous schedules and richer, more complex foods, it has turned out that my way through the thick and thin patches in life, the worldly and spiritual places of life, has been a sensual one, one that needs hands, soil, smells, and food for fodder, for direction. Looking back, I'm not so surprised that a bowl of rice, a few sesame seeds, the sour and salty tastes on the tongue, were what opened the world of Zen practice for me.

Away from my simple family life of food, my own austere college meals, and postgraduate meals of peanut butter and brown rice, I had been finding pleasure in getting as many of the sweet, soft foods in my mouth as I could. But what about that family life at the table? It hadn't prepared me at all for what was to come in my life.

3. Family

Our parents influence us enormously, even when we think we've finally gone out on our own. It takes a while to see that influence, though. Thanks to my parents, I have come to conclude that my past experience with food is oddly bifurcated. I grew up a jerky girl, a girl yanked between plenty and scarcity. There was pleasure and abundance at one parent's table, tension and lack at the other. How could two parents be so different from each other when it came to food? The reasons probably run as deep for each parent as they now do for me. It was not surprising that I began life with a schizoid inheritance: one that said there was never enough (Mom) and one that found there was plenty (Dad).

My father had wanted to farm since he was a boy, and he began once he returned from World War II, in 1945. First he and my mother had a farm in Avon, Connecticut, then one in upstate New York, and later one in Ohio. To me these different places are merged into The Farm. All were farms, none was exactly like the others, but there were cows, goats, chickens, orchards. The Farm was a wonderful place to be a child in, but an isolated and lonely place for an urban woman like my mother. I try to imagine living far from others without the Internet to connect us however flimsily, and I have to admire my mother's courage. I suspect that it was a grand adventure at first, but one whose excitement soon wore off. As for me, although I was just a toddler, then a young child, I loved living on a farm. I wheeled a bantam chicken around in my baby carriage, snuggled up to the soft, caramel-colored cows, their breath sweet and vegetal. I recall with pleasure the smell of water flowing over the flat rocks of a creek and the smell of grass being mowed for the cows on our dairy farm. And the cows themselves. It all left a strong impression and I suspect it's one reason why farms still hold such an allure for me.

When lightning struck the last barn and burned it down and the cows within, farming ended for my father. After this trauma and loss for both my parents, I don't think that there was enough emotional or financial reserve to recover and start over. Instead, my father took advantage of the GI Bill to go to graduate school. He moved his small family into graduate student housing in Ithaca, and eventually got his doctorate in botany at Cornell.

A graduate student's life in 1950 was not an affluent one. There was not a lot of money, and there wasn't a lot of food either, at least the way we know it today, and the way my parents had known it on their farms. For them, the good foods must have simply gone away, because I remember squeezing the dye into a plastic pouch of dead-white margarine to give it a buttery glow, and items like roasts and "real" butter appeared only when grandparents came to visit. I clearly recall a cat being thrown out into the snow for licking a precious cube of butter that had been set out for one of these rare company dinners and another cat who was nailed for dragging a liver off to a corner for her own private feast, a liver that was supposed to be our family supper. There's a photo of my mother shucking corn in the yard, a bunch of small kids playing around her. She looks happy, but later she told me that her truly happiest moment was saying goodbye to her pressure cooker and canning equipment when we all left for California. She did what had to be done until she didn't have to anymore.

After my dad got his PhD we got into our canvas-walled Willys Jeep—my parents; my infant sister, Jamie; my brother Mike; and I—and drove to our new home in Davis, California. We camped along the way. Each night my dad set up a big, heavy green army tent and that's where we slept, often in the company of mosquitoes, with trains roaring nearby, and highway sounds tearing into precious sleep. I was eight years old when we made this move.

When our Jeep at last emerged from Donner Pass and headed down toward Auburn, Sacramento, and finally Davis, there was that first place where we caught a glimpse of the Central Valley and its broad, flat expanse. I was thrilled, curious, and drawn to it. My mother, however, was not. To her, as she told me later, it just looked dry and way too flat. It was nothing like the green rolling terrain of the places she had always lived. She didn't have to say anything then, for I could see doubt on her face, and anger too, to think that she had been brought to live in this horrible place. It was summer. It was hot and the wild grasses had turned from their brilliant February green to gold. For a long time I thought that's why California was known as "the Golden State." It was only later, when we took school field trips to Sutter's Fort that I learned about the Gold Rush.

My parents were born within a day of each other. Both went through the Depression and both had fathers who kept good jobs and neither had a family that stood in breadlines. Yet my mother embodied the Depression mentality of insufficiency— that and an immigrant mentality, although her family had been in America for at least three generations. She cooked and ate from a sense of scarcity that was largely imagined. Still, she loved to have people over for dinner, often made gifts of food, welcomed new neighbors with a loaf of bread and salt, and cooked for herself and others into her mid-nineties, when she finally died of old age, not disease, not hunger. But at no time in her life was money squandered on things to eat. Even when she was very old, she spent less than twenty dollars a week on food for herself, shakily walking from Safeway to Longs because the eggs were a few cents cheaper there. Never mind that my brother Mike was an organic farmer and brought her eggs from his chickens, real food that nourished.

Years earlier, on shopping forays to San Francisco, my mother and I would stop for lunch at the Woolworth's on Powell Street. I learned to read menus by scanning down the price column, my eyes poised to catch the lowest number, instead of reading the menu items themselves. Invariably the cheapest lunch was an egg salad sandwich, not something I was terribly fond of since I had so many of them in my lunch sack. Our conversation would go something like this:

"Have anything you want!" my mother would offer. She was generous and upbeat, but a trifle anxious. I could hear it in her voice. She was probably afraid I'd want something expensive.

"Umm." I would scan the menu carefully. It was true, I was looking for an adventure.

"I think I'd like the crab salad." I'd never had crab.

"Oh? Crab?" my mother would say, her voice more clearly nervous. The crab is expensive, even at Woolworth's. "Are you sure you want that? Wouldn't you like an egg salad sandwich instead?"

I knew it was about the cost, so I ordered the egg salad sandwich. It was fine. And I also suspected that she might have wanted something other than egg salad, too. While ordering by price wasn't a method for encouraging adventurous eating, I understood my mother's situation, that everlasting imprint of the Depression and at this time, the competition from other areas deemed more important than food, like art and music. Money was tight and lunch wasn't for adventuring but to keep us going. Still, I would have far preferred that crab, or better, to go to Blums nearby on Union Square for a slice of coffee crunch cake.

Even today I still tend to order what's least expensive when eating out. It's a hard habit to break. I learned my lesson well.

My father was a roller of pie dough, a generous eater, and a good cook in a meat and potatoes way. He embraced butter, cream, lard (olive oil came later), and all the foodstuffs that make food melting and succulent and desirable. My father's way with food—his appetite for it, his botanist's knowledge of taxonomy and plant characteristics, his affection for old varieties, his passion for growing plants, and the pleasure he took in searching in the wild for those that resisted cultivation—shaped my own interest in cooking, farming, and foodways. I didn't notice it as it was happening, but over time his actions quietly ebbed and flowed in and out of my life until one day I looked up and saw that I was indeed, at least in some respects, my father's daughter.

My mother had a different sort of appetite than my father, one that never allowed for much pleasure around food, although she very much liked the *idea* of food. Food, plants, and flowers were entwined subjects that filled my mother's colorful paintings and batiks—figs and their articulate leaves, little schools of fish perched on ice in a market, melons, lemons hanging off leafy branches, glossy eggplants—the luscious foodscapes of the Mediterranean, of California farmers' markets, even of our yard.

Not one to be described as a person with a lusty appetite, my mother, when offered something to eat, usually muttered a modest refusal, her hands fluttering up to her face in a faint gesture of protection, as if to push the offering away. When she finally came to Greens, where she could order whatever she wanted as my mother and our guest, she had a cup of soup and a green salad, completely ignoring the rest of the menu.

I am utterly different from her about food. I reach out for it, always. At least I used to. One day I was horrified to find myself taking a sandwich at the Toyota dealership while having my car serviced simply because it was there and it was free food and for no other reason. I didn't want it. I wasn't hungry and I didn't even like what was in the sandwich. It was such a purely animal gesture that I shocked myself.

A small black-and-white photograph with scalloped edges shows my father standing in the long summer grass on one of my parents' farms. In his early thirties, he was a handsome man with strong clear features and thick wavy hair that remained so throughout his life. In other photographs he is playing his guitar and singing folk songs, or he is playing his flute, or the recorder. But in this one he is holding fruit. In this photo taken shortly after World War II, he is wearing a nightshirt that comes to the ground. The hem is wet with dew. His feet don't show so he appears to be floating over the grass. It is dawn and just light enough for my mother to have snapped this picture. Behind him is the orchard. The fruit he is cradling, should it have been peaches, would later be sliced over cereal then covered with the thick cream from our small herd of Guernsey cows. Later in the day more fruit would become a pie. My parents made and ate a lot of pies before they had a family.

When we moved to California, my father still had cream over his morning cereal, but it came in bottles, rising thick and yellowish above the milk. In bed, I heard the milk bottles jiggling in their metal basket as the milkman ran to the front door, followed by the slap of his feet and the sharper jiggle of the empty bottles on the return trip to his truck. These were the sounds that often infiltrated my dreams during the last moments of sleep.

4. Young Life in Davis

W e moved to Davis in 1953, one hundred years after
the Concord grape was developed in Concord, Mas-
sachusetts. My father planted blue, seeded Concord grapes in
Davis and every September he and my mother made Concord
grape pies. Now I make one at least once a year, partly to honor
my parents, but also because Concord grape pie is one of the
best pies ever—rich and berrylike. I've always included some
variation of this pie in my cookbooks. I can't help it. I really
want people to experience it.

First we lived in an apartment house, then in a rented farmhouse in the country where my brother and I went barefoot all
summer and stepped on nails and other pieces of rusty metal,
which meant a visit to the doctor for tetanus shots. We also
stepped on hills of red ants, which meant momentary stinging
pain. Mostly, my brother and I had dirty feet with scabs and cuts
and no one cared. There was a water tower behind our house

where a family of barn owls lived. We visited it often to watch them cluck at us as they dipped their heads and moved them menacingly from side to side. Water gushed in the irrigation ditches that wound through the walnut orchard next to our house and we spent many summer hours floating in them. Navigating our way in these ditches took us far from home into the shade of the enormous trees as the ditches curled around and through the orchard. At some point we outgrew them and willingly rode our bikes three miles to the swimming pool at the university in what felt like an oven's heat—and three miles back.

At the end of summer we gathered black walnuts and sold them, by the gunnysack, for a dollar a sack, which was a fortune to two small kids. We earned thirteen dollars one summer! The walnuts left stains on my hands that were practically indelible.

Our parents splattered colored paint on a gray floor and my father built Calder-like mobiles for the living room—the same room with the Jackson Pollock–like floor. Come Christmas they stuffed our gifts into panty hose, which stretched and stretched until they held them all—including a jar of green olives for Mike and a box of chocolate-covered cherries for me. Aside from the food, gifts were practical and for our betterment: pencils and socks, books, a recording of the Kreutzer Sonata one Christmas, binoculars for bird-watching and a book of Audubon's birds on another. I collected feathers, eggs, and dead birds galore and learned to stuff them. I was a budding taxidermist with horrid results, but I was a child with a serious interest in birds. The first "thing" I wanted to be was an ornithologist. Hence the book of Audubon's birds.

We didn't really have neighbors, but not too far away, at

the intersection of two country roads, the grandparents of a school acquaintance had a house. There was a big cactus garden in front of their home, probably to keep people away. I doubt that it was planted as an ornamental garden, but it gave the area its name, Cactus Corners. If we told a friend in town that we lived near Cactus Corners, they'd know where it was. Once my brother and I rubbed our hands over the cactus pads so that the embedded needles meant we wouldn't have to practice our instruments—Mike's the cello, and mine the violin. It took only one time to discover what a bad idea that was. Our hands prickled with pain and we still had to practice.

We stood by the side of the road in the fog in winter, waiting for the school bus and anticipating the moment when its yellow headlights could just be made out. We watched them get stronger and larger until the bus finally stopped and we got on. The bus ride lasted an hour and the route wound through the countryside, through walnut, almond, and citrus orchards, ending up at the school, which was just a few miles away from our house. I saw many orchards felled then replanted over time.

Our move into town did not hamper our pleasure even if there were no more water towers filled with barn owls or irrigation ditches to float in. Instead, there were the annual trips to the auto dealers to see the new models and gorge on the donuts put out for potential customers. I often went to the dump in search of treasures, like old kerosene heaters. Once, I was bitten by a snake. "What were you doing at the dump?" my doctor growled, incredulous, as he gave me a shot.

With all its floats, marching bands from all over California, sheepdog trials, and the freedom to wander into the labs of my parents' friends and see what they were up to, Picnic Day, UC Davis's open house, was the best day of the year for me, even better than Christmas.

On other days the university was still a lot of fun for us kids. There were great places to ride our bikes, musty old buildings, and a grand library. Mayten trees grew in the quad. Our father paid us a modest sum to strip the pink berries from their stems once they ripened. His plan was to sell them to a nursery for a lot of money, a plan that failed. UC Davis had a pretty famous vet school even then, and I made so many visits to the horse barns to watch gelding operations that the people in charge finally called my dad and asked him to come get me. When I went to the chemistry auditorium to see art movies there were lots of people to say hello to—mostly my parents' friends. Even today I harbor a remnant of the expectation that I will know a lot of people at the theater. I almost never see anyone I know.

My friends and I swam in Putah Creek, where two of my siblings now live. We plunged into the waters of a cold green creek lined with plants that were home to giant yellow and black spiders and their webs. Later there was waterskiing above the creek, where the waters that formed Lake Berryessa were vast and deep. Before the lake, there was the little town of Monti-cello. It had been flooded in 1957 to make the lake and the resi-dents were forced to move. Dorothea Lange talks about this in the movie made recently by her granddaughter, Dyanna Taylor, *Dorothea Lange: Grab a Hunk of Lightning.* When I was sixteen, I spent a few months living with a woman who had photographed this little town before its demise.

I lusted for good clothes and learned to sew from an expert who taught me all about bound buttonholes, French seams, and invisible zippers. I made my own "Lanz" dresses in lieu of buying them, Nina Ricci suits, and prom dresses from Vogue patterns. But I came home from those dances in tears because no one wanted to dance with me, despite my elegant clothes.

High school was misery, but my junior year I decided that I had to have a pair of sandals from Sandals Unlimited in Berkeley. Once I had those, they were all I wore. Every season, every day of the year. And I wore the same clothes week in and week out. I was the first in my class to smoke pot, I skipped the sports assemblies in favor of taking classes at the university, and I played in the college orchestra. Secretly I wanted to be a cheerleader more than anything, but that was such an impossibility that I just went all the way to the dark side. I've never been to a class reunion, but I have done several book signings and readings in a Davis bookstore where I've met many of those I grew up with, those who stayed.

I failed to see why people screamed about Elvis Presley, even though I did go see *Love Me Tender*. Friends and I went to the drive-ins in Sacramento, where we'd watch four films in a row. "When is Ray Milland coming back?" I'd ask. "Oh, he was in the first movie." We were on our third or fourth.

I rode horses and donkeys with my girlfriends and later, when I had a job working on a catamaran in a barn out of town and was earning some money, I bought a motorcycle, which I gave up only when I was out of college. I was sure my time had come for an early demise, so I sold it as soon as I graduated from UC Santa Cruz. But it was great fun while I had it.

My parents were Unitarians and I belonged to the LRY, or Liberal Religious Youth. We were liberal and young, but not very religious. I was in a group with four boys and we spent our Sundays doing things like bicycling to the "frog pond" with our adult leader, who was probably a professor at the university, to collect pond scum to study under a microscope once we returned. My mother, who taught religion classes to younger kids, thought we should learn *anything* more religious than that, but our religious education consisted of learning about our teacher of the week's research and going to his lab—or the frog pond.

I didn't know a Republican until I was in my twenties and living elsewhere.

What I especially loved, and I still do about Davis, was the smell of jasmine and the mockingbirds' song in summer. Today, come summer, I splurge on a five-gallon plant of blooming jasmine to put in my office. We have a few mockingbirds where I live now, but they aren't persistent the way they were in Davis. They appear for a few weeks in June, then leave. The scent of the jasmine lingers longer. To me that smell is the smell of the future, the unknown, of promise.

We played outdoors endlessly. We had adventures. We explored, we did stupid things like putting nickels and nails on a railroad track then watching the train run over them from a few feet away. We pulled up surveyors' stakes for a cannery that was going to be built but that we didn't want. We rode Flexies, a low sledlike thing on wheels, bikes, horses, and donkeys. We played hockey with croquet mallets. We ran behind the DDT trucks as they sprayed for mosquitoes. We were kids. We knew nothing. It was a good youth. Then we grew up.

. . .

For years my father sent me boxes of single apples from trees he had planted on the California coast, their names written on papers that were twisted onto their stems, their descriptions penned in his elegant script: "King David: Turns a beautiful red in August but is as acid as a barrel of vinegar. By Thanksgiving it will be full of translucent sugar spots." Or "Sidsport. Hate to waste postage on a yellow delicious especially when it is still a couple of weeks early, but if it mellows on the trip it will be a grand apple." It was. "As for Ashmead's Kernel," my father's note read, "better organized in its flavor than Golden Russet, in my opinion." When he penned his opinions for Cox Orange Pippin, Cornish Gilleflower, Winesap, Wykins, and other old varieties, he had the eloquence of Edward Bunyard's writings on fruit.

In his eighties my father concluded his late-life travels to set-tle near Ithaca, New York, the site of his first farm. He bought an old farmstead called Windy Hill, where he proceeded to plant hundreds of apple trees on a hillside that sloped to a river. It didn't seem to have mattered to him that he would probably not live to see any fruit. For my father, age was never a reason for not moving ahead with life.

Between the first tastes of cream and the last gifts of apples that arrived in the mail, my father was the supplier of countless other good things to eat. When we went to the beach to escape the heat of California's Central Valley, he emerged from tide pools with his hat full of mussels, a crab, an abalone, clams, and sea urchins, which he cooked into a briny stew. The night before

I married for the first time, he joined our two families with a paella made from crustaceans both familiar and strange that he had gathered from his home at that time on the Northern California coast.

One Saturday afternoon, when he was a new professor at UC Davis and Mike and I were children, my father put some golden syrup in a petri dish and offered us the chance to taste something deliciously sweet. Because it was in a petri dish and we were in his laboratory, we were highly suspicious, but we finally did taste it, putting just the smallest drops on our tongues. It was sweet, just as he had promised. Another time he asked us if we wanted to taste pure brown sugar, and when we said "Yes!" he brought out a spotted banana and directed us to the mushy brown places. "Pure sugar," he said, "that's where it is." We were disappointed, of course, but he was right. He also taught us about eating the skins of kumquats and how to suck out the flesh of the pineapple guavas that grew under the campus water tower. We had to climb over a fence to get them. He wanted us to enjoy these tastes, but I believe that he was also teaching us to overcome our prejudices (the petri dish, the rotten banana, skins not flesh, climbing over fences for fruit growing under water towers), to become open-minded people. At least that is how I think of it now.

On campus he planted corn, which is a grass, after all, even if it's not turf grass, for his students to observe. He grew one patch using conventional methods with the usual doses of fertilizer and pesticides. The other was planted in organic soil, without fertilizers and pesticides to help out. The organic patch thrived beyond the conventional. This was in the 1950s. My father was an early proponent of organic agriculture even though this was not in step with the University of California. I don't think he saw any virtue in destroying soil to raise food. He became a charter member of *Acres USA* magazine, the kind of publication that still makes me feel that finally, here's where sanity lives, in observations, comments, and stories of intelligent (albeit sometimes cranky) people engaged in growing good soil and raising food right. My dad was that combo—the grower of soil and the cranky doubter of modern methods. At a late point in his life he became, as Mike put it, a cross between Santa Claus and Willie Nelson with his long silvery braid and crackpot ideas, although that's not really fair to Willie.

I didn't know, until I read my father's obituary, that his interest in plants extended well beyond the boundaries of our family garden. Mike knew this and he wrote that our father practiced his own brand of guerrilla horticulture, planting trees wherever he thought they were appropriate without concern for whose land it was. A fig tree planted by my dad in the northwest corner of Redwood Park in Davis is still there. In the schoolyard behind our house he ripped out one kind of apple tree the city had planted and replaced it with a better variety. Forty years later my mother still picked fruit from this tree. And as for our own garden, it was a forest of edibles—apricot, fig, quince, apple, plum, almond, peach, apricots, and bamboo (which we ate), corn, melons, berries, and vegetables. His academic specialty was actually turf grass, and true to form, we had the homeliest lawn in town. But we had the greatest fruit.

. . .

I know I am putting my father in a rosy light. Of course he was also difficult—remote, oddly aggressive, and stubborn. Certain things were *his:* the Dutch gingerbread and Gouda cheeses and licorice bought from a traveling man who drove around California with his van filled with Dutch treats. He squirreled these away in his home office. They were his. A dog he bought in Scotland, a Skye terrier, was his. He did share boxes of matches that were bright red and had *nematodes???* (the bad kind) printed on the front. They were around for years as none of us smoked or lit incense. And the Citroën he bought in France, the one that rose and fell on its own hydraulic accord—that was his too.

I was sixteen when he got the Citroën, and for Jamie and me, it was mortifying to go anywhere in that car. At that time my dad had a long, waxed Salvador Dalí–esque mustache. He wore a pith helmet while driving and took great pleasure in explaining the works of his softly hissing beast as it rose and fell on its hydraulics to astonished gas station attendants. Jamie and I really just wanted to disappear but we couldn't. It was the family car. We both gloomily wished that our father would want something more ordinary, like a Ford or a Buick, but that never happened.

Every August my mother went back to Connecticut to visit her mother and relatives in West Hartford. When my father returned from the Sacramento airport his arms were filled with shopping bags, and for one week the food in our house changed.

Instead of shredded wheat for breakfast, we had bacon and fried eggs, the hot bacon fat spooned over the yolks to cook them. At dinner my father brought out hearty fare such as chicken and dumplings, pot roasts, and short ribs, followed by pies and cobblers for dessert. It was usually around 110 degrees outside but that didn't stop him from indulging his taste for the robust wintry foods of his Iowa upbringing. It was unlike anything else we ate the rest of the year and it was wonderfully good. But once Mother returned, those foods receded into the background, where they became the uncertain memory of an interrupted routine. Only when Mike came home from his terms at Andover and Harvard did we have a pot roast, ostensibly to celebrate his return. He, of course, had been eating large pieces of roasted meat every Sunday for months and was not at all interested in eating more of the same, but his homecoming provided a way for my dad to bring a big piece of meat into our household. It was tender and delicious. Falling off the bone. It was just about the only meat I knew and remember from childhood with pleasure.

My father died in 2005 in an upstate New York town so poor that food was purchased at the gas station. By then he had dementia and was living with a couple who truly loved him, although they couldn't have been more different from each other. At his funeral there were many funny stories about my father's little quirks, and everyone had wonderful things to say about him. It was obvious that he had touched all of their lives.

I arrived with a suitcase of some of his favorite foods from when we were kids—Irish Cheddar, Dutch licorice, an aged

Gouda, a honey cake, walnuts, avocados, Meyer lemons from California, and more. I brought napkins and candles for the table to make it special, and after the small service we—there were only six of us—sat around the table and nibbled and talked. All at once, I was spent. I looked down and saw a bottle of single-malt scotch. I asked if that was Dad's, by chance, and when his teetotaler caretakers said yes, I poured myself a glass, raised it, and said, "Thanks, Dad. For everything."

My mother was born in Pawtucket, Rhode Island, into a family that was large, Russian, Jewish, and East Coast. Her parents were respectable and middle class and my tiny, elegant grandmother was the mistress of the rich, succulent dishes that put distance between the hard times of the past and the better life of her present. Not surprisingly there were always plenty of good things to eat in my grandmother's kitchen—and in those of her sisters, my great-aunts. I recall the searing of briskets, the use of sour salt, the raisin squares she sent us every year, Aunt Anna's brownies, and the Passover dishes the few times I got to make the trip to West Hartford for that meal. The food back East was plentiful, meat laden, and delicious, but my memories of it are few and that generous table wasn't really mine, as much as I want to stake my claim there. I was only a guest, a visiting relative whose mother had temporarily left the fold of Judaism. With the extended family three thousand miles away, I didn't grow up learning to cook alongside my grandmother or her sisters, or any other women in the family except, on rare occasions, my mother, to whom I'm grateful for telling me not to be afraid of baking with yeast. She was so right. But not everyone has cozy memories of learning to cook alongside a grandmother. I certainly didn't.

My mother's name was Winifred. She was gifted with a strong creative bent that emerged early in her life, a bent that was not encouraged. It was incomprehensible to her family that a girl might want to express herself when she was just going to get married, the goal for so many young women of her generation. Despite her elders' expectations, she managed to go to Bennington and later to Oberlin College, study modern dance with Martha Graham, play the violin in chamber groups and orchestras, model hats in New York, meet Russian men who claimed to be princes in exile, and pose for famous artists. She published fourteen books for children and young adults and wrote many more for full-fledged adults. She drew microscopic organisms in the geology department at UC Davis, and had many shows of her paintings, the last at the age of ninety-five. She made a home for four children, a succession of animals, and a husband, *and* managed to live a rich, creative life. She also decided to complete her college degree and she graduated from UC Davis the same year I graduated from high school. She was a Phi Beta Kappa.

To us kids she was quirky, often irritating and hurtful, but to others she was an amazing woman and much admired in our town. Still, the work and time it took to fulfill her many ambitions—art, music, and writing—meant that there was a lack of nurture for us kids, especially in the feeding area. Food, as she frankly owned, was somewhere on the (far) edges of her world, not at its center. She cooked every day, but cooking was something she fit in after her own work, hurriedly, with distraction and occasional irritation. Only now do I appreciate that she cooked at all. And although I too admire her and miss her terribly, it's difficult to paint her full portrait. As her daughter, what I recall most are the hard parts, that kids to her were a bother, that she said things that were just inappropriate, like asking a man I was dating if he'd ever thought he might like to be a mountain goat. "Mom!" The thirteen-year-old's whine comes out and explodes until the very end, regardless of my actual age.

My mother lived such a long life that I had begun to think she would always be here. The reality of her aging sank in only gradually. I'd open the mailbox and suddenly realize that I would never get a Valentine or birthday card from her again. When her caretaker asked if she could have one of the books I had written that was in my mother's kitchen, I of course gave it to her. The rest, I thought for some reason, my mother might still cook from, even though that was highly unlikely. I guess I didn't really think at all at that time. Her attitude toward death and dying had long been fairly upbeat. She'd tell us not to worry. She'd joke that she'd lived past her expiration date. And then, her life was over.

I was so disoriented. While I had felt that my father had lived a long and good life, I was struck more by my mother's death, far more saddened. My father left few possessions, almost nothing behind. My mother had a house with four bedrooms crammed with things that had to be gone through. Her horrible cooking didn't really matter, but it was too late to tell her that. Other things did matter, but their power had diminished. My siblings and their spouses along with my husband, Patrick, and I gave her a great send-off in a room filled with her many admirers and friends, music that she loved, food that contained no meat, at her request. We set up a room with her paintings and invited everyone there, her friends, to take one, and they did, with joy.

While my parents' approaches to food were irreconcilable, together they did something good, something that was adventurous: They hosted dinners in which they explored "foreign" cuisines. There was the cheese fondue party, the beef bourguignon party, the spanakopita menu, curry dinners with their little bowls of raisins, chutney, and roasted peanuts. The Time-Life Foods of the World cookbooks did not influence this era of experimentation, for they would not be published for another few years. Rather this exploration was launched by a book called *The European Cookbook for American Homes* by "The Browns, Cora, Rose and Bob." Published some twenty years before my parents were using it, it's a good and useful book. Whoever this family was, and there's no clue on the dust jacket, as there would be today, they were keen observers of the different places they lived. Every time I look through this book, I come away with a few good ideas. (Since having my mother's copy on my bookshelf, I've learned more about the Browns and their other books through Omnivore Books on Food in San Francisco.)

My parents' repertoire grew when the Foods of the World series finally did come out in 1968. This was, perhaps, one of the first times that "ethnic" foods, so often hidden by immigrant families, came out of hiding and made their appearance in the larger culture. Writers who were well qualified to discourse on the foods of Japan, Provence, Sweden, or wherever their assignment took them wrote these volumes. And they were full of pictures. A lot of my parents' friends, all of whom had spent sabbatical years living abroad in one country or another, had these books and gave parties from them. As children, we looked on and later sampled any leftovers. I was drawn to *The Cooking of Provincial France* more than any other volume.

Moving from upstate New York to California must have been quite a food adventure for my parents. The beneficent Mediterranean climate that made formerly exotic foods available literally in our own backyard, and the international community at UC Davis, plus the closeness of San Francisco, contributed streams of culinary possibilities that they couldn't have imagined in the cold Northeast.

Once a month, my dad would fill up our larger, new maroon and orange Willys Jeep with "five dollars' worth of regular" and we'd go to San Francisco for the day. There were fixed places along our route—the Crystal Palace Market, Golden Gate Park, a museum or two, a bakery, and the City of Paris department store, which had a French pastry shop in the basement. If we were lucky, we might go home the long way, which meant stopping in Sausalito, where we bought butterscotch ice cream cones, a tremendously exciting taste long before the days of Baskin-Robbins and its myriad flavors. We sat on a barge licking our ice cream as seagulls shrieked and the barge rose and fell with the waves made by passing ships. For kids, this was terrific.

The Crystal Palace Market on Mission Street in San Francisco, one of the great public markets of that era, was the most exciting place we went. A glass ceiling floated high above its spacious interior, which was filled with rows of small, family-run market stalls. It was a keenly aromatic place full of bustle and conversation. I loved it from the first time we went there. There's no doubt that my love of markets started at the Crystal Palace.

At the entrance there was a long, polished wooden bar where Anchor Steam beer was sold. It was my father's prerogative to pass a solitary half hour with a stein of beer and a handful of pistachio nuts while the rest of us wandered around the huge hall. Gunnysacks of grains, beans, and nuts were stacked in front of some booths; turkeys and other fowl hung off the racks of others. Looking at photographs of the market, one can see that these were not the big-breasted white turkeys of today, but smaller, more oblong-shaped birds, perhaps one of the heritage breeds that are now making a comeback.

The vendors bent down and stuffed our little hands with red-dyed pistachio nuts, dates, or pieces of candied fruit. But even more than receiving the sweets, what Mike and I liked to do was go to the meat counter and stare at sheep's heads, calves' tongues, brains, pigs' feet, and other animal parts. We wondered if people really ate these things, and we wallowed in the thrill of disgust that such a thought provoked. Actually, our own father was a customer here and *we* ate those things. Some of them, anyway. He bought pigs' feet and turned them into gelatinous sweet-and-sour "pickles," and we often ate boiled tongue, a cut one hardly sees anymore. He also bought kidneys and liver. Certainly the Crystal Palace Market catered to a variety of ethnic tastes, but perhaps these were simply more the traditional tastes of that time, for people still ate offal and didn't balk at the cuts of meat that are seen as unusual today, although they are slowly making a comeback. Still, we never saw the head or neck of an animal simmering in a pot in our house. In fact, I didn't see one until I was in my fifties and a Welsh friend transplanted to Colorado cooked a lamb's neck for us one visit. He traded with the local Navajos for sheep, and there was always a joint in the oven or a neck in the pot or something we didn't recognize. My husband, Patrick, was somewhat uneasy about this food and he'd always ask, "What kind of squirrel are we having tonight?"

My parents bought a lot of their food at the Crystal Palace Market—bags of bulgur, beans, lentils, rice, nuts, candied fruits for holiday breads, dried figs for snacking, sesame seeds, and olive oil. My father always managed to secure a nice piece of cheese for himself.

The Crystal Palace wasn't expensive nor was it a fashionable place to go. It was where the common people shopped, often for the foods of their ethnic pasts. Replacing the grand old public markets that have been lost over time in our country has come slowly and at a great cost, as people have had to be awakened from their supermarket stupor to the value and vitality of what public markets have to offer. San Francisco once again has something of a public market at the Ferry Plaza, where a weekly farmers' market and various shops and restaurants coexist. The Ferry Plaza Market is a popular, bustling place—and it is extremely expensive. You can pay several dollars for a peach, and happily, if you can afford it, because it will be worth it. It will be not just a good peach, but a memorable one, and that is rare enough in the world of stone fruits today. But all the stunningly beautiful, well-grown, and smartly crafted foods found here are certainly unaffordable to many. The Crystal Palace market was funkier, but it was accessible to all.

After the Crystal Palace was demolished to make room for a hotel, we started going to a Greek deli on Market Street for many of the same foods and a new product, filo dough. Filo dough had entered American middle-class consciousness about that time, along with recipes for spanakopita from the Greek volume of Foods of the World. For years we always had a package of filo dough in the freezer that my parents used for their "Greek" parties.

Another regular San Francisco stop was at a bakery where my parents bought broken cookies. How they knew about this golden opportunity, I don't know, but they always picked up a bag for each of us kids. We mined through them, first fishing out the largest pieces, then working our way down to the bits of chocolate and raisins, and eventually the crumbs. Recently, reading through a book of essays written by my brother Mike, I was surprised to find that he too had memories of—and strong feelings about—these broken cookies. Sensitive to their cheapness, he viewed them as a flawed gift and felt that it would have meant more if the cookies were whole. I didn't think my parents were trying to pull the wool over our eyes. I thought that the broken cookies were a little treat—and a bargain at that—a whole bag for each of us. But those crumbs did inspire me to improve the quality of their lifestyle, at least with regards to food, an endeavor I persisted in for many years.

One day, with the money I had saved from mowing the neighbor's lawn, I bought a pebbly pink box of *whole* cookies for my parents' anniversary. After successfully hiding it for a few weeks, but opening it at least once a day to stare at the columns of different cookies, I couldn't resist making a little slit in the cellophane and pulling one out. I ate it slowly, savoring its "store-bought" flavor, that cheap, sugary taste that was so alluring. But now, with one stack shorter than the rest, I had to go to the opposite corner of the box and eat from a similar stack to balance things out. Eventually, of course, I had to even out the entire first row before finally giving the box to my parents. Not one of the cookies was broken, but a fifth of them were gone. My parents never said a word about the missing layer. And nothing changed. We still got broken cookies when we went to San Francisco.

The usual routine was to go to Golden Gate Park, have a little picnic, then finish it off with pastries. After reading the paper, my father would do gymnastics on the iron horse while we rode that fantastic old carousel of wooden lions, tigers, and ostriches. Invariably we'd feed the ducks. We often went to the de Young Museum or the aquarium, and on nice days we'd go for a row in Stow Lake or sip tea in the Japanese tea garden. But when it was hot in Davis, San Francisco was often foggy and cold. An old photograph captures the mood that generally pervaded these visits: We're all sitting at a picnic table wrapped in our jackets, shivering and looking as if we can't wait to get in the car and go home.

Once, when it was raining and going to the park was out of the question, my father decided that we would have our picnic in the car. We were parked on Geary Street, right in front of Gump's, a stylish home furnishings store just off Union Square. We unwrapped and ate our sandwiches and hard-boiled eggs, then opened the box from the City of Paris. The pastries were passed around the car so that we could try all of them. Powdered sugar and flakes of mille-feuille shattered over our clothes. While we ate lunch, drivers would pull up and stare in the window to see if we were leaving, only to discover that we were *eating*. My mother sat rigid in her seat, mortified. I thought she wanted it to look as if she had gotten into this car by mistake and couldn't get out. She acted as if she didn't know who we were and she would not eat her lunch in a car like a bunch of hicks. Frankly, I didn't blame her.

Because my parents would never buy them, I stole both Hostess cupcakes and Twinkies on a regular basis from the State Market until I was finally caught. Mr. Lee chased me out of the store, yelling at me for stealing while I insisted that the Twinkies had been in my lunch bag all along, a blatant lie that I hated telling. I jumped on my old fat-tire bike and pedaled off as fast as I could in fear and in shame, my heart beating a path out of my chest. I never stole again, and if the State Market were still there, I'd go and try to make amends.

That we didn't eat like everyone else, that my mother didn't buy Twinkies and Hostess cupcakes, has, however, in the long run, been beneficial. We had soft drinks once or twice a year, on occasions: root beer or ginger ale when my mother sold a new children's book or had a show of her batiks and paintings. Chips, Fritos, Oreos, processed meats, and candy didn't have a place in our house, not because they were junk but because they were expensive. Our relationship with white bread disappeared the moment there was an alternative, when my mother agreed to paint the portrait of a neighbor's many children in

exchange for heavy but wholesome breads. Some of my friends
had mothers who were also of the Adelle Davis persuasion and
who made sure we had a glass of "Tiger's Milk" after school.
The friends I wanted to have would have been drinking Coke
and watching TV—another item we didn't have. The "health
foods" listed in *Roget's International Thesaurus* are exactly what
we had in our cupboards: molasses, wheat germ, whole-wheat
flour, cornmeal, and bulgur.

It wasn't all grim, though. My mother did make us cakes,
soothing custards, and cinnamon rolls. My dad was great at fudge
and pie. There were treats of all kinds from the traveling Dutch-
man, Corti Brothers in Sacramento, and other places far better than Safeway. Still, if we kids said we were hungry at night,
hoping for another bite of dessert, my dad would say, "There's
shredded wheat in the kitchen; help yourself." He always saw
right through us, and we were never hungry enough for that.

My mother was not a terribly good cook, but she would get
high marks for her feeding efforts today when it came to the
lunch box, for she used that wholesome bread for sandwiches
with their vegetarian fillings and a piece of fruit for dessert.
There are many of us who would love to see such options in
today's cafeterias and lunchrooms. But left to my own devices,
I reveled in making less healthful food choices. For my birthday
I always asked for Wonder bread and sweet and sour spare ribs,
both of which I got. When my grandparents came to visit I hov-
ered around the breakfast table in an annoying fashion in the
hope that some of the store-bought pastries procured for their
breakfast might also be mine. Elementary school field trips took
us not to farms, as they might today, but to the Hostess cupcake

factory in Sacramento, where we stared at all those squiggly white lines of icing being set down over the shiny dark domes of a thousand cupcakes. I lusted for them.

Despite feeling deprived as a kid, I never developed a taste for soft drinks or potato chips, fast food or junk food, or cigarettes, which were also forbidden in our household. None of this ever tempts me, for which I'm grateful. It always strikes me as odd that when I'm being interviewed, there's inevitably the moment when the interviewer says, "Okay, confess. What is your favorite junk food, your guilty pleasure?" I have to confess: Junk food is not really on my horizon. But I have other temptations that do harm in excess—mainly good cheeses, cashew nuts, and cream.

My first kitchen forays were focused on sweets. By the time my brother Mike and I were eleven and thirteen, we were accomplished at whipping up a white cake from an old edition of *Joy of Cooking*, to which we added poppy seeds. We ate about half the batter and baked the remainder, yielding a one-layer cake for dessert on any given night. Our father had taught us how to make frosting out of margarine, powdered sugar, and vanilla, and we made it whether or not there was a cake to be iced. And he taught us a kind of short-cut praline we made out of margarine and brown sugar.

After cake, frosting, and pralines, crêpes became a favorite, and my best friend and I often made them after school. Following crêpes suzette as our model, we folded them, put them in a pan with butter, then added whatever liquor her parents had, as mine had only wine. Gin was not especially good with crêpes, while sherry could be tolerated. Once we got to use Grand Marnier, which was the best, and this pretty much constituted our modest foray into booze as well as French desserts.

At thirteen I made my first pie, one for my mother. It was a dreadful thing, the crust made with hot water from the *Joy of Cooking*. I have no idea why that recipe was included in that otherwise venerable book. It seems to me if you're that intimidated by making pastry, you should probably be encouraged to make a crisp rather than mess around with a tough little crust that will only disappoint you. Making piecrust, regardless of the recipe, was a painful ordeal for me for a very long time. I hated that it stuck and tore, and working with pie dough made my temper suddenly mean and short. The first time I swore was while making piecrust, that *first* piecrust. Even today pie dough can be a bit dicey for me. If my husband walks into the kitchen and sees I'm rolling out dough for a pie or a galette, he quietly goes out to my office for the duration. But I'm not so bad at it now. In fact, it usually goes pretty well. I very seldom swear, and I never think twice about making a pie because of the pastry. With practice, one can learn.

After my first pie failure, my mother, who was actually a pretty decent bread baker when she took the time it required, introduced me to the joy of working with yeast. She taught me to make cinnamon rolls that were loaded with brown sugar, walnuts, and raisins and completely free of healthful pretensions. Again, I thank her for never suggesting that anything could go wrong with yeast. Yeast is really quite easy to work with, yet so many people are scared that they'll kill it, forgetting that in the end, it's just a package of yeast and some flour we're talking about, not a huge investment. Making breads and rolls is such a pleasure that it's a shame to miss out on it just because someone once overcautioned you about using water that's a degree or two too hot.

Not only was my mother a good baker, but so was our neighbor June Halio, who used to make challah every Friday afternoon for Shabbat. Its enticing smell would drift from her yard into ours. It was so deliciously eggy, seedy, and yeasty that I asked her if she would teach me to make challah and she did. I made it every week for about two years and eventually came to turn out some pretty handsome braids. I traded my weekly excess to a few ceramicists at UC Davis, Robert Arneson and Dave Gilhooly in particular, in exchange for some of their pieces, which is how I began to build a pottery collection. Unfortunately I gave away those wonderful, wacky pieces during my ascetic Zen Center days, but I still have a love for clay, which, when you think about it, is not unrelated to bread and to food itself. Food and clay are both gifts from the earth, and both dough and clay get kneaded. When I became an art student at UC Davis, one of my short-lived majors, parties were held after bronze castings, and I often hosted them and did the cooking. That's when I really developed my challah-braiding techniques alongside my piroshki-making skills, as well as my attempts in ceramics. I even ventured into making homemade noodles rolled out with a rolling pin to plump up in chicken soups. They were never quite thin enough, but were more like dumplings. Wrong but good.

Since, as a teenager, I wanted to have a larger food experience, for my fifteenth birthday I asked to go to a restaurant. My father chose a Mexican restaurant he knew in Daly City, and we all went. I was enchanted with the large paper flowers, the mariachi band, the tortillas and enchiladas, which would soon enough become common food for my friends and me. But that was the first time, and it was transporting.

Soon other restaurant experiences followed. My high school French class ate at the Lion d'Or in the Tenderloin in San Francisco. The room was dark and smoky, the very stuff of adventure, but I can't recall one morsel tasted. Later I ate at the Old Poodle Dog Ritz with my boyfriend and his well-traveled academic parents, who knew their way around France and a French menu. The father was impressed when I ordered sweetbreads. I didn't tell him that I was curious about what kind of bread the French might serve as a first course; it seemed so odd. Plus, I was baking a lot then so I really did want to know. When they came, I saw that sweetbreads were not bread at all, and I found them too revolting to eat. The father gallantly asked if I might trade my dish for his sole—my sweetbreads looked so good. I still marvel at what a gentleman he was. The entire experience was fraught with mistakes and confusion, and although I wanted to be, I was not enchanted.

Another boyfriend and I went to a hotel, again in San Francisco and again for a French meal. As we were settling into our seats, we noticed a large table of women pointing at us and looking our way. Eventually one of them came over with a platter of crêpes suzette. They were all on diets. Would we like them? Of course we would! We were nineteen and hungry.

By this time I had formed a more or less distinct image of what I thought French food should be, thanks largely to the Foods of the World cookbook series, in particular the volume *The Cooking of Provincial France*. But the hotel's menu was what we used to know of as continental; and there was not one of the gorgeous, lusty dishes that the pictures in the Time-Life book had promised. Whatever we ate—seafood with béchamel sauce pinked up with tomato paste I believe—there was nothing memorable about it, except the crêpes. To be fair, our dessert appetizers could have affected the rest of the meal, but my disappointment was a big one. I didn't really recover from it until I went to Chez Panisse for the first time many years later. That's where I experienced the food I had thought of as French all along.

When I was about sixteen I started going to San Francisco on my own via the Greyhound bus. There I spent hours hanging out at City Lights bookstore and less time trying to enjoy espresso in North Beach, or taking the bus to the Surf Theatre out on Irving Street to see foreign films. It was a thrill to discover the dense poppy-seed-filled pastries in the Russian neighborhood on Clement Street and the piroshki stuffed with moist, ground beef. After eating my first piroshki I longed to learn how to make them. With practice (and help from the Time-Life volume on Russia) I became pretty good at these tender savory pastries, which I made by the hundreds for all kinds of occasions.

Once I discovered a fortune cookie factory in a Chinatown alley and watched from the doorway as an enormous wheel with little griddles on the end of each spoke moved jerkily over tiny flames until the batter on each griddle was cooked just enough for a seated man to deftly lift the hot cookie off its grill and fold it into quarters around its paper fortune. I also discovered dim sum during this time, along with Chinese pastry shops that featured endless versions of steamed sponge cake, and the Japanese shops where pastries were made of glutinous rice stretched over sweetened bean pastes. San Francisco offered a carnival of flavors and possibilities.

Sacramento, thirteen miles from Davis, was our other, less exotic city, but it had its own interesting personality, and it too was accessible on the bus. Part of Sacramento's allure had to do with its place on the Sacramento River, which, until the levees were built and the flat rice-growing floodplain established, periodically caused severe flooding and big trouble.

A Chinese neighborhood was clustered around the train station. It was not a bright bustling Chinatown like the one in San Francisco, but a more somber place with shabby old buildings and restaurants with creaky wooden floors. Frank Fat's, a fancier Chinese restaurant that stood a block or so from the state capitol, served as a meeting spot for politicians. It was also where kids went on their prom nights, that and a Polynesian restaurant called the Tiki Hut, which served scalding bits of chicken wrapped in tinfoil; they were terribly exotic and burned your fingers as you unwrapped them.

Sam's Hof Brau, next door to the bus station, was also considered special, like Tommy's Joynt in San Francisco. You took your place in a line that snaked past all the meats sitting warm under their heat lamps, containers of sauces and pickles, baskets of rolls, and barrels of beer. I went to Sam's on my first date, and as I knew little about meat and nothing about dating, I just ordered what my date ordered, a rare roast beef sandwich. The stringy meat was bloody and impossible to chew, and I was scared that it would lodge in my throat, which made me even more nervous than I was already. It ended up in my purse, folded in a napkin. *Food!* From the get-go, I didn't have an easy relationship with meat, and for a long time it was somewhat of a mystery to me. It still is.

Old Sacramento in the late 1950s and early 1960s was funky, but not dangerous. There was no mall and no Macy's, but there were places like Beers bookstore, a giant old barn of a building that had that musty smell of used books and dust. The state capitol was elegant and grand, and you could just walk into it to gaze up at the white and gold dome. A display window for each county on the ground floor showed what it produced. Around the time of the state fair, in September, the windows would be filled with pyramids of fruit and vegetables, showing off the incomparable treasure of food that amassed each summer in California.

When I was a young teenager, I had a huge fascination with all things Japanese, which came from meeting my father's Japanese graduate students, who occasionally joined us at home for dinner. They always brought plates of inari sushi and other treats, and they were by far the nicest people I had ever met. In addition to these visitors, porcelain Japanese teacups, fans, sumi-e paintings, and other Japanese foods all became extremely compelling. I fell in love with Japan in the way that a young, naïve person can—passionately and without discrimination.

Sacramento had a Japanese community and there were a few Japanese restaurants scattered along the river. When I was fifteen or so I used to eat there by myself in little cafés with half curtains, or *noren,* strung up at the entrances. There were just a few tables in small dark rooms, and the customers were Japanese people speaking Japanese. The menus were also in Japanese, so I had no choice but to point to what someone else was eating, or say the only useful word I knew: "sukiyaki." The Iris Café was where I encountered braised tofu for the first time. Nestled in a dark salty sauce among the yam noodles, a raw egg, and sliced beef, it was the most tender, subtle food I had ever eaten. With its faintly nutty flavor mingled with the lingering salty broth, the tofu possessed this remarkable silkiness. Unlike today's tofu, which lasts for months in its packages, this was utterly fresh. Here I could look into the kitchen and see the tofu in its large buckets, the big white cubes floating freely in water, unbound by plastic. It was probably used the same day it was made, the way it was in Japan. Later when I went to Japan, I recognized the immediate, clean, unsullied flavor of the tofu there as being the same, and a few years after that, when I was cooking at the Zen Center, the tofu I ordered also came floating in five-gallon buckets of water just as this had, only it was a coarser Chinese-style bean curd.

Since tofu arrived in the mainstream culture and received its unfortunate designation as a health food, it has become durable and long lasting, practical, and endlessly versatile, baked and smoked, flavored with Thai or Italian seasonings, fashioned into hot dogs, sausage, turkey, and more. "Exquisite" would be among the last words I'd use to describe this food that has strayed so far from its origins. But the bean curd I was encountering in these little cafés that were soon to be razed and replaced with touristy shops had the distinct and delicate mark of impeccable freshness, which is one of the qualities that makes tofu tofu.

Today it's hard to find tofu like that, but recently in Sacramento, I had a good tofu experience when visiting Suzanne Ashworth, an organic farmer, author, and seed saver who farms along the Sacramento River. We had gone to the wholesale produce terminal to make a delivery, and as soon as we unloaded her organic tomatoes and tiny bell-shaped peppers, a smiling Japanese woman ran up to Suzanne and thrust into her hands a plastic bag that held two blocks of tofu swimming in water. We took them back to the farmhouse, where Suzanne made a stir-fry with the tofu and some greens from her garden. It was exquisite.

5. My Mother's Recipe Boxes

After my mother died, I found two boxes filled with recipes. I was surprised that she had squirreled away so
many—*any* recipes for that matter—given her general apathy
in the kitchen. Her collection was a mishmash of handwritten
notes and other recipes torn from magazines, mainly *Sunset* and
Gourmet and occasionally *Good Housekeeping,* which was kind
of ironic since, by her own admission, my mother was hardly a
good housekeeper. These folded bits of printed paper and yel-
lowed cards, most of them typewritten recipes, introduced my
mother to me in a new way, and they helped me to see her as
a person I had not known or even imagined. I had to wonder,
Why *these* recipes? Did she ever make them?

Her handwritten categories weren't necessarily related to
the recipe contents. Filed under "Meat," for example, were reci-

pes for pomegranate jelly, orange jellies, orange breads, cakes, pickles, guava preserves, and even a guava chiffon pie—none of them meat and none of them foods we ever ate. The many recipes based on oranges were labor-intensive undertakings that involved taking apart, then reassembling the now highly sugared fruits, something my mother would not have had the patience to do. Maybe she wished, at least a little, that she were that kind of a person, a woman who spent hours in the kitchen instead of at her typewriter writing or at her easel painting. I suspect the real reason there were so many orange recipes was that my parents had moved from the cold, snowy East to California in the early 1950s, and the orange trees there must have seemed miraculous. As a small child in upstate New York, I treasured the orange snuggled in the toe of my Christmas stocking. It *was* miraculous with that mist of oil that sprayed into the air as the skin was pulled back from the wet, juicy flesh. Once we lived in California, my siblings and I choked down sour orange compotes on Christmas mornings for years because the oranges were from our own trees, even though they wouldn't be truly ripe and sweet for at least another month. It was as if my mother could never get over the miracle of California.

Where were the meat recipes, I wondered. Elsewhere. My mother was not a fan of meat and was, in fact, a fin-and-feathers vegetarian. Perhaps the meat recipes were dutifully collected for our father, who did enjoy meat, like the recipe for roasted lamb neck. That my mother, a person sensitive to the lives of other beings, my mother, once a young farm wife back East who couldn't bear the thought of a difficult goat being slaughtered, would even have such a recipe was surprising to me. I'm sure we never ate such a thing. The meat dishes that we did eat were mostly in her "Armenian" file, which also contained dolmas, shashlik, kebabs, and a miscellany of curries. There was a recipe for *köefte* from the 1950s, long before Paula Wolfert introduced us to more than fifty kinds. It was more like a fried meatball, but there it was, coming into our consciousness. On one card there were instructions for preparing pickled tongue with raisins. Again, I doubt my mother made the tongue, but we did eat tongue (and kidneys and liver and pigs' feet); my father was the one who bought these meats and cooked them, but never with raisins.

The substantial meat-based dishes that graced my grandmother's table never found a place on ours. We never had a brisket, and only once did we have a steak. The steak came from the animal science department at the university. We had to fill out a questionnaire as we ate it. Was it tough? Was it dry? What color was it? I remember that it was tough and dry and gray, and why it was special was a mystery to me. I was ten years old, and what I really wanted was a horse, not a steak.

Meat was costly, and my mother was loath to spend money on food in part because the food budget was what she dipped into to make sure we all had music, dance, and art lessons. At one point my mother and her three eldest children could have had a quartet if we were all in the same room at the same time. Even a quintet. My sister and mother played violin, I played violin as well but also viola, and Mike played cello. He also took up the tuba, which was, I see now, a slap in the face to my mother. Sadly, the result of her efforts to better her children culturally was that her three eldest became involved with food: Mike is a farmer, I have been a chef and food writer, and my sister, Jamie, is an excellent cook, although she is now an artist and not as interested in cooking as she once was. Or so she says. As for the last child in our family, my kid brother, Roger, my mother claimed that she was simply too worn out to insist on music lessons for him. He, of course, is the only one of us who plays an instrument. He's played jazz guitar in various bands for years, and he's a good baker, too. He mills his own flour and he owns a finca in Costa Rica.

For the most part, my father was patient with the way my mother managed things, but sometimes a bitter word escaped, letting her know that he could tell the real from the ersatz and that he wasn't always happy about substitutes. On one such occasion she had made a cheesecake using cottage cheese instead of cream cheese, a recipe I found copied twice in her files. My father said, "So, this is what the rich eat!" This was a comment I heard on more than one occasion, and I saw that it hurt my mother. I winced when he said those words, because I knew it took extra time and effort and money to make a dessert that wasn't Jell-O. But I don't think my mother could imagine the importance of making the voluptuous version my father knew, whatever it was.

I remember her cottage cheese cake as good, and I know that it can be quite a nice thing in its own right. I make a cottage cheese pie that is fragrant with nutmeg, and there's nothing lacking about it. But I've learned that you can't let anyone think you've made a cheesecake when you've used cottage cheese or they get all confused and upset. Cheesecake is just a different animal altogether. It's seductive, creamy, and caloric, and you can't stop eating it. One made with cottage cheese is not that. It's too light and not as seductive. But it is very good.

On an early spring day my mother and I took an aimless drive to look at the green foothills of California and the blossoming orchards. At ninety she no longer drove, so this was a special excursion for her. She was thin and fragile, but also alert, curious, and full of ideas. We talked about Judaism, about books and novels that we'd read or wanted to read or write. Suddenly out of nowhere—perhaps she stole a glance at my profile—she exclaimed, "My God, my children are so old!"

And we were. I was sixty-one, my brother was fifty-nine, my sister would turn fifty-four the following day, and our kid brother was hardly a kid at almost fifty. Still, it was a funny thing to say.

"You should talk!" I teased.

My mother knew she was old, but thinking of us, her children, as also old was another kind of mirror, a way of seeing herself and her age.

As we drove along I thought about how long we can keep our stories going—especially our anger at our parents. Even as an "old child" I could raise a righteous indignation about some thoughtless comments of hers, but when I heard my mother's astonishment at where we've all landed in life, she at the doorstep of death, which could be true for the rest of us for that matter, we don't know, suddenly my anger fell away. Whatever issues remained, they were now wholly mine to deal with, not hers. And I could even see them with humor. Spaciousness filled the confines of the car and our relationship, and we enjoyed the ride. Any edge that was in my voice seemed to have vanished. It was a miracle.

The practice of Buddhist meditation, zazen—watching thoughts and feelings come and go without judgment—was good for everything, including thoughts and emotions stimulated by powerful mother actions. But it was seeing my mother's bony arms, watching her courage in the face of the daily dimming of her senses, seeing the perhaps foolish but nonetheless rising mind that made her invite a Mexican man who once rented a room from her to dinner—a meal that was a challenge for her to make at her age—was humbling. Of course she was forever stubborn and resisted doing the simple things that could make her life easier, but in the end, that's just who she was.

The trade-off of food for lessons meant that in place of real butter we ate Coldbrook margarine, which came in a yellow carton and cost ten cents a pound. Instead of a whole farm chicken roasting in the oven, we had the lesser parts of mass-produced poultry. Wishbone dressing was poured over iceberg lettuce— "the only kind of lettuce there was," my mother rightly pointed out—and packaged puddings and Jell-O showed up repeatedly for dessert in place of the pies she and my father had made on their various farms back East. The hastily made Jell-O, never stirred long enough for the gelatin to dissolve, had a thick leathery skin on the bottom and was thin and wobbly on top. When it came to the lemon pudding, we ate our portions with trepidation until one family member's face showed the rest of us a mighty grimace. Then we could relax. The pill, that sour lump of tart citric acid, was seldom thoroughly dissolved, and part of the thrill of that dessert was to see who got it. If you got "the pill," you tried to hide it, but you couldn't because it was so sour your face curled into a pucker. Clearly my mother was distracted in the kitchen. Carrots were burned. Fish sticks were as well, but still frozen in the middle. The Jell-O didn't set, the "pill" wasn't dissolved.

Marion Cunningham, who redid the Fannie Farmer cookbooks and wrote some wonderful books of her own, when we talked about family meals, used to say, "Well, something always happens at the table. It might not be good, but it is something." The pill was one of our *somethings,* and so was the leathery Jell-O, but so were the occasional chocolate pudding cake, custards, and the yeasted cinnamon rolls my mother made. The atmosphere at dinner wasn't frightening, but it was sometimes perilous when the tension between my parents was high or the north wind had been beating against the house for three straight days. I recall a cast-iron skillet hurling through the air toward one parent or the other.

Our table, made by my father, was attached to the wall to maximize the space in our small kitchen, so instead of sitting around a table, we sat *at* the table, my parents anchoring the two ends, us kids on benches facing the wall. The wooden benches my mother made in a shop course she once took were such that if one sibling got up, the other suddenly sank down while the free end of the bench flew up in the air as if they were on a seesaw. Dinner was punctuated by unscheduled risings and fallings of the benches as one kid or another got up to retrieve milk or some other necessity. There was talk of school and this and that. Family chatter. We hid the bits of food we didn't want under lettuce leaves that we claimed we were just too full to eat. We asked to be excused and Mike and I did the dishes. Evening meals were at 5:15, and we were called to the table by an old cowbell from one of the farms. Meals did not last long. They weren't especially pleasant, but they weren't horrible, either. They were ours, for better or worse.

6. My Central Valley—Flat and Fertile

If you grow up in California you are ruined. No other place is so fertile, so beautiful, so varied, so fragrant, and if you grew up in the Central Valley, so flat. I once wanted to buy a walnut orchard near Davis, and when I took my husband, Patrick, to see it, he looked at it and simply asked, "Why?" Yes, it was flat, though I did point out the Coast Range and Sierra Nevada, both visible on that day, and the diagonal pattern of the trees, if you viewed them in a particular way, was handsome. It mattered not. "But why?" he asked again.

Today I live in a beautiful state in the West, but even after thirty years home is still, somehow, California. Yet when I return I don't really like what I see—the prices, the traffic, a harsh and harried aspect I never noticed before, the terrible poverty in the smaller, more rural and affordable towns. The drought. The fires. The sheer numbers of people. My hometown, which was such a wonderful place to grow up, is both boring and booming. The crappy little houses we all grew up in are now selling for almost a million dollars. In fact, I don't love California now nearly as much as I do my memory of it. Maybe we always feel that way about the places where we grew up because growing up is such an exciting thing to do. When we've had a good childhood, our home is the place that smells right, where the food tastes right, where the nuances of language and behavior are right. It is the right place. It is *the* place.

And if our experience growing up was not good, we maintain anger for that place. Distance.

A friend and I were talking about these qualities of place recently when she suddenly emoted, "Nebraska! I long to be there!"

"Really? Nebraska?" And then, like Patrick, I could only ask, "Why?"

She added that she was a fifth-generation Nebraskan. "But my husband reminds me that I don't really want to live there."

Still she longs for it. It's the same story.

When I'm driving out to California I often have to stay in Barstow because I know I'm too tired to go onto CA 58 and make it to Mojave. Sometimes there is jet fuel in the water and you can't drink it, so the motel gives you bottled water for your teeth. Barstow is ugly and limited, but I always give myself the exercise of looking out over the town and finding something I might fall in love with, a view I might look forward to seeing each day, a way to live there. But I can never find it. On the other hand, the stretch between Needles and Barstow, which was once hateful to me, has become a drive I look forward to because I once drove it in the moonlight and suddenly saw that its bare geological bones revealed a rugged beauty. Now I see that beauty in the daytime, too. Maybe Barstow can become a new heartthrob, but somehow I don't think it will.

I do, however, thrill to names like Bakersfield, Delano, McFarland, Fresno, Ceres, Stockton, Modesto, Sacramento, and all the small agricultural towns in between. I suspect that not everyone feels this way. "Oh, Fresno" is what most people think. Not "Oh! Fresno!" Actually, I don't like Fresno much either and I even tried to live there once with my first husband, Dan. The move lasted three days. I couldn't go from Rome, Italy, to Fresno—it was impossible. Once we realized our error, we moved to Berkeley. That was better. We two, former valley kids, thought we could return, but we couldn't. Still, I thrill to the names of the towns that fill the Central Valley.

7. Dashi Days

My siblings and I were expected to go to college, and we all did. But during high school I spent far too much time fooling around outside the classroom to get the grades I needed to go to an East Coast school, so I went to UC Davis. I had been to some teas where we young women were introduced to the Seven Sisters colleges, and I had decided that Smith was where I wanted to be. But I didn't even apply. My mother had made the point of saying that Mike, who went to Harvard, would have to support a family one day, whereas I would be supported.

At UC Davis I knew all my professors, having babysat their kids while I was in high school. The first year I lived at home, but my sophomore year I moved into an apartment in downtown Davis above Whitey's shoe repair store. The Spudnut shop was next door, and it became the source of warm, wonderful mouthfuls of soft, sweet maple bars, cake donuts with icing and sprinkles, and jam-filled Bismarcks. Fresh donuts, I discovered, were divine. While they weren't exactly good for you, you didn't come away from them with your mouth coated with strange grease and the feeling that you'd just taken five years off your life either. Compared to Krispy Kremes, these were real food. And doesn't the "spud" in Spudnut refer to a potato?

I made a clearly more wholesome discovery when some fellow actors in a college play showed me a little carton of creamy white stuff and handed me a spoon. They said it was milk but somehow soured, and that it was really good for you and that I should try it. It took a long time for me to work up the courage to put that first spoonful of yogurt on my tongue. I expected it to be like spoiled milk but it was surprisingly pleasant. I don't remember where this carton came from—I think that one of the men had brought it back from Europe. It was still awhile before yogurt would be easy to buy in the United States and people no longer needed to have their Salton yogurt makers going full-time to keep them in good supply. Yogurt was known then, but mostly it was the province of health food folks who made it at home.

It's hard to imagine now that there was a time when yogurt was just breaking into our collective awareness, but as with arugula, fingerling potatoes, tofu, and goat cheese, there was a moment when yogurt went from being something only a few eccentrics ate to being something everyone eats. Today we've managed to fill our yogurt cups with ingredients of dubious merit—corn syrup, jam, sugar, sugar substitutes, and vegetable gums. But to balance out the horrors of overprocessed yogurts that are sucked out of tubes and spooned out of cartons are all those great organic yogurts, and especially good are those made from organic, non-GMO whole milk.

In addition to donuts and yogurt, I was ingesting other interesting things, like LSD. The drug craze was just starting and LSD wasn't scary yet. No one had jumped out of a window believing they were flying. Rather, LSD was seen as something that had great possibilities for spiritual discovery, and it certainly gave me what I would call a spiritual experience with clear Buddhist overtones, or undertones, even though we later learned not to mistake drug-induced states with the real thing. This life-changing psychedelic journey was, for me, accompanied by the heavy perfume of sandalwood incense and the even more mysterious fragrance and taste of tamari, a condiment my boyfriend at the time served with the brown rice and vegetables that greeted me when my first trip finally ended.

Understandably my parents were dismayed when I—at last an A student—decided to take a break from school. My father, who was normally very supportive of me, was furious that I had taken acid—and here I'd thought he'd approve and even be interested in some for himself. Nonetheless, one January day he drove me downtown to the train station and I got on the Feather River Canyon train. It took me to Vancouver, where I switched to the Canadian National Railway and rolled across Canada to Montreal. It was a wondrous cold white journey over icy moonlit passes and thousands of miles of snow-covered plains dotted with solitary churches.

Dinners on the train—roast chicken, warm biscuits or rolls, fried trout, blueberry cobblers and pie, all served by handsome French Canadian waiters—were on the same level of goodness as my father's summer pot roasts. But after dinner, at night in my cabin, I lit that sandalwood incense, unscrewed the lid on the tamari, and took a whiff. The sweet incense smoke entwined with the rich fermented notes of the tamari provided a thread back to my "spiritual" experience, and I wanted to keep that spell going as long as I could. The problem was, I didn't really know what to do. I knew it might have to do with meditation, but what was that? Eventually, I would find out.

Once in Cambridge I got a job as a research assistant for the assistant to Dr. Jerome Bruner. Basically I showed out-of-focus slides to students and noted the point at which the images became clear to them, when what started out as a slab of meat became a bunch of red flowers. My brother Mike was there, along with other friends from Davis who went to Harvard, so I got to know him better. And being in the midst of urban East Coast life was exhilarating. So much was going on for me there—playing in the Harvard-Radcliffe Orchestra, rock climbing at Quincy Quarry, exploring my new landscape, and work, which I loved. The Sergeant Pepper album came out while I was in Cambridge. There was something dark about it, something that portended change, something exciting and mysterious.

I didn't miss California at all.

One of the great joys of being in the Boston area was discovering Haymarket Square, the huge outdoor market in the North End. When I was last in Haymarket, the market was broken up by Boston's seemingly endless road and tunnel construction— now finished—and it wasn't nearly as vibrant as I remembered, but when I was there in the sixties it was an intense Italian market that was crowded and noisy with shoppers and vendors. I rode over on the MBTA with an empty Kelty pack and brought it back crammed with vegetables, bags of pine nut macaroons, bundles of pasta, and bottles of Italian syrup. These weekly visits made it necessary to cook nightly for my one roommate, myself, and whoever else might drop by our Somerville apartment for dinner if I were to actually use everything I'd bought. I know that I must have cooked a lot of vegetables simply because I had so many of them, but nothing stands out as remarkable or adventurous except for my roommate's recipe for halibut baked with sour cream and onion dip. I did know that it was exciting to be cooking, but I don't recall any particulars. I was just starting out, and probably making very basic things, but nothing that was very memorable.

After the excitement of living in Cambridge, I couldn't imagine going back to Davis so I transferred to the new UC campus, UC Santa Cruz, which had opened while I was away. Norman O. Brown was the campus hero, and a few professors whose classes I had sat in on at Harvard would be teaching there, so UCSC seemed like it would be an interesting place. Plus you had to love a school that chose the banana slug as its mascot.

The low tuition made a California university a real possibility and I was ready to go back to school. I was ready to study.

Instead of living in a trailer on campus, I chose to live downtown, across from the boardwalk, in the second floor of a summer beach cabin. Everything about it was miniature. The little rooms had low ceilings, which I navigated in a slightly hunched-over posture. The kitchen had a tiny sink, a tinier stove, and a little table with two low chairs. This miniature house was directly across the street from the roller coaster and on weekends it trembled to the cascading fall of the train, the screams of the riders, and the whoosh of the wheels.

A Portuguese couple lived on the ground floor. When both were home, they fought. With no insulation to muffle their shouting, they might as well have been in my rooms. Apparently when the husband, a fisherman, was away at sea, his wife was entertaining a lover. I was probably at the library during their trysts, but afraid that I might talk, she bought me off with mackerel when her husband returned. It's really too bad that I wasn't more interested in cooking because her bribes of fish offered a great opportunity, now that I look back on it—all that fresh fish and the wild fennel growing nearby. But I was studying hard and working; I knew no one; and I didn't have a clue about what to do with a whole fish. I managed to cook many mackerel, but that was about it, managing.

Mostly I got through college supping on little packets of soups, which could be found in Japanese markets. These perforated strips of dashi packets contained bits of freeze-dried scallions and fish cakes. Once you stirred them into hot water, they blossomed like those Chinese paper flowers encased in a smooth shell that you dropped into a glass of water. They probably weren't terribly nutritious meals, but they provided a cheap way for a work-study student to feed herself, albeit rather minimally. Ramen was a heftier indulgence, but I scarcely remember eating in college, other than these thin soups and the occasional mackerel.

Apparently something was happening somewhere, though, because to celebrate my graduation (with high honors, no less), in which Ravi Shankar and Alfred Hitchcock spoke to my class of one hundred students, I hosted a party for my family in the backyard of an actual house I had rented for my senior year, having bid goodbye to the roller-coaster apartment. I covered a huge platter with boiled crabs, asparagus, and artichokes and doused it all with lemon vinaigrette and fresh herbs. There was a crusty loaf of sourdough bread, and I made a big strawberry shortcake for dessert. It was a beautiful lunch and all of it came from nearby. The vegetable stands near Santa Cruz were the source of the berries and vegetables, lemons grew in the back-yard, and crabs could be found down at the pier along with the bread. This was the first version of what has turned out to be one of my favorite things to make, what I call a platter salad, an ever-changing collection of foods in their season, usually diverse and always colorful, resting on a platter and covered with some sunny vinaigrette or *salsa verde*.

I don't know where the idea for this big platter meal came from. But my mother told me about something her mother used to do. "She sliced a round loaf of rye bread the wrong way [crosswise rather than lengthwise] so that she had large circles of bread, which she covered with softened cream cheese and then decorated geometrically with anchovy paste out of a tube, sliced green olives, pimentos cut in strips, and black caviar. Not only was she an excellent cook but she also played with food to make it beautiful."

I remember my mother doing something similar with tomato aspic, which she made in a French copper gratin dish, covered with a thinned mayonnaise to make, in effect, a canvas, which she decorated with delicate sprays of scallions, finely sliced rounds of carrot, black olives, and thin strips of peppers. While the salad I made was quite different from either of these, I thought that it showed a similar exuberance and sense of style that was somehow passed on to me from my ancestors. No one taught me to do what I did. It just happened, though it may, indirectly, have had something to do with Alan Chadwick and his amazing Biodynamic French Intensive garden on the hill above Cowell College.

Alan Chadwick was an eccentric Englishman, a brilliant horticulturist, a student of Rudolf Steiner, a wild man, and the creator of the most beautiful gardens I have ever seen. He practically scared me away from gardening forever, though. When I finally went to see his garden, he flew at me from the opposite end of the acre plot, running and shaking his arms and screaming that I was stepping on one of the beds and to get off and get out! I knew enough about gardens, having been brought up by a gardener-botanist, not to do that, and I'm pretty sure that I hadn't, but that's how he saw it. I flew from this crazed man, fueled by fear and humiliation, and never dared to go back. (Many people talk about having had these kinds of experiences with Alan Chadwick, but not everyone had them.)

However, the vegetables and flowers that grew in that garden were picked and placed in buckets by the bus stop for people to take home with them. I often slipped some edibles into my backpack before riding my motorcycle down to the beach cabin, where I cooked them to augment my soup packets. It wasn't the flavor that struck me—their goodness was a given—as much as the appearance of that food and those flowers. Everything that emerged from that hillside acre was so vibrant and alive. It almost pained you to gaze on the buckets of dazzling blue delphiniums, the glow of shiny summer squash. You just couldn't argue with their beauty, even if the gardener was a frightening being. Their clear, pure colors and forms completely seduced me. Sadly, I didn't take advantage of what Alan Chadwick was teaching then, but gardening and cooking were not yet on my horizon. I was studying sociology and writing a thesis on trailer parks.

I met up with Alan Chadwick years later under somewhat less intimidating circumstances, at Green Gulch, the farm owned by the San Francisco Zen Center. Alan came to live with us very early on to get a garden started. As a body, we combed the hillsides for cow patties, which became compost, but when 5:30 came and it was time for zazen, we abandoned the garden for the zendo. While a gorgeous garden was made, I think Alan despaired that we were not sufficiently sincere if we were just going to run off to meditate. He left for Covello, further north, and we continued to garden, but also to stop for zazen.

While I was still in high school, Cesar Chavez had organized the United Farm Workers. Even after the protracted Delano grape strike, tension over farmworkers and their lack of rights did not go away. One New Year's Eve I marched in the cold with a group of Quakers in support of Chavez and the UFW. I marched because I was sympathetic and angry.

When we lived in the country, just outside of Davis, the "bracero" program, which brought workers up from Mexico for seasonal fieldwork, was in place. About twenty *braceros* worked the tomato field across the road from us, and they ate their lunches in a grove of black walnut trees near our house. On Saturdays they put on clean clothes, walked the three miles into town to send their money back to their families, and walked back. They were shy, hardworking men and our family liked and admired them.

During my senior year in college, someone organized a field trip to visit the farmworkers' quarters on the farms in nearby Salinas, where so much of the country's lettuce is grown. I looked at this so-called housing in dismay. The workers were given the meanest of hovels to live in, rooms that were no better than shacks, the only running water, if any, was from a hose that filled recently used pesticide containers. There were no latrines, no kitchens. In fact, I don't think they were given these shacks—I think they built them themselves from whatever materials they could find.

I've always been a sucker for agricultural landscapes, having grown up in the Central Valley, which was pretty much agricultural. I especially loved the soft green vistas of all those lettuce fields in Salinas, as well as the fields of strawberries and artichokes nearby. These scenes, enveloped in fog and mist that softened all the edges, made it look beautiful rather than gritty. But after I'd seen firsthand, without that softening mist, the meanness with which the workers were "housed," the prettiness of those scenes vanished and I could never look at them in the same way again, or look at lettuce in the store in the same way or, eventually, any mass-produced vegetable. This glimpse made a deep impression on me, which resurfaced years later when I found myself involved with food and farmers' markets.

I moved to Berkeley after graduation from UC Santa Cruz, and befriended a young woman who showed up on my doorstep one rainy night with a note from a man I had met just once, a man who revolted me by eating raw chuck roast, which he carved off the bone with a knife. The note said I should welcome her. She was a French-speaking Anglo from Morocco, a *Pied-Noir*, and she moved in the night she arrived. That's how we were in the sixties—ready and willing to open our doors to strangers. Who could turn away a wet person standing in the rain holding a damp piece of paper with an address written on it and an anxious look on her face? Maybe it was a gesture from the hippie era, but I've also been grateful for offers of rides or places to stay by strangers in France, Mexico, Japan, and other countries, none of them hippies or even young.

At that time my postgraduate diet consisted pretty much of brown rice, yogurt, walnuts, and peanut butter. This was my austere and stingy period. But shortly before Evelyn arrived, something compelled me to buy a French, tin-lined omelet pan. Maybe with school out of the way I had come to a moment where I could pause, look around, and remember that it might be enjoyable to cook. Maybe I was ready to eat something else besides brown rice and peanut butter. Or perhaps it was just that the pan was a beautiful object. Whatever the reason, that pan was the first of many culinary acquisitions. I still use it on a regular basis.

Being both French and Moroccan, Evelyn had certain basic expectations about food, plus she could cook. She found the contents of my refrigerator pathetic, but she could put my new pan to good use. After a while, to find something good to cook other than omelets, she went to Chinatown and bought whole fish, chickens, and vegetables. Evelyn also found chiles, coriander, cumin, cilantro, olive oil, and other foods that were new to me, and then she cooked. Our apartment took on a rich and spicy smell as Evelyn produced tagines and a battery of other Moroccan and French dishes. Had I been a food person at that time, I would have been all over her taking notes, asking questions, and trying to duplicate flavors and dishes. But I wasn't. I was just thrilled that she was there introducing me to new things to eat. I cooked alongside her, but mostly I was focused on my new, first out-in-the-world job.

My college degree had been in sociology and I wanted to be helpful in the world. I was attracted to city planning, an exciting new field at that time. I applied for a job at the Department of Housing and Urban Development, but when I saw the lunchroom filled with people leaning on their elbows and wolfing down sandwiches at narrow little counters, I couldn't imagine working there. Instead I got a job carrying out a study for a professor in the architecture department at UC Berkeley, where I felt much more at home. In Berkeley, I worked for that professor in urban studies for a year or so, which eventually brought me to Japan and, afterward, to San Francisco and that first sesshin at Sokoji.

8. My Buddhist Family: Living and Eating Together

A row of Victorian houses stood across the street from Sokoji, and Zen students lived in quite a few of them. I moved into one right after sesshin. Some students who lived in these old Bush Street houses were dockworkers; some were writers and poets; others had regular jobs downtown. One worked for Standard Oil. I got my first and only retail job, selling koi in the Japanese trade center a few blocks away. We were a diverse group of young people and it was a free and improvised time where each household figured out what it wanted to eat, whether it was vegetarian or not, whether shoes were left at the door or not, and the other little details of shared living. But details of living arrangements aside, we were all there because we wanted to be at Sokoji early in the morning to sit with Suzuki-roshi, the priest whom the Japanese congregation had brought over from Japan. It was the young Anglo students who wanted to sit zazen with him. He was a gentle and kind person. The American man who became the next abbot was hawk-like in appearance, smart, and connected. He was the one who negotiated the purchase of Tassajara, Page Street, and Green Gulch and who had the vision for the Tassajara Bread Bakery and Greens.

A few months after I moved into one of these apartments, the San Francisco Zen Center, which was funded by donations and the summer income from Tassajara, our guest-season resort and monastery, bought a large residential building across town on Page Street. As Sokoji had once been an Orthodox Jewish temple, 300 Page Street had been a home for young, single Jew-ish women who could experience chaperoned forays into the world, safely but apart from their parents. By 1970 there wasn't much call for chaperoning young women anymore so the build-ing was available and it was perfect for us. A lot of us had Jewish backgrounds, but we wanted more intentional lives than what our Jewish communities had offered when we were growing up. There was still a mezuzah on the door when we first acquired 300 Page Street. We moved in and quickly adopted a sleek black cat, whom we named Huey, for Huey Newton.

Each of the fifty or so residents had a small room with a built-in dresser, a mirror, and a small closet, which seemed appropri-ately monastic, except for the mirror, which the more zealous students covered. The basement housed a library, the zendo where we practiced sitting meditation or zazen, and a "Good-will," where we swapped clothing with one another in lieu of shopping in stores. Above the basement, on the first floor, was a large kitchen and dining room, offices, a very funky student lounge, and the Buddha Hall, where services and ceremonies were held. Above that there were two floors of bedrooms and finally a rooftop that was a good place to go for a view and fresh air when the Zen life below became too much, as it sometimes did for me. Those of us who staffed the Zen Center received room, board, and small stipends. It wasn't what we think of as making a living today, but taken together the room, board, and stipend were sufficient.

Julia Morgan, the architect who is famed for having designed Hearst Castle and many beautiful buildings in Berkeley, also designed 300 Page Street. She endowed it with a feeling of amplitude, and nothing about it was cramped or stingy. The windows bore gentle curves, the halls were wide and generous, there was a lovely courtyard with a fountain and shrubbery. This was one of the most gracious buildings I have ever lived in.

But there were questions about how to live as a group, such as how would we eat at Zen Center once we all moved in together. At first we ate anything and at any time of the day we chose. Then came Thanksgiving. One student, a nurse, was given a turkey by her hospital for the holiday. It was a gift and she shared with everyone. It was roasted in the kitchen and put out along with the brown rice, candied sweet potatoes, and other dishes on that day. Some students dug in, but a number took offense at seeing a turkey on the table. They felt that it was completely wrong for there to be meat in the building at all.

"What about the Buddhist precept against taking lives?" they asked. "Aren't Buddhists supposed to be vegetarian?" "Wasn't the Buddha himself vegetarian?"

Maybe.

The way I saw it, recalling Alan Watts's program on KPFA,

begging was the way of the Buddha. His followers and Buddhist monks for generations thereafter offered their bowls for others to fill. Begging didn't allow much room for picking and choosing. If meat went in, then it was eaten. You wouldn't put your bowl out to be filled, then peer into it and say, "By the way, I don't care to eat carbohydrates, or gluten, or meat." Isn't there a reason for that adage "Beggars can't be choosers"? While this may have been inconvenient for anyone with strong dietary preferences, for a monk it would offer a rich opportunity to become free of the dualistic this-not-that thinking that normally fills our lives. Maybe begging could help us step outside the difficulties that come with the separation of self and other and help us to be at one with the world.

"What did the Zen monk say to the hot dog vendor?" "Make me one with everything!"

Sure, the monk was buying the hot dog, not begging for it, but even in this joke the monk leaves it up to the vendor to decide what everything is, at least as it pertains to the hot dog.

Years later in Venice, Italy, I was struck by a beggar I passed daily for a period of time, a man who knelt on the stone street, his body upright, hands outstretched, eyes cast down. His was not a soft, sinking-on-the-ground-comfortable kind of kneeling, or a lively standing posture, but a far more energized upright posture. I suspected it was hard on the knees, as well as the back and outstretched arms. This could not have been a comfortable pose to sustain. With eyes lowered, the beggar wasn't even relieved by the entertainment of watching people passing by. Should you give such a supplicant money, you weren't rewarded with a glance or a cheerful "God bless you, have a nice day!" or even a nod. What you gave and how you felt about it were entirely your business, not his. His immobility helped you see what your own expectations might be when you offered a coin, which might be more difficult than being the one begging.

But here we were in 1970, far from the time of Buddha and almost any tradition of begging. We had to answer the question of whether or not we were vegetarian in terms of our own realities, and certainly we couldn't ignore the first of the precepts, which warned against taking life. (The commandment about not committing murder is number five in the Christian lexicon.) We finally decided that the main kitchen, the one in which all our community's food was cooked, was to be vegetarian. There was a little side kitchen and that was where people could cook and eat what they wanted. Still, it was offensive to some students to get a whiff of someone's breakfast bacon, so eventually the small kitchen became off-limits to meat as well. In time we became a vegetarian community. (Of course, once you were out in the City, you could eat whatever you wished and no one would mind or know.)

Intentional communities are somewhat like families. What we eat and drink shapes us into one kind of being and we want the parts that make up this being to be roughly similar. It helps to be on the same physical page with regard to food if you're engaged in certain activities. Farming, playing sports, or living a life around sitting meditation all have their own physical requirements. It would be, I imagine, odd if some members of a monastic community tucked into steaks at dinner while others found thin vegetable soups to be sufficient. Not that both can't practice sitting meditation, but the meat-eating contingent might want more digestive time before evening zazen. Practically speaking, eating the same foods is a smart thing to do.

So once we figured out we were vegetarian in the City Center, one of the first orders of business was to figure out how to eat so that fifty people weren't trying to cook their own meals several times a day. A student named Loring Palmer offered to take charge of the food in the first weeks of our moving in together. Loring was an exceptional cook and he was calm and focused in the kitchen. He also happened to be a macrobiotic cook, but not in some half-baked, brown-rice-only way. His repertoire went far beyond brown rice. His dishes were truly balanced, deeply nourishing, and delicious. In particular he was a master at making succulent stews based on vegetables that most of us didn't grow up eating, like burdock (*gobo*) and lotus root and daikon. His cooking inspired me to take classes from his macrobiotic teachers in San Francisco, but even though I liked Loring's food tremendously, I didn't really want to sign up for the whole macrobiotic lifestyle. Still, I learned something in those classes about how to hold a knife, and how to look at and generally consider a vegetable.

Loring hadn't planned on being the head cook for long, so one evening at a house meeting, the question was asked if there was anyone who was interested in taking over the kitchen. My hand shot up. I hadn't realized that I wanted to do this, but at that moment it felt that the kitchen was just where I wanted to be. For one thing, it looked like the most interesting place to be. Two, I wanted to cook. But, three, I wanted to be around food because I had my own anxieties about being hungry.

No one else seemed to want the job so it was mine and I overlapped with Loring just long enough to learn a few basics before he went on his way. I knew hardly anything about the foods he cooked, but I learned how to make brown rice for sixty, miso soup, a few arcane vegetable stews, *gomasio* (sesame salt), and pancakes without the benefit of baking powder, sugar, eggs, or milk. I had never seen myself as a vegetarian, but since meat hadn't occupied a particularly large place in my prior life, it didn't really matter to me what I cooked. Dry lamb burgers, experimental steaks, and those rarely met with pot roast and chicken-and-dumpling Dad dinners hadn't made me a serious carnivore. I suspected that there were plenty of things to cook aside from meat, and the way I saw it was that I just happened to have gotten myself involved with cooking vegetarian food for a while.

In the 1970s we were taking a stand against TV dinners, processed food, and the white bread of our parents' postwar generation. Our mothers may have felt liberated and we may have longed for those TV dinners where you could eat dessert first and Mom wouldn't care. (TV dinners were hearsay for me—we didn't have them, or a TV.) But here we were sincerely trying to replace these new convenience foods with all those wholesome grains, beans, and other foods that promised good health. Our collective intention was to return to eating whole foods, nutritious foods, *honest* foods, unprocessed foods. The problem was that we didn't really know that much about cooking anything at all, let alone these foods. Whose mother had cooked soybeans with sesame paste? Whose dad had strolled out to the barbecue to grill a slab of nut loaf or tempeh? (We didn't even have tempeh then.) Who knew how to cook wheat berries or, for that matter, who knew what they tasted like or, even more fundamentally, what they were? Not terribly astute when it came to food and the kitchen arts, we were exploring new territory with varying degrees of success and without the advantages of cooking classes or cooking shows to tune in to where experienced chefs might show us the way. Cooking classes had not yet started being offered in the San Francisco community, except for Jack Lirio's French cooking class, which I did take. I remember his cream puff swans. Aside from this, there weren't really others.

The results of our kitchen efforts were not very appetizing and this was indeed the era of stodgy, heavy, hard-to-digest, dull but meatless food. The bad rap that came with vegetarian food was well deserved. It would take time and a great deal of accumulated experience to learn to handle grains with a light touch and cook beans so that they were digestible and to explore deeply the world of vegetables. But in the process, many students did become adept bakers and cooks, working at places like the Good Karma Café in San Francisco, or writing books like Edward Espe Brown's the *Tassajara Bread Book*.

Back at 300 Page Street quite a few students didn't care for macrobiotic foods, either Loring's well-developed dishes or my less well-developed ones. Breakfast was an especially tough sell. Miso soup, soybeans cooked with molasses and onions, and brown rice cream just didn't cut it for a lot of students, who ended up bypassing the kitchen altogether and drifting down to the Lum's Café two blocks away on Market Street. There they could be found sitting at the counter reading the paper and enjoying fluffy pancakes, fried eggs, bacon, and white bread toast or home fries—standard American food—accompanied with coffee and sometimes a cigarette. Something had to give if we were going to eat together.

A lot of distinguished guests came to eat with us at Zen Center and the abbot told me that as the head cook it was my job to cook food that most, if not all, of us, guests and students alike, enjoyed eating. That meant the food had to be familiar. Recognizable. The question What is that? should never arise when dinner was served. About the same time I figured that if we persisted with a strict macrobiotic menu, only those Zen students who were indifferent, hungry, or passionate about macrobiotic food would show up for meals, and that didn't seem like the most inclusive way of feeding a community of people interested in practicing Buddhism. I sensed that Zen practice wasn't as much about eating a macrobiotic diet (despite the word "Zen" in the macrobiotic cookbook that was popular then) as it was about the attention and care brought to cooking and eating. If we were going to sit down and break bread or eat rice together, meals had to be appealing enough to bring people to the table in the first place. In our case, the food itself had to change. It was already something that we were vegetarian. Not everyone in the community even wanted to be that.

Gradually I began to include butter and cheese in our menu. I put baking powder in the pancake batter and used white flour so that the pancakes would be lighter and maybe even fluffy. Cinnamon and vanilla entered the kitchen along with pasta and tomato sauce. We had desserts on Saturday nights and cinnamon rolls for breakfast on Sundays. Bit by bit, I fashioned dishes that were familiar and appealing enough that we could all eat together without giving up all of our former foods or those counterculture foods we were striving to eat for better health. As a result we enjoyed a rather hodgepodge menu, which might have us eating brown rice cream, soybeans, and pickles for breakfast one morning, muffins and scrambled eggs the next.

Some of these changes were not in the interest of overall health, especially as we've come to see it today. Our original diet would probably score well for many, and I have heard that the Zen Center kitchen has gone through a vegan phase. We knew then as we know now, that whole wheat was better for us than white flour. Oil was (maybe) better than butter but butter was better than margarine, plus it tasted better. Popular thinking at that time suggested that it might be a good thing not to eat eggs, and here I was putting them back in our diet. Coffee gets mixed reviews today, but we sure wanted it then. Sugar? Sugar was rife with problems, but there it was. We wanted that, too. And we really wanted cheese.

I never saw a Zen student turn down chocolate cake, buttery mashed potatoes, or a plate of cheese enchiladas. Foods like these were powerful attractors to the dinner table. Later we'd get it right again, but for the moment it was necessary to make a kind of backstitch to secure the fabric of community. How to balance change with intention and nascent kitchen skills was a question that was answered only by constant cooking and fine-tuning. In the meantime, people liked eating pancakes washed down with coffee, putting butter on their bread, and having cheese on their pizza. Eventually there was way too much cheese. There was cheese on everything. When I started Greens I added cheese to classic recipes that didn't even call for it because I was so nervous about our nonvegetarian customers not feeling fed and satisfied with meatless food. I wanted them to feel good, and cheese helped.

. . .

Being the cook in any community is a challenging job. For starters, it's hard work and there's a lot about food that requires constant care and attention if it's not to be wasted or mistreated. It can mold, it can dry out, attract bugs, sour, and lots of other things can go wrong. But what was especially difficult for me was learning that I couldn't please everyone. People didn't hesitate to tell me when they were unhappy with the food, so I was always failing at least a few people at a time. There was never a point in resting on some imagined laurel garnered by an especially successful meal, for someone was sure to let me know exactly why it was wrong—for them.

People had their own ideas about what was good and what wasn't concerning food, and there were plenty of food trips disguised as allergies and other health conditions that were used as arguments and defenses. As anyone who has cooked in a restaurant knows, while some allergies are quite legitimate, others become a person's way of saying, "I don't like that" or "I'm special." Some special conditions were real at the Zen Center, and even if I thought they weren't, I tried to treat them as if they were, but I wasn't always as sympathetic as I might have been. Sometime I just wanted to say, "Oh, you're just making that up!" (I do admit that I am forever grateful that I have missed the antigluten, -grain, -dairy phases we humans are going through.) At the same time, I was quite aware that unlike the person pleading for more cheese or less miso, being in control of the food meant that I didn't have a reason to be anxious. I could, after all, dip into the cookie jar if I wanted to. Or cut off a hunk of cheese. I was at the source.

Traditionally in Japanese Buddhist monastic life, the job of head cook, or tenzo, was given to a senior monk, not a beginner like myself. There is a famous Buddhist guide for the tenzo, called the Tenzo Ryokan, written by Dogen-zenji in the 1200s. We didn't know about it then, so I wasn't using any guide, just feeling my way. But somehow, the business of sitting zazen every day and going to service and chanting and all of that filtered into my kitchen consciousness. My mind may have been racing around like crazy while I was sitting on my cushion with a straight back and aching knees, but at least sitting was bringing attention to that discursive mind. Eventually that attention came to bear in the kitchen as a kind of tenderness for both food and people. It just happened. It was a very slow process. I mostly failed but even so a sense of care grew bit by bit.

Just recently I was sitting at a dinner table with a man I was ordained with decades ago when, in the midst of our reminiscing about Zen Center, he suddenly blurted out, "I'll never forgive you for serving hijiki and carrots in the third bowl during sesshin!" This had been in 1970. We were now in the teens of another century. He didn't mention the brown rice and miso soup that were served with the hijiki and carrots. I was also pretty sure that he hadn't really been harboring this nonforgiving resentment for the past forty years, but I was taken aback to learn how offensive a dish that seemed good to me (and many of us at Zen Center) was to a young man from Kansas in 1970. But another friend asked, when he heard this story, wasn't it already strange that this Kansas boy was assuming a cross-legged posture for hours at a time?

· · ·

Not everyone was comfortable with the Japanese food inspired by our Japanese teachers, or by macrobiotics, or by some of the "new" ingredients, like hijiki and tofu, though the response wasn't all necessarily negative. "That was the most tender chicken I ever tasted!" exclaimed a student from New York City upon tasting tofu for the first time.

Food disappeared fairly reliably from the Zen Center kitchen so the cooks were always putting signs on containers pleading, "Please do not take!" The best ruse was to say it was for Suzuki-roshi—no one would take that. Sometimes there was a forest of signs protecting leftover desserts and whatnot for Suzuki-roshi. I had to wonder if he really was intending to consume all this food. Yet I hesitated to throw it out when it was time to clean the reach-in.

There were always little trails of stolen chocolate chips and raisins in the storeroom, cheese whacked off the main block. Even tofu got it. Arriving in the kitchen around 4:30 one morning to start the breakfast cereal before zazen I encountered a block of tofu sitting on the cutting table in the semidarkness; a knife was plunged into it and liquid was seeping out and dripping over the edge of the table. It was just water, of course, but it felt like blood, as if the tofu had been murdered. Why anyone would want to eat raw tofu in the middle of the night or at four in the morning was hard enough to understand, but it was also hard not to take it personally.

Another morning I found a note on the reach-in door. Someone was apologizing for having taken some plums. Actually we didn't have stewed plums, we had stewed prunes—this being back in the day when there was a difference—so I thought it was an interesting liberty the author of the note had taken. Although his poem seemed like a good one, I was annoyed at the theft. When I asked him about it after breakfast he laughed at me— didn't I know that poem of William Carlos Williams's? I didn't, then, but I do now. It goes like this:

This Is Just to Say

I have eaten
the plums
that were in
the icebox

and which
you were probably
saving
for breakfast

Forgive me
they were delicious
so sweet
and so cold

I was not unfamiliar with food theft, both long before my Zen Center years, when I stole Twinkies because my parents wouldn't buy them, and much later, near the end of my Zen Center years. I was then living at Green Gulch and was sitting a sesshin. It was the third day, often the hardest of the seven days. One's body ached, one was tired and often discouraged. The time that remained before the sesshin ended seemed endless. We might at this point wonder why we were even there and not somewhere else more pleasant. So when the tea came in midafternoon, it mattered. It was going to be warm and soothing; it was going to wake us up, and there was going to be a treat, and on the third day one still cared about treats.

The treat for this particular tea break was a walnut crescent butter cookie dusted with powdered sugar. Tea was poured at a fast clip, the clappers were hit, and we nibbled and sipped furiously before the cups were collected and tea was over. When I bit into the cookie I thought that it was the most perfect cookie in the world—the texture, the flavor of the ground walnuts, the scent of the vanilla peeking through—the whole thing. It was perfect. I wanted to clear my throat and announce to everyone in the zendo how utterly stellar this cookie was. But I didn't. I behaved and enjoyed this little moment of perfection quietly.

Once the cups were collected we left the zendo for a break. I walked through the kitchen on my way to my cabin and there, alone and unguarded, was a platter of the walnut crescent cookies dusted with powdered sugar. I didn't even look to see if anyone was watching—I just took one, tucked it in my deep Japanese sleeve, and left. Once in my cabin, I retrieved the treasure and took a bite. I expected the same magic to flood over me, but there was nothing. Yes, it was a good cookie, even an excellent one, but it had lost its power to move me, let alone the world. Where did its power go? I took another bite, but it didn't return. It was gone. It had somehow evaporated.

Is the magic in being given something, not taking it? I'm

sure there are times when that isn't true, but I concluded that if you were not starving but merely aching and tired then the goodness and magic might just have to come from a gift. Later I thought it was the context—the fatigue I felt in the zendo, the discouragement, the quick serving of the tea and treat, the spaciousness surrounding the event, perhaps these were the conditions that allowed me to experience the miracle of that cookie. All that was missing in my little cabin.

9. Shopping for Food

For all the familiarity I was trying to introduce to the Zen Center kitchen, our shopping habits were quite different from those of our parents, as were the ingredients we used. Soy, our major oil at first, was supposed to be good for us, but it was not particularly tasty and it easily became rancid, that is if it wasn't already. Olive oil became our new oil when I made contact with Mr. Sciabica, an olive oil producer from Modesto, and he put 300 Page Street on his delivery route, showing up every few weeks with a five-gallon tin of his golden Mission olive oil. A cheerful and vibrant man, he wore without fail a bright cap and matching vest knitted for him by his wife, Gemma. When Greens opened, in 1979, I was still buying oil from Mr. Sciabica. Twenty-five years later, when researching my book on farmers' markets, *Local Flavors*, I ran into Mr. Sciabica at the Modesto farmers' market, where he was selling his family's now several kinds of olive oils and vinegars, many of them prizewinners. He was still wearing a matching knit hat and vest made by his wife. As we talked about those years when I began to buy from him, he told me that his family started selling their oil in 1936, and that they were the first in California to produce olive oil commercially. It's taken more than eighty years to get to the point we're at now, a place where many people are making olive oil, though often, but not always, on a much smaller scale than the Sciabica family does. Even my brother makes olive oil. His brand, Yolo Press, has won many competitions, too. But as his is an entirely one-man hands-on operation there isn't as much of his brand as of the companies we see at Trader Joe's or the Sciabicas.

Giustos was the source of all the whole grains and cereals we used, from wheat to barley flour, buckwheat, rye, corn, millet, cracked brown rice, wheat berries, and soybeans, along with cashews, almonds, raisins, and other fruits and nuts. Many orange Giustos bags filled our pantry. In business since the 1940s, they delivered products that were—and still are—regarded as healthful and unadulterated. At one point we acquired a mill and started to make our own flour. It was a very noisy, long process to grind enough grain for bread, and it never took off in a big way for us, but it did produce some tasty foods. Pancakes and quick breads made from freshly ground flours are special indeed. Today I have my own stone mill, a Mockmill 200, which lets me mill with quiet ease flours from ancient grains.

Our vegetables came from the San Francisco produce terminal and the Alemany farmers' market in South San Francisco, California's first farmers' market. The latter was a very different market than today's farmers' markets with their fair-like atmosphere. Going to a farmers' market wasn't a hip thing to do then. Foods weren't labeled organic, and in any case, growing organically wasn't something the mostly Filipino farmers and shoppers seemed concerned about. Rather, it was the price, which was low, and the types of vegetables available to that population. But the market energy was high, exchanges loud and energetic with everyone shouting and thrusting their dollars and handfuls of produce at the vendors, like in a market you might find in another country. There were greens, vines, herbs, and tubers I had never seen before. None of it was particularly standardized and there were no frills, no T-shirts or coffee stands or bands. The Alemany market was a very down-to-earth place. It was always invigorating to shop there, and while confusing, it was a walk in the park compared to going to the produce terminal.

The San Francisco produce terminal had its wild side, too, but it was a different kind of wild and it wasn't an easy place to figure out. It was a tough, loud, and occasionally violent market with lots of forklifts whizzing around and men shouting in what sounded like code. Some sheds were frankly hostile to small-fry buyers, like us. (I often went with another person.) Others weren't but we had to figure out which was which by wading into the fray. Whether we got helped or not depended on who was working that hour, or how the day, which was just ending for the sellers, had been going. We had to be fast and decisive about what we were buying and few sellers were willing to take a little extra time to help us. It was get it or get out of the way. We managed to learn the ropes and do all right.

My helper and I were expected not to dally at the market, but we usually took a half an hour to catch our breath over break-

fast at the terminal, where we could observe from a safer distance, over eggs and toast and coffee, those burly men tossing
crates of "grass" or moving palettes of "chokes," and listen to
all the interchanges that go on, the insults, the threats, the kind
of rough camaraderie that unfolds when working to keep the
energy up at the end of a long shift moving food. Then it was
back to Page Street to unpack it all and put it away.

When I first started cooking at the Zen Center, in 1970, there
were scant resources to turn to outside of those few vegetarian cookbooks in existence, like the Seventh-day Adventists'
book *Ten Talents* or the recipes that were collected in *The Farm
Cookbook*, some books on macrobiotic cooking, and a few other
oddities I picked up at yard sales. The former was heavy on
meat analogs and the second on nutritional yeast-based gravies.
And macrobiotic food was, well, macrobiotic. As none of these
approaches were what I was looking for I turned elsewhere for
information and inspiration.

To augment the recipes in the cookbooks that were lying
around the kitchen, I bought one of my first cookbooks, *The
New York Times International Cook Book* by Craig Claiborne,
which I pored over in search of ideas for dishes to cook in the
Zen Center kitchen. I also used a chunk of my stipend for a sub-
scription to *Gourmet* magazine. I read my *Gourmet*s religiously,
especially Caroline Bates's reviews of California restaurants.
Here was this woman who, month after month, ate in places,
some not far from where I lived, where she had ecstatic experiences that were simply inconceivable to me. She was a wizard at

describing food and I was particularly entranced by her frequent references to silken sauces "napping" pieces of fish and other foods. I had no idea what she was talking about most of the time, and I despaired at not knowing what it was to have a gourmet experience. Had I had one? Would I know it if I did?

I gathered that the main thing is to be transported by something you're eating, but how far and where to, I was unsure. Unable to answer the gourmet question for quite a while yet, I was, in the meantime, getting the idea that food might be terribly exciting, just as it had been for me when I lived with that couple in high school who were not my parents. And even if I was going to cook vegetarian food, couldn't it also be good enough to be exciting, if not transporting? I was sure it could be if I could just somehow figure it out.

More practically speaking, I got a lot of useful ideas from Craig Claiborne's international collection, partly because some of the countries he included had very vegetable-intensive cuisines. A number of recipes were already worked out, such as spanakopita, crêpes, curries, and ratatouille. They could, I discovered, with some tweaking, become vegetarian main dishes if they weren't already. What's more, they could be paired with other foods from the same chapter so that there was some sort of cultural integrity within each meal, and this was a great help. At this time I hadn't yet begun to travel, but I knew I didn't want a mishmash on the plate with bits and pieces from all over the world.

It helped that there weren't endless choices in this book; it kept things from getting confusing and gave me something of a base to work from. For example, once I got spanakopita figured out, I could take a next step and come up with other ways to use the idea of filo dough layered with a vegetable to make a dish that departed from the spinach-feta mixture. Today there are books that cover Greek cuisine and culture in depth, and with them in hand it's possible to see still other, yet traditional, ways of getting some vegetable matter between those flaky layers of filo pastry. But when I first started cooking, this wealth of information hadn't yet come to light. Given a template, I pretty much figured things out as I cooked. In short, I made things up based on recipes and approaches that already existed in our limited lexicon. I didn't consider myself to be an especially creative cook as much as I was a person who was alert to possibilities. And that's true today, too.

Other books entered my life at that time as well. Escoffier's tome, *Ma Cuisine, Larousse Gastronomique,* James Beard's books on American food, and others of the classic French or American variety: *Joy of Cooking,* Henri Pellaprat's gigantic volume, and Fannie Farmer. I already had *Mastering the Art of French Cooking,* which my father had given me for a birthday, along with a good knife. *Larousse Gastronomique* was a book that I mined for ideas as well as basic information about cooking itself. In effect, *Larousse* pretty much became my cooking teacher, and from its hundreds of pages of little entries I learned the names of techniques, methods, equipment, dishes, even foods themselves. When I finally opened Julia Child's books and started to cook from them, all that information from Larousse came to life.

Escoffier, along with Pellaprat and Mapie de Toulouse-Lautrec, also gave me ideas, especially for appetizers, soups, and desserts. I appreciated the detail Escoffier went into about, say, innumerable potato dishes, egg dishes, savories and toast dishes, and so forth. I still go to Escoffier now and then and always come away refreshed by some recipe, some approach he's taken, even though *Ma Cuisine* is now a very dated book. His flavor pairings, especially for desserts, hold up well, despite the new fruits, herbs, and spices that we have and our tendencies to merge sweet with savory flavors, some of them downright whacky (bacon ice cream?). Still, a bowl of peaches with a champagne zabaglione and wild strawberries is always exquisite.

Marcella Hazan came to San Francisco in the mid-1970s to teach a class that I took. That's when I first learned about risotto, but risotto didn't really get going in the culture, at least my corner of it, for a while. Sun-dried tomatoes from Italy arrived about the same time Marcella gave her class, and I remember tasting them for the first time at Carlo Middione's shop, Porta Via. They were plump and moist, dripping with the olive oil they were packed in. They came from San Remo and were very costly. Carlo had invited a bunch of Bay Area chefs to come taste these succulent bits. We swooned. We certainly weren't using them at Zen Center, at least not those tomatoes. We did later, when sun-dried tomatoes took off as a new product among the more sophisticated members of the farming community, but they were nothing like these gems that Carlo was offering. The tomatoes were usually just dried in the sun, the succulent (and costly) bath of olive oil forgone. While useful as an ingredient and a great way for farmers to make use of their excess tomato crop, these dried-in-the-California-sun fruits never reached the height of lusciousness that those from San Remo did. Although I have never come close to even liking the inevitable sun-dried tomato, goat cheese, pine nut combination, I occasionally buy sun-dried tomatoes packed in olive oil when I'm in Italy, and then I'm reminded all over again of what all the excitement was about.

Being Americans, we've added our own twists and turns to this product, just as we have with tofu, hummus, and other foods that have entered the culture from elsewhere. Texas farmer friends in Austin grew, dried, then smoked their tomatoes before packing them in olive oil. These were delicious in their own right, and even more important, they provided a way to introduce smokiness without heat to vegetarian cooking.

Another friend dries his heirloom tomatoes in a dehydrator until they are crisp. They aren't attempting to be anything other than crisp, dried tomatoes, but you can crumble them into stews or braised greens, where they give their bits of color and sharp flavor to the dish. They are a different beast altogether than those from Italy.

In turning to classic French, Italian, and American food for inspiration, I often found that if I looked hard at a meat-based recipe, I could ferret out some aspect of it that could be translated into a meatless dish. Something *à la forestière* had a mushroom component that I worked into a mushroom ragout, for example. That's a dish we take for granted today, but it didn't exist then except as a traditional garnish. I had to extract it from the beef or the chicken it was paired with, then give it an additional component that transformed it into a vegetarian dish, such as—turning now to Italy—risotto or polenta. This is how I came up with vegetarian dishes that were outside the tofu–nutritional yeast realm, by going back to more classic culinary sources and working out techniques and flavors from there.

I didn't encounter Edouard Pomiane's charming book, *Cooking with Pomiane,* until long after I left Greens although it first came out in 1962. A new edition had come out in 1976 and I could have gotten some good help from a great cook and writer. After some 178 pages of classic French recipes, which are presented with such wit and humor that they are rendered utterly fresh and appealing, Pomiane broached the subject of, surprisingly, the vegetarian diet. It was posed as a penance, a temporary cure for immoderate eating, certainly not as a lifestyle, but he approached his vegetable-only days cheerfully and with optimism, which was surprising for someone who had just given us reason to savor all manner of rich, flesh-based dishes. He pointed out what his doubtful reader already knew, that vegetables were used as garnishes in French cooking; they were not what you brought to the center of the plate.

"A dish," Pomiane wrote, "when it arrives at the table, must always charm one's eyes as well as one's palate," which was, I believe, the main reason for garnishing meat dishes with those foods that contain color and beauty, that is, vegetables. He then went on to muse, why not apply the same idea to vegetables and combine them in ways that were also attractive and appealing? It came down to visual and gustatory harmony. Certainly a single vegetable seems lacking, this he understood full well, but what about combinations of vegetable dishes? He then gave the reader some suggestions, such as tomatoes à la crème on a potato puree; fried potatoes garnished with watercress; braised turnips with croutons; mushrooms in cream on toast. Pomiane also included a vegetarian menu in his book, a meal that began with a vegetable soup thickened with rice, went on to include fried salsify, sautéed porcini with watercress, fresh garden peas with cream, and pineapple and cream cheese for dessert along with more fresh fruit. This was hardly a lean, Spartan meal, but I would have loved to sit down to it.

There was one vegetarian cookbook that did what I was attempting to do, and that was Anna Thomas's *The Vegetarian Epicure*. It felt as if Thomas just dropped out of the sky with a basket full of goodies. She didn't come by way of any counterculture group; she just appeared via her book, which was vegetarian, but not strange vegetarian. She was smart, she traveled, she liked to cook and eat, and she happened to be vegetarian. She was fun to read—you could get on the boat right with her, or join her in a favorite French café, and taste what she had tasted. Her recipes were the ones we made for special occasions. They took more time and used richer and more expensive ingredients than those we used every day, but they were always well received. They made people happy and they inspired me. They also provided an avenue to more possibilities, for other ways to think about creating vegetarian dishes and building a menu.

As I pored through the little cookbook collection that I amassed in those years, I wasn't looking for recipes as much as I was hunting for pairings and combinations of foods and flavors, sequences of steps, and basic techniques like deglazing or reducing. Since I didn't have a lot of experience eating out in the world at that time, I didn't have very well-formed ideas about what things tasted like. Later, as I began to eat out, I ate everything, including meat. Eating meat helped me discover what normal food tasted and felt like. It showed me saltiness, texture, balance, and harmony, qualities that I strived to build into my own plant-based cooking. Since vegetables tend to be sweet and lacking in anything that approaches the texture of muscle, it was a huge challenge to create vegetarian dishes that could get outside the sweet and soft ranges. It's still a challenge. But the Zen Center kitchen is where I started to meet that challenge. Today I find that I really don't care so much about meeting it or not.

10. Twenty Missing Years Again

I was being interviewed at the Social Security office when my interviewer peered into her monitor, hit print, then held up several joined pieces of paper for me to see. They were spattered with a record of my work history. She pointed out a gappy-looking area on the first page where there was no income, no taxes paid, no Social Security contributions.

"Is this right?" she asked. "It's about twenty years that you didn't work. Or is something missing?"

I told her that it was right. But I didn't explain that those gappy years reflected the time I had a stipend at the Zen Center, about fifty dollars a month, whether for cooking, for being a director, or for whatever other position I held, except when I was chef at Greens. Then I was given a little more because I had to have my laundry done. She didn't ask me what I was doing during those years, which was a relief. I didn't want to tell this civil servant that I was a Zen student in California and then try to explain what that meant. She probably assumed I was young and married and raising kids. In any case, she didn't ask and I didn't have to say.

Zen Center had—and has still—a monastery, known as Tassajara Hot Springs. Once an Indian camp, Tassajara is located deep in the Los Padres National Forest, not far from Big Sur should you be able to fly like a bird. It had been a resort when the Zen Center bought it, in 1967, and it still is, during the summer months. People came and paid to be there, whether as work students or full-fledged guests, and they still do. But after Labor Day, it was closed to the public and became our monastery, a place that mimicked the Japanese schedule for monastic events, like sitting meditation, work, study, sesshins, and Buddhist ceremonies. Some period of time spent in a place of monastic practice was expected for Zen Center students. It was a place where one could really focus on practice through a strict schedule of meditation and, one hoped, come to know oneself better. Unfortunately I didn't have too many stays there over the twenty years I was at Zen Center, but I did enjoy a few practice periods.

I went to Tassajara as a student for the first time in 1971. When I arrived Tassajara was an austere and virtually comfort-free place, except for the bath period each day, a welcome soak in those hot sulfury spring waters. The previous winter the Tassajara Creek had flooded and the road had washed out, leaving students stranded and living for a time on nothing more than brown rice and wheat berries. A residue of nervous excitement over this recent winter was still palpable when I arrived and I in turn was nervous that I wouldn't do well with such austerity. But the road never washed out while I was there, and although we did eat a lot of brown rice and chewy undercooked wheat berries, we ate other foods as well.

We were, all together, about fifty souls in this isolated place at the bottom of a steep canyon at the end of a treacherous dirt road marked with signs that said "Impassable in Winter." The winter hours of sun in the deep, narrow valley were few. We weren't hungry, but we were cold. We got chilblains on our fingers and toes. No one had money to spend on down coats and silk underwear to make life more comfortable, as students later would. It was a little like camping—in winter. Still, time there was encased in a magical atmosphere and everything was extremely vivid. There was the musky perfume of Japanese incense mingled with the strong smell of sulfur from the springs. There was also the sharp crack of oak limbs breaking under too much snow, and the softer crack of the mallet hitting the *han*, urging us to get up and get dressed for zazen or to stop the work we were doing and go to the zendo for sitting meditation. The quiet intimacy of the zendo was also vivid, and so was the anxiety that was often there for me along with the pain in my legs. The landscape—the plants, the smells, and the sounds—revealed itself gradually over time. I learned that it was possible to become intimate with a world I had scarcely noticed before.

The hundred-day fall and winter practice periods that followed the very busy, hectic guest season were, at first, a relief—the quiet, the work, the return to practice. Later they became difficult, but difficult-wonderful, the way hard things often are. We followed a traditional Japanese monastic schedule and remained at Tassajara without leaving for three months. We sat a lot of zazen, worked hard, slept little, kept focused and mostly silent. Both practice periods ended with a grueling seven-day sesshin.

When the weather turned cold, we figured out little ways to make life more comfortable: If I rolled up my sleeping bag around a hot water bottle before going to evening zazen, it would be warm and toasty when finally I slipped inside and blew out the kerosene lamp, a fleeting moment of physical comfort. I figured out that certain things could be toasted over the narrow funnel of the same kerosene lamp. There was the deliciousness of Horlicks malted milk powder mixed with hot water and the welcome relief of hot tea during sesshin in the zendo. There was a special pleasure when my Stanley thermos finally arrived in the mail, which meant I could enjoy hot drinks in my cabin as well as in the morning study hall. There were the oddly mingled smells of the kerosene, since we didn't use electricity in our cabins, and the sweet scent of tatami mats. Sometimes there was the call of a wildcat in the woods and we were grateful for the protection of our flimsy redwood cabins. There were stars of crystalline brightness and the sound of the wake-up bell tinkling its way into my sleep. There was the work in the kitchen, the sweeping of paths, and the turning of compost. And there were studies, lectures, and the practice of zazen.

Glancing at the moon on my way to my cabin after evening zazen, and seeing the same moon just hours later upon rising, was startling. It wasn't really a new day just because I was waking up, but a continuation of time that I was once again slipping into, more or less awake. Or was it? Our usual reality shifted. We questioned.

After practice period ended, it was quite a shock to take that first drive over the mountains and up to San Francisco. As much as I might have longed to be back in the world, when I finally got there it was too fast, too shiny, and too weird. But after a week or so, everything seemed pretty much normal and Tassajara was that faraway place and time.

Summer was when we turned our practice inside out to accommodate the guests who came from Memorial Day through Labor Day. We cooked and cleaned and welcomed them into our monastic home, which was suddenly no longer ours. Nor was it quite as monastic. We students doubled up and the guests lived for short periods of time in our eccentric little cabins. They were enchanted by the rusticity of Tassajara. Sometimes we fell in love with a guest, or with their better food. One summer I worked as a guest cook, a grueling job to be sure, but on my breaks I managed to read most of Proust while also hoping to be rescued by some knight from San Francisco. That never happened.

The summer was just as vivid as the winter, only with the intense heat gathered in that narrow valley. The blue jays grew increasingly bold as they joined us at our lunch table under the trees and helped themselves to the food on our plates. I once caught two of them, one in each hand, as they flew all blue and brazen through the guest dining room. The intensity of work made a wonder out of having an entire day off to spend alone, hiking away from the tight grip of our valley, over one rise to another, less-visited part of Tassajara Creek where I could quietly eat my lunch. I fell in love not with a guest but with fellow residents, the plants of the California coastal chaparral and their particular smell. I got to recognize plants the way one knows friends. I started to spend my time on the *zafu,* the round black meditation cushion, imagining hillside plantings of clarkia bordered with toyon. I was not such a good Zen student perhaps. I was extremely interested in words, cooking, and plants. But Patrick reminds me that everyone was probably thinking about something, so maybe plants weren't so bad. Plants or not, we were all interested in eating. Obsessed. Take away movies, music, the city, and sex, and the only things left are food and the Dharma. And for a few of us, plants.

11. Three Nested Bowls

Each person at Tassajara ate from three black lacquer bowls that started out nested within one another. A folded napkin, a lacquered paper "place mat," and a cotton packet of utensils sat on top of the bowls, and all were wrapped up in a cloth to make a single, tidy unit. There was also a mysterious stick with a cloth end called a *setsu*. The setsu was for cleaning our bowls and it was right there, nestled with the chopsticks and spoon. The entire package was called an *oryoki*. It was easy to carry to the zendo and stash by your cushion. When it was time to eat, you placed the oryoki in front of yourself on the wooden edge of the sitting platform, then unfolded and set it up for a meal with a few minutes of origami-like activity.

The Zen monastic way is to eat quickly and silently in the meditation hall in cross-legged meditation posture. Once everything—the bowls, the utensils, the lacquer place mat, the napkin, the setsu—is in place the food is silently served. But before that, there are drum rolls on the big *taiko* drum, food offerings made to the Buddha, bells rung, and clappers clapped to announce the first *gatha*, or chant.

Actually our meals were anything but silent; it was just that there was no talking. For example, one never served oneself, but instead received from others. If I wanted the gomasio that had been placed near me but was out of reach, say on the other side of the person next to me, I'd raise my hands in a formal *gassho*— palms together in front of my chest—rather than pointing or going *"pssst."* I would be at the mercy of my neighbor to notice my raised hands and I'd wait until he or she did. (And if I had the gomasio and I didn't notice my neighbor waiting for me to pass it, I'd feel like a jerk once I did notice.)

As for eating, we would lift the lacquer bowls to ourselves. Soups were sipped; morsels were lifted with chopsticks and brought to the mouth. Cereal and grains were eaten with the shallow lacquer spoons from the largest lacquered bowl. The bowls became extensions of the body, whereas our everyday plates and dishes seemed more like extensions of the table. It was a very different orientation, one that held connection and intimacy with our food.

Chants and offerings, a kind of extended grace, began, ended, and punctuated the meal, which helped keep the mind focused on gratitude and appreciation rather than sensual enjoyment. The meal chant during the time I was at Tassajara opened with the words "Seventy-two labors brought us this rice, we should know how it comes to us." The wording has been changed many times since. Over the years it seems that the entire Buddhist lexicon, both short verses, or gathas, and the longer *sutras,* has been translated and retranslated in an effort to make it more relevant and meaningful to practicing Americans. But it's possible that the poetry of a chant was sometimes lost in doing so.

I was and am, still, especially taken by the idea of seventy-two labors. "Innumerable," the first word that replaced "seventy-two," is almost too big to reckon with, so there's a tendency to dismiss it. But seventy-two is a number that catches. Seventy-two? Not more? Not less? Where did this food come from and what was involved in producing it, in cooking it? What *were* the seventy-two labors? As I thought about what they might be, I realized that I knew almost nothing about the labor food entails. Perhaps a student who worked in the garden would know something of these labors, someone who had dug beds, made furrows, planted seeds, covered them, and watered them daily, then protected the emerging plants from birds and animals. Then the mature fruits would be harvested and sent to the kitchen for washing, chopping, cooking. It wouldn't take much to get to seventy-two labors just for the basil in the salad or the zucchini in the soup. Like using food miles: we commonly say that our food travels fifteen hundred miles to our table, but if we looked at everything on the plate (or in the shopping cart) we'd have to keep multiplying and soon the number would be huge—far in excess of fifteen hundred miles, or seventy-two labors. And what about tea, or miso, or cheese, or rice? Although I had a sense of the labors from cooking, the idea of these seventy-two labors caught my attention and has held it for a very long time.

Between the chanting, unfolding of cloths, formal serving of firsts and then seconds, followed by the cleaning of the bowls with warm water, and finally, drying and reassembling them in their cloth packaging, monastic meals took a while to get through, but the actual time spent eating was very little. We didn't linger and daydream, but ate with purpose and attention.

Even though I've been away from monastic life for many years, I still eat too fast and it has been difficult to learn to slow down and interlace bites of food with the conversation that is a part of most meals.

Given the structure and form of the zendo meal and the dishes themselves, it was not surprising that monastic food was simple. The food was not about variety or complexity, although it could be varied and complex. It was also not about style and presentation, although a soup might be stunning in its black lacquer bowl. And while great importance was placed on the role of the tenzo, or monastery cook, the food was not intended to provide the kind of culinary experience that a chef provided, nor was cooking about obtaining the rarest and finest ingredients, as a modern chef might do. Rather, the tenzo labored to acquire the monastery's food, cared for it so that it wouldn't spoil, tended to it so that it wasn't wasted. There was a fine line between providing enough nourishment to sustain students through hours of outside work and more hours of meditation indoors, but not so much food that a surfeit of calories would make the monks feel sluggish and sleepy. Similarly, the tenzo wouldn't want to serve combinations of food that were hard to digest: It is difficult to sit in meditation with a stomach that is knotted with indigestion. There were many challenges for the tenzo to consider, but they were not those of the restaurant chef. The tenzo was more like a mother caring for the welfare of her family, making her budget stretch where it needed to go, making sure her children were well nourished for the business of growing up and that they remained safe from harm from the food they were fed.

I'm sure my mother felt that this was what she was offering her kids. She even said as much. "You kids were well nourished," she told us firmly and more than once. She mentioned custard in particular. Of course we kids knew she was frugal, but custard *was* nourishing. A tenzo might have to be frugal as well, but he or she wouldn't have to deal with the importance of conformity that comes with the territory of childhood, of peer pressure.

When we were still new to California and living in the country, my family got six loaves of white bread delivered every Monday afternoon by the baker, Mr. Vienna, a pasty-faced man with a sweep of thin black hair across his forehead. But when we moved into Davis proper, all that changed. My mother made a deal with a neighbor to paint portraits of her six children in exchange for healthful, heavy, dark brown loaves of bread. That bread became the stuff of my sandwiches throughout junior high and high school. I eventually saved up some money, threw my lunch away, and ordered a bologna sandwich in the cafeteria. I mispronounced its name, but the cafeteria lady knew that I meant "baloney." I was so happy when I got that squishy white bread and a circle of thin pink meat with a swipe of mustard. Finally, I was like everyone else.

I didn't taste real bologna or mortadella for many, many years, and then it was, where else, but in Bologna at a Slow Food meeting. When I bit into a collapsed circle of utterly thin, pink meat, a peppery mist enveloped my mouth. It was truly a most

astonishing food. Of course we didn't have bologna at Tassajara
or any place in Zen Center, for any meal.

Breakfast at Tassajara went something like this: The first
and largest of the three bowls was filled with a warm cereal,
maybe soft nubbins of brown rice surrounded by their soupy,
glutinous sauce, seasoned only with a little salt, but gomasio,
that mixture of toasted sesame seeds crushed in sea salt, was on
hand if anyone wanted more seasoning. On cold mornings it
warmed the hands to hold this bowl as we ate from it. The second bowl might have held miso soup with tender cubes of tofu
bobbing in it along with spinach crowns, the pretty root ends of
the spinach that are so often thrown out, or sea greens. Placed
in the last bowl were slivered carrots sautéed in sesame oil with
ginger and hijiki, a delicious black sea vegetable.

Or the menu might have been less Japanese and more Western, containing, say, oatmeal in the first bowl, stewed fruit in the
second, and a boiled egg or yogurt in the third. Regardless of the
specific foods served, the sequence of dishes followed a progression from large to small and from bland to intense. You can eat a
lot of bland food but not very much food that is rich or strongly
seasoned. Moderate portions—the second bowl contents—were
right for foods that lay between these extremes.

Zendo lunches tended to consist of more grain, maybe millet, white rice or brown, buckwheat; soup—split pea, lentil, vegetable, or pinto bean—and a salad or vegetable, such as sautéed
sweet potatoes or stir-fried winter squash and cabbage. Brown
rice, miso soup, and hijiki and carrots (again) was a menu that

I still have a fondness for today, although usually for dinner. Whatever it was, the food had to fit easily into the oryoki bowls and be easy to manage with chopsticks or the fairly flat and therefore essentially useless lacquered spoon.

When boiled eggs were offered, someone announced from the back of the zendo whether they were hard or soft. I had a deep dread of the soft-boiled egg. A runny yolk was pretty much inedible in my estimation, but when it came to the zendo meal, you couldn't pick and choose. You could ask for a little of something, but you had to commit to the whole menu, or not take anything at all. A soft-boiled egg wasn't something you could ask for a little of—an egg is an egg—so during those meals when one was offered, I just sat there, hungry, without eating. At one point I decided I should toughen up on this matter, so when a soft-boiled egg was next announced, I put out my bowl. A brown speckled-shelled egg appeared on the black lacquer dish. I gave it a whap with my spoon and got ready for the yolk to spill out, just as it was spilling into the bowls of those on either side of me. My egg, however, was hard-boiled. I was just lucky. But maybe a little disappointed, too, that I still hadn't confronted the runny yolk. I have gotten closer to it with time, but always with caution and a piece of crisp toast in hand to offer a textural contrast.

Dinner, known as "the medicine meal," was also eaten in the zendo, just as breakfast and lunch were, except that the zendo dinners were pared down, the chanting omitted, and only two bowls were used for food. One was filled with gruel and the other with a vegetable.

Gruel was an interesting concept. Essentially, it consisted of the day's leftovers put into one pot and heated through. It could be quite delicious, but it was the kind of thing that sounded utterly off-putting and easily could be if it were not built with care. I had to hope the tenzo didn't just throw everything in a pot willy-nilly and leave it at that, but kept the idea of the evening's gruel percolating as each day unfolded so that a righteous combination of elements could be noticed, then brought together in a good way. (I admit that this is a cook's perspective.) A good gruel, for example, would be one made with rice, leftover pinto bean soup, and the addition of some Cheddar cheese and minced scallions. If you just poured beans over rice and garnished it, you'd have rice and beans, a dish you'd be happy with. The gruel version just mixed it up a little more and was made from leftovers. But it was delicious. Another good gruel might consist of brown rice with sesame soybeans thinned with a little miso soup, flavors that went well together.

Bad gruels weren't held together by any culinary logic at all. For me, a bad gruel included leftover scrambled eggs mixed into, say, oatmeal and miso soup. Everything about it was unappealing. Nothing went together, not the colors, flavors, or textures. But I found that if I was truly hungry, I appreciated it. Sometimes I could anticipate a good gruel, or a bad one, based on what we had been eating for lunch and breakfast, but whichever it was, I had to face it the same way. It was a kind of archaeological gamble. I encountered bits of things and remembered the meal they came from. If you were a person who was interested in cooking, you might even get some ideas about combinations you'd never thought of.

Gruel was a lesson in the value of familiarity—the more familiar the elements, the easier it was to like. But even if it were very good, I would never, ever, serve gruel to friends should I make it in my own home. Gruel is personal. At Tassajara it was something I could push against to look at my discomfort and anxiety. And gruel pushed back at me and asked me to be open. I might find that I could just relax and accept what the evening meal brought without saying it was good or bad. In any case, I couldn't send it back once I had it. I had to eat whatever I had taken. We all did.

One summer I was teaching at a conference in Utah when the cook for our lunch announced that he had a special treat: he was going to introduce us to gruel, and he was very excited about offering us this experience. His version of gruel was cold, stiff polenta covered with a lukewarm stew made with vegetables from a local garden. I was not too excited about this gruel, especially since it was tepid and we were chilly, but also because we were to eat it with our fingers. (For some reason, the teachers were given spoons.) But sure enough, as I poked around trying to make it all adhere, some goodness emerged that exceeded the promise offered by its appearance and temperature. And it was easy to discover the moment when I was full because the gruel wasn't so tasty that I wanted to keep on eating, regardless. That's kind of how monastery gruel was.

It was not surprising that the evening meal was referred to as a medicine meal, one we partook of if we needed food to get through the evening meditation periods. But we all partook, whether we needed it or not.

Days whose dates ended in four or nine—another tradition imported from Japan—were our days off, like the nineteenth of November or the fourth of March. But days off weren't really "off." Rather the schedule was modified so that we could wash our clothes and oryoki cloths, re-cover our setsus with clean cloth, fill and clean the kerosene lamps in our cabins, enjoy an extra bath, maybe take a hike, write a letter, take a nap. Regardless of how you spent your time, the days off ended with a sumptuous dinner, followed by a period of zazen. Lunch fixings were put out right after breakfast and we could make our own bag lunches—sandwiches on thick, heavy bread, fillings of miso and peanut or sesame butter, and cookies. Before I got to Tassajara, I had heard that there was a day-off tea when cookies were served. One student was completely undone by the cookie, weeping, because he wanted to join the group but he didn't want the sugar. In 1971 we were fine with sugar, and when I was there, we got to take a cookie or two—or none.

I usually made two sandwiches and ate one in the privacy of my cabin immediately after breakfast, then the other around noon. Others did the same. Eating these hefty sandwiches so soon after breakfast had nothing to do with hunger. I'm not sure what it had to do with—maybe the pleasure was found in eating by myself in my own way without the drumroll, chants, clappers, bows, and all of that. It was a bigger kind of hunger those sandwiches were attempting to assuage.

One practice period I was the *anja*—sort of a glorified housekeeper to the priest who had come from Japan to introduce us to a variety of Japanese monastic practices. On days off he wanted soba for his lunch and he taught me how to make buckwheat noodles, rolling them out with a long cylinder of wood, not a pasta machine. Rather, he showed me once, then I was on my own. I got better as the practice period went on, but I'm sure my noodles were never really up to snuff. I did find it a challenge to do the same thing every five days and see the results of my efforts change. The noodles did get better. But fortunately the visiting priest joined the rest of us for day-off dinner.

The day-off dinners were the treats of the four-day monastic week. Because we ate in the dining room from plates, the kitchen crew wasn't limited to foods that fit in oryoki bowls. And the fact that we used forks and knives made even more things possible. We could have baked potatoes or spaghetti; blintzes or lasagna. And of course there was a dessert, most likely something dense, sweet, and caloric, like a thickly frosted chocolate cake. These rich and elaborate dinners felt as if they were the products of all the collective food fantasies that had accumulated during the previous four days. This one dinner was in extreme contrast to the zendo meals. But these meals were a bit odd. We'd sit down to a feast then eat it in silence, at least at first. Try to imagine setting the table with cheerful red cloths and vases of flowers, covering it with all these beautifully prepared, delicious, rich foods, and then not talking for the first ten minutes. It may be hard because it's just not something most of us do. It was strange for me, too, but it showed me how much the pleasure of a meal has to do with sharing conversation—and the degree to which conversation covers up who we are when we eat. In the zendo we didn't talk, but we didn't face one another over a table, either. At day-off dinner we did face one another. It always seemed so strange that with all these dishes—the foods you had longed for and probably obsessed about the past four days, and all the work that went into preparing them—there was silence when you really wanted to be able to say, "Yum!"

Still, it was interesting to see what happened when the talk was taken away. I don't know about others, but for me the silence served as a kind of mirror in which I viewed my own expectations of pleasure, what I thought my needs and wants were, and why I heaped my plate so high that I would surely regret it. People tended to eat so much that evening zazen following the day-off dinner was painful indeed. Eventually the clappers sounded, announcing the end of silence. Talk ensued, and a more comfortable kind of unconsciousness took over while eating.

The overall atmosphere surrounding food at Tassajara was vaguely to intensely anxious. Would we run out? Would there be enough? Would it be good? And mostly, would it satisfy some impossible longing? One way in which individuals' anxieties and desires were allayed was via the town trip. Once every five days a few older students who had already done practice periods and could therefore be trusted to leave Tassajara without going nuts or escaping, drove a truck into Monterey. There they picked up groceries for the kitchen, tools and equipment, kerosene, and other things that Tassajara needed in order to run. It was also possible for students to order things like soap, ChapStick, razors, flashlight batteries, and best of all, food. The morning after the town trip, which always coincided with a day off, everyone's purchases were set out on the dining room tables—boxes of Mystic Mints and Oreos, jars of Horlicks malt, jars of peanut butter, chocolate bars, and bags of candies, nuts, more cookies, and even the occasional bar of soap or flashlight. Once a student ordered—and got—a bucket of KFC. Who got what was on view for everyone to see, a public display of the secret feeding frenzies that were going on outside the austere zendo meals. I saw who had a lot of cookies, and before I knew all the wonderful things that could be made out of malted milk, I knew whom to ask. This all tapered off come guest season, when suddenly there was lots of food all of the time, including sweets. Guest season was like one big (leftover) day-off dinner.

But before students could experience any of this—the gruel, the bag lunches, day-off dinners, the daily schedule, zazen, the zendo meals, town trips—they had to prove their intention to practice by doing *tangaryo* for a period of five days. Historically, tangaryo referred to the days a monk spent sitting outside the temple gate to prove his intention to practice. At Tassajara tangaryo involved sitting in the zendo from the predawn zazen period into the night, without moving. You could not talk, walk, wash, or do anything but sit. There were no breaks for walking meditation, as in sesshin. Tangaryo was excruciating; but it wasn't an empty form. During this period I projected a life story for myself of a perfect marriage and children, then as I retold it to myself, it started to fray here and there until it fell apart and I had to conclude that there were no guarantees for happiness. Lots of other stuff about my life came up that firmed my intention for the practice period to come, and I'm sure that was true for others. Otherwise why not leave? In short, tangaryo was a good thing to do.

While I was sitting during tangaryo, I could hear the students having their work meeting just outside the zendo, after breakfast. They could be talking about lost socks and to even imagine taking part in such a conversation seemed like the most enviable thing in the world. Ordinary events were infused with the miraculous when there was absolutely no possibility of taking part in them.

During tangaryo, I was faced with the monastery's food for the first time. Tassajara food was different from city food, at least in 1971; it was more austere and even somewhat strange. One day we were served a lentil soup in which stale croutons of Tibetan barley bread were submerged. The bread was so dark and chewy that I was sure it was beef, and I couldn't believe there would be a beef stew at Tassajara. I was also a little relieved because I hadn't been thriving that well on my new strictly vegetarian diet and here was this beef and it was so nourishing and good. That I couldn't tell bread from beef already said a lot about my ability to discern grain from flesh, but I couldn't wait to make this stew for my parents when the winter break came, this and other good foods, like hearty split pea soups and strange new breads, for instance bread made from gruel—gruel bread, in fact, was what it was called. When I finally did go home, I tried out these new foods on my parents, who were only marginally impressed. Now, of course, I realize that they had their own ways of eating and were not very interested in adding new ones, especially those from a Zen monastery. I probably should have known that then, but I was so excited by these foods that I didn't think about it. I was keenly disappointed that they weren't more enthusiastic.

12. Guest Season at Tassajara

When we first acquired Tassajara, in 1967, we continued running it the way it had been run before Zen
Center's ownership. Which is to say, the kitchen served meat,
a practice that continued for a short time. Imagine what it must
have been like for these hungry, hardworking, not necessarily
vegetarian students smelling the lamb chops they carried out of
the kitchen to the guests in their dining room. Within a season or
two, we decided to serve our guests vegetarian meals.

This was a very daring thought. Vegetarian food was still
pretty primitive at that time, but we had some advantages: Our
guests had absolutely nowhere else to go unless they wanted to
take a very long drive out and back on that treacherous road,
which they didn't. They were relaxed, and they were hungry.
Plus Tassajara was rustic enough that being there in the summer
was a little like camping, and as we all know, everything tastes
better out-of-doors, or something like the out-of-doors. Sitting

in a large screened-in dining room that was perched over the rushing Tassajara Creek was not a bad dining situation for the guests, and all of these factors made the transition to a vegetarian menu that much easier. The food itself evolved year after year as we became aware of new dishes and recipes and how to cook them, changing ingredients and bettering our cooking skills—in short, accumulated experience. For the most part, our guests were accepting and happy.

Although it was vegetarian, guest food was not like the student food eaten during practice period. It was more familiar to the guests and far richer. Most every meal was an occasion for biscuits, fresh breads, rolls, cakes, and other kinds of baked goods. They were so delicious—especially the breads—that many guests asked if they could buy a loaf to take back with them to the City. Extra bread was always made for that purpose. At some point, we started hearing people ask if we could open a bakery in San Francisco. This was long before Acme bakery and the era of slow-rise levain breads and there weren't many bakeries making tender whole-grain loaves and blueberry muffins. Eventually Zen Center opened the Tassajara Bread Bakery on Cole Street. It was a hugely successful adventure that gave students the chance to work in an atmosphere of their own (Buddhist) making instead of having to go downtown to work. Its income helped support the Zen Center, and it provided many San Franciscans with loaves of bread along with lemon bars, those muffins, poppy seed cake, and other pastries.

The Tassajara Bread Bakery closed some years ago. A friend recently referred to it (and Peet's Coffee in Berkeley) as "so twentieth century." Now there is a very different reality concerning bread and baked goods, a reality that involves growing grains or sourcing them from smaller growers, milling them, using cold, long rises, sourdough starters, rustic shapes, higher hydration levels, and so forth. That the bakery on Cole Street was so twentieth century was true. But it served a purpose during the years it was open, which was to provide customers with better bread than they could buy elsewhere at the time, and some old- and new-fashioned American pastries.

As with the baked goods, guests were increasingly impressed with the food that Tassajara was serving. Again we heard them ask if we couldn't cook this food in San Francisco. (Most of our guests were from the Bay Area.) Could we open a restaurant? It didn't happen right away—Greens opened in 1979—but the Tassajara guest season served as an opportunity for us to learn our craft. And as we became better cooks, the divide between student and guest food began to narrow somewhat, and not only in the summer. Remnants of that good food served to the guests strayed into the practice period as well, especially once Greens opened.

One of the last zendo meals I ate at Tassajara before leaving Zen Center altogether struck me in an odd way. At that time, Laura Chenel's goat cheese was one of the hot new foods in the San Francisco Bay Area and we often served it at Greens. It was special and expensive, and unlike today, it was pretty much the only goat cheese available, except for the French Boucheron. During a zendo lunch on this fall day I held out my third bowl and the server carefully set in it chopped radicchio and arugula dressed with olive oil and a piece of Laura's goat cheese. It looked stunning against the black lacquer, but I was taken aback. I was, essentially, eating a miniature version of a Greens first-course salad. Of course it tasted good, but somehow I didn't want to have a restaurant dish in the zendo. It made everything the same, and what had been special about eating in the zendo was the opportunity to experience food that was truly modest, even humble, and maybe not very well prepared, and have it be okay. Even more than okay. For me zendo food was about having less and discovering that it was more. It was never about having a dish you might get in a Bay Area restaurant. For all its goodness and prettiness, this dish seemed out of place in the zendo. Perhaps guest food and student food, or Tassajara food and city food, shouldn't merge in the meditation hall. Or perhaps it was fine that they did and it was my work to come to see that it was, indeed, all the same. Perhaps today that salad would seem ordinary and unproblematic. Maybe even "so twentieth century." Maybe I didn't have to get involved in the issue. Questions abound when you make room for them.

About ten years later I returned to teach a cooking class to guests at Tassajara and I ate with my students in the guest dining room. The food seemed stagnant, the cereal was rancid, and the menu was essentially a repetition of what had worked in the long-ago past with scant regard for new tastes, new ingredients, and new preferences for foods, such as those that wouldn't put five pounds on a guest over the course of a brief stay, or foods that were better suited for hot weather than nut loaf and chocolate cake. I was not impressed. I was shocked.

13. Also in the Seventies

BREAD

Someone recently sent me a wonderful gift. It was an issue
of *Life* magazine from December 11, 1970. The cover depicted
a robust young woman with long blond hair. She's smiling
over her shoulder and hefting a backpack that's stuffed with
vegetables and, of all things, stalks of rice. The cover headline
declared, "Organic Food; New and Natural." "The Move to Eat
Natural" was the title of the article.

There were photos. One showed a display of sixteen seeded,
dense-looking dark breads. Another showed bowls of brown
foodstuffs, including cranberry beans, millet, soybeans, toasted
buckwheat, sunflower seeds, and lentils. A smaller photo showed
students at my alma mater, UC Santa Cruz, who, having chosen an organic, vegetarian meal plan, were helping themselves

to condiments like kelp, nutritional yeast, and bean curd. I just missed being one of them by two years—I graduated before that was an option. There was also a picture of Alan Chadwick's garden at UC Santa Cruz. The caption said that students could relax from their studies there by working on the Garden Project. (Ha! I thought. That is if Alan himself wasn't screaming at them to get out, as he did with me.) But there it was, a school garden. Forty-plus years ago. And the garden looked magnificent.

The article explored the incipient movement toward the embrace of organic foods through the development of food co-ops (Berkeley's Food Conspiracy) and health food stores (Nature's Children in New York), a restaurant in Los Angeles that juiced carrots, tomatoes, and watermelon to order (the Source), and the emergence of four successful under-thirty entrepreneurs nervously embracing capitalism (owners of Wholly Foods, also in Berkeley). It also considered compost, vegetarianism, unleavened breads, beverages without added sugar, and brown rice.

It ended with the words of Iowan Ervin D. Jaspersen, who was, at that time, trying to get organic farming methods taught in agricultural schools, "where," he said, they "might start future farmers in the organic direction." He believed that what stood in the way of schools doing this kind of teaching was that much of their funding for research came from the chemical industry. (My dad, who spent years developing thornless long-stemmed roses that would bloom on Valentine's Day and bicolored gerbera for the UC system, would have agreed.) He also claimed to have "irrefutable proof that a farmer can run a profitable operation without the use of chemical fertilizers or pesticides." Jaspersen was right, of course, on both counts, and today many land grant colleges finally do have small farm and organic components, and plenty of farmers have been able to make decent livings without resorting to the use of petrochemicals. Many also struggle. But this magazine cover story proved to be an encouragement. We could look back and see that in some respects, we had actually gone forward.

Still, the photographs were dark and those chewy-looking breads must have seemed pretty scary if you were one of those who knew only fluffy white bread. Finally we have come to see that breads like these, though far better crafted, are beautiful in both their appearance and their promise of nourishment. One of the most gorgeous displays at Slow Food Nation in San Francisco in 2008 was one in which tables and walls were heaped and hung with just such robust seed-studded breads from the ovens of the nation's foremost bakers. And a more recent issue of *Food & Wine* (September 2017) again depicted gorgeous deep brown breads. But when I looked at the photos from the magazine, what I saw was earnestness merged with the idea of health painted in big, broad brown strokes. I wanted to sigh. The notion that vegetarian food, or health food, was brown and ponderous came from just such images, and this very vision was what I was working against when I started to cook at the Zen Center. I caught myself asking, Wasn't it meat that was the brown food? Why did we have this idea that vegetarian food has to be so drab? But then, I remembered: It *was* drab, at least at that time. Although I struggled with this image of organics and health, I saw that even this article was in fact attempting to shed a preexisting image, mainly that of bodybuilders and exotic eaters, such as fruitarians.

HEALTH FOOD STORES

The smell in a health food store in the 1970s was nothing like the smell in regular grocery stores with their lingering odor of floor cleaners. The closest smell I can come to is silage, the fermented vegetable matter that is stored in silage silos and fed to livestock during the winter. Silage has a green, grassy fragrance, something like freshly mown hay, but with the odd undertone of fermentation. A feed store smell came close, too, and those grassy, grainy odors mixed up with wheat germ and molasses somehow conspired to promise freedom from whatever ailed you, whether you had a special health drink, took home some vitamins, or bought a bag of dates. Java Juice could not be further away in mood, look, or concept. In the health food store of the 1970s you sat at the counter while your drink was frothed up in a blender. You quietly drank it. There was no cell phone to check. Bob Marley was not to be heard. The experience was subdued.

Before the 1970s health food stores catered to building wellness via the big, strong bodies of weight lifters and bodybuilders. A store on Sutter Street in San Francisco was one that I popped into on occasion when I felt I needed a nutritional boost. There you could buy that wheat germ and those dried fruits, but also grains, nuts, Tiger's Milk, Loma Linda meat analogues, honey, and of course, molasses. You could also buy vitamins and powders for gaining weight. There was a counter where you might order a health drink, made and served by women dressed in white, like nurses. The nurse image was appropriate, for these women dispensed knowledge about what was good for you along with your health food drink. They were ready with advice.

A few years later the old health food stores of the Sutter Street variety were giving way to the new organic model described in the *Life* article. The new model was more about girls with long hair, big smiles, and embroidered peasant blouses than about dour women in white uniforms. The new stores had more things to eat and fewer pills to swallow. There was tamari; Swiss *bircher muesli*, the only "health food" cereal for a time; whole soybeans; and bulgur. There was tofu, miso, *umeboshi* plums, brown rice, and other staples of the macrobiotic kitchen. There were no nutrition bars, vegan cookies, instant Indian dinners, or grass-fed beef. In fact, there was no meat of any kind, for these stores were usually vegetarian. When natural food stores—the eighties incarnation of the health food store—started carrying meat, some customers were deeply offended, feeling that meat didn't belong in that setting. But it stayed.

As for vegetables, triple-washed bagged salad greens were not even on the horizon of the most vivid imagination. Rather, there were more solid vegetables and generally they were sad things to encounter. I still vividly recall bunches of beets in a health food store near the Zen Center that were so limp and sad your heart went out to them. They were also expensive. I wondered who would buy them. Vegetables would not entice a shopper until the new small-scale organic farmers and store owners figured out how to get produce right—not just how to grow it and sell it, but how to keep it cool, clean, firm, and fresh, too.

. . .

In addition to food, one could also find Indian incense, something tie-dyed, steamers, juicers, and Dr. Bronner's all-purpose peppermint soap with that label that lists, in the tiniest print possible, its multitude of uses. As for that wholesome food store–silage smell, it lingered but was nearly buried under a layer of patchouli and sandalwood.

We were, in the seventies, still a long way from today's gigantic "natural food" supermarket chains that feature aisles of organic cereals; huge meat, fish, and produce counters; rows of protein powders; vitamins and homeopathic remedies; shampoos; recycled paper goods; and organic pet food. There are organic versions of almost everything you can imagine from kale to toothpaste, and as much space given over to processed and prepared foods as in any supermarket. That silage–feed bin smell has disappeared completely, buried under a complex of scents emanating from the wood-burning pizza oven, the roasting chickens, the open cheese counters, the bakery, the takeout, the espresso and juice bars, the flower shop. Other smells are kept in check by packaging; tough plastics keep all odors, should there be any, locked in. But the produce, even without packaging, doesn't have that much smell, especially the fruit, which is scentless, picked when hard and green, and shipped from afar. Today shoppers don't know to bring a plum or a peach to the nose to assess its promise.

Except for some co-ops and the very occasional family-owned market where there's an owner who cares, the big stores like Whole Foods don't do as much as they claim to support their community's local farmers and food producers. The words are right, but it's not always clear that there's much follow-through. The old hippie health food stores might have been funky, but there was a sincerity that prevailed, and there was follow-through. Workers seemed to listen when you asked a question, then considered their answers. I miss that. Yet I also appreciate that in my small town I can find good olives and olive oil, a favorite American farmstead cheese and a good chunk of Parmigiano-Reggiano, along with more than decent wines. But because most of the produce is labeled "conventional," much of it is from far away, and organic is almost always "big organic," I go to my farmers' market for my vegetables when I can't harvest something from my garden, to my local bakery for the best bread in town if I'm not baking at home, and to my local co-op.

My repertoire of foodstuffs is narrower than in the past, especially my California past. But I don't mind. It's still excessive, especially compared to what native New Mexicans have known. When I'm asked questions about the sustainability of our foods, I often respond by saying it might be a good idea to stop thinking we should have everything all the time. Could we be happier with less, but still have more variety than we have had? It's hard with food, as it is in all realms, to find the middle path. When I first visited Santa Fe the farmers' market offered a few carrots, some uninteresting tomatoes, chile, posole, and chokecherry jam. Now the market teems with variety, much of it heirloom, and most of it good. Of course, supermarkets continue to have even more as they draw from all the seasons of the world.

MARRIAGE—A JALAPEÑO IN HIS POCKET

Another thing that happened in the 1970s was that I got married. I married another Zen student, Dan Welch, just a few

months before Greens opened in July 1979. Ours was a huge
Zen Center wedding. My sister made the cakes at the Tassajara
Bread Bakery and there were thirty-five of them, all in the shape
of hearts. Some were large, some were tiny, and there were many
in between. They floated over an enormous linen-cloaked table
and were themselves covered with raspberry-tinted whipped-
cream icing, which in turn was embroidered with scallops, dots,
and swirls of white frosting so that each heart appeared to be
draped in lace. They were gorgeous. We each broke off a piece
of our heart, awkwardly fed each other, then toasted our mob of
friends with imaginary champagne glasses because somehow we
were overlooked when the glasses were passed around and the
bubbles were poured.

Before we married, Dan and I enjoyed cooking together,
mostly at the home and woodsy camp of Nancy Wilson Ross,
whom you'll meet in the next chapter. We had had a few wor-
thy cooking adventures as well. Our Zen Center palates had
already been teased into a rough awakening through an invitation to come eat dinner at Chez Panisse. It was the goat cheese
that did it at that dinner. Its simultaneous creaminess and tang
made Dan's eyes open wide and forced his eyebrows to shoot
up. *What was that?* I could practically see his taste buds waking
up, stretching, then doing a little dance. I'm not sure, but that
first taste of goat cheese might have been what got Dan interested in eating and cooking.

After the goat cheese discovery, there was Gorgonzola,
another "What was that?" kind of taste. But it was cilantro that
really launched Dan into the heady atmosphere of big funky flavors. When we went to see *One from the Heart* during its brief
showing in San Francisco, we came away so buoyed by the film

that we wanted to celebrate it. Toast it. Being Zen students, we had no money, but we did have a key to Greens and we let ourselves in. In the dark kitchen we made ourselves sandwiches, layers of bread stuffed with cilantro, Gorgonzola, and goat cheese. We ate them seated at a table with a view of the Golden Gate Bridge and we toasted the movie. Why not put all your favorite flavors in one bite? And take the best seat in the house? That was Dan's approach that night.

Dan's first job as a cook in his own right was at Green Gulch, where he was the tenzo, or head cook. Students loved his food at first, but they ended up complaining after a few months, saying that it was *too* good and could he please tone it down?

About that time there was a big scandal with our abbot. We couldn't stay and go through the community soul-searching, so we left Green Gulch and Zen Center and cooked at Chez Panisse, where I made desserts and Dan made pizzas with great flare and lots of chile, at least for the staff. Next we both cooked in Rome, where we spent a year at the American Academy making special meals for the director and various academy events. That year was followed, for Dan, by a stint as a mobile Santa Fe pizza man who drove his pizza oven around in the back of his red pickup truck and made extravagant pizzas for people under the moniker Spaghetti Western, a homage to *Once Upon a Time in the West* and other films of that genre. Returning to his Zen practice, he became the head cook at Crestone Mountain Zen Center in Colorado, where he was also the assistant abbot and ofttimes a great many other things. Today Dan is enjoying a lay life in Santa Fe, where he can cook all the things he's dreamed of cooking and eating and then some. Pork has loomed large in these dreams but he also crafts sublime pizzas and has generally broadened his repertoire to take on a great many other foods.

Before he had his own kitchen, Dan cooked in mine, plunging in with no second thoughts about using up my best ingredients, not to mention dusting my kitchen stove, counters, and floor with salt, flour, and olive oil. Nothing ever came out of a jar, except some very good anchovies and my brother's olive oil. Everything began fresh and ended up big, gorgeous, and dramatic. Dan tasted everything as he cooked, slurping up big fingerfuls to make sure there was enough salt or another crucial ingredient. He held up his stained napkin after a meal and asked, each time, with an earnestly raised eyebrow, "Who had the most fun?" He has built a pizza oven during the day and cooked pizza in it that night. And he keeps a log of all the meals he's served to his friends.

After so many years—forty or so?—Dan is still so unbelievably enthusiastic about food that it makes me tired just to watch him cook. And now that he's cut his monastic ties, he has become even more excited, expanding his repertoire on a daily basis. Now we're likely to enjoy a *donabe* as well as a pizza, or a slow-braised pork shoulder cooked on the hottest day of the year, followed by a cake from *The New York Times* that he is trying to perfect. Essentially, Dan is over-the-top in the kitchen. He is enthusiastic, always energetic, and constantly paying attention to details to the point of obsessing over the tiniest ones. When he cooks, he goes for the greatest amount of color and drama possible. How do you tone that down? You don't.

Over the tenuous time of our breakup, now decades ago, our food tastes diverged. We were both committed to quality and doing things right, but there our similarities ended. I was drawn to Mediterranean flavors and American dishes, while Dan was increasingly ramping up the flavors and heat with chiles, garlic, tapenade, cilantro, robust blue cheeses, bacon, and anchovies. When we were living in different states, but still visiting each other in the hope of finding common ground in our fractured lives, our ability to nourish each other lessened with each visit. When Dan arrived at my house in Berkeley and I'd serve, say, an almond soup with chervil for starters, he would take a sip, then say something like "Ummm, Deb, your food is so delicate, so subtle." There would be a pause, then the question I learned to expect: "Do you mind if I put some chile in it?"

He'd get up and dice a jalapeño, which he just happened to have in his pocket, then doctor things up to his liking. It was hard not to take it personally. When I went to visit him in Santa Fe, he too cooked a good meal, only it was so hot I could do little more than sputter and cough. Since I was a chile wimp, that didn't work, either.

Eventually, when we could no longer feed each other and neither our lives nor our kitchens were mutually nourishing, the marriage ended. But the friendship continued—it was just too old to give up. After all, we first met when I was in high school and he was working for my dad after his return from Japan, and later at the Zen Center. Today we eat together frequently and feel free to add chiles or scrape them off. Or we just happily eat what's served, or we might teasingly complain about the other's cooking, with no hard feelings.

14. Three Diversions Before Greens

Before opening Greens or even knowing about the possibility, there were three side trips: the time I spent with the writer Nancy Wilson Ross, the all-important years with Alice Waters and Lindsey Shere at Chez Panisse, and my first trip to France. Each of these interludes took me away from Zen Center and each of them introduced me to new foods and ways of experiencing the table. Ultimately, their influence came with me to Greens.

NWR

Those were her initials and how we often referred to her. Otherwise she was known as Nancy, or Nancy Wilson Ross, an author of novels and some of the first books on Buddhism, most notably *Three Ways of Asian Wisdom*. Her husband, the playwright and publisher Stanley Young, had died recently, and the abbot of Zen Center, who was a friend of Nancy's, had been sending students to help her with the cares that come with a big house, car, travel, and so forth, cares that she had never had to be involved with. She lived in Old Westbury on Long Island, and in 1975 I was sent there to be her "slave," as she liked to call us skinny, awkward people from San Francisco. I was thrilled to be her slave. It wasn't that I was unhappy at Zen Center, but I was longing for a more worldly life, one that promised the inclusion of books, trips to Manhattan, even a longer journey to Europe.

Strong, self-assured, and somewhat intimidating, Nancy was also smart and sophisticated in that East Coast way. Of course she had her own ways of doing things, her house rules as it were, which were sometimes quixotic and hard to decipher. I was in trouble when a mouse made a nest and had her babies in the vacuum cleaner. Somehow it was my fault and Nancy was furious because the karma of killing those baby mice would fall on her shoulders. At the same time she was a very loving person and generous with big hugs and words of encouragement. I actually felt her love and support even when she got cross at me for not knowing how to do things like hail a cab or keep that mouse from having her babies in the lint of the vacuum cleaner.

When I brought coffee to her each morning, where she sat propped up in a large bed that was strewn with books and papers—"my other office" as she called it—Nancy often would say something like "I've been really wrestling with how to treat so-and-so." It could be a shoddy mechanic, a publisher, a friend—anyone she was feeling a lack of compassion for, someone for whom there was a little friction or a larger anger that she wanted to turn around. She took the Buddhist meditation of loving-kindness very seriously. It was her practice, her focus.

We sat zazen every afternoon. I was there to support this practice, as was another student who arrived shortly after I did, Dan Welch, the same Dan whom I eventually married. We met at the end of the day in her sitting room and sat not on zafus, the plump round cushions of the zendo, but in big, comfy wingback chairs. At least ten minutes passed before I heard Nancy clear her throat and say in her gravelly voice, "Make me a Manhattan, would you, dear?"

That request was not unlike the bell ringing in the zendo at the end of a zazen session. I stretched my legs, stood, then brought in the cocktail tray from the dining room, readied with the ice bucket, glasses, bitters, whiskey, vermouth, and canapés. This was my—and Dan's—first experience with a cocktail hour, and while it wasn't exactly assuming the cross-legged posture, it was a calming period. The main problem with this form of meditation was following those Manhattans with a trip to the kitchen to make dinner, followed by another trip to tidy up. Trying to get by drinking club soda and bitters, or tonic water without the gin come summer, wasn't acceptable.

"You kids are going through an awful lot of tonic water," Nancy grumbled when we switched to gin and tonics.

Nancy's food tastes were very much those of the 1950s. Sometimes she pulled out a recipe card from her file and gave it to me to figure out, or she showed me how to make a favorite dish. One was a butter that was seasoned with garlic, anchovies, and mustard, which one spread over toast followed by a little cheese. Actually this butter was good on, over, or in just about everything savory. She was fond of slices of ham wrapped around asparagus, floury cream-based chicken soups and chowders, linguine with clams, roast chicken with paprika, and sole wrapped around a filling of creamed spinach then cooked in clarified butter until golden. Spinach soufflés and hearts of palm salads with canned baby shrimp were also on her list of favorites. I relied a lot on James Beard for guidance and found that cooking these retro dishes was like learning a new language. Except for the soufflé, Nancy made no requests for vegetarian meals.

There was a camp in the Adirondacks that Nancy talked about frequently. We would be there from May until September and we would have to row a boat across the end of the lake to get to her place. That was all we knew. Dan and I, who were both from Northern California and knew about camping in the Sierras, were sent out to buy such things as a new record player, cases of wine, and other supplies that neither of us associated in the least with camping and backpacking. We thought that maybe her tent was on a platform and therefore more houselike, but somehow camping in any form didn't seem at all Nancy's style. We were mystified.

When we finally did arrive at the lake, there was the flat-bottomed boat as described; we loaded it, then rowed across the lake to the camp, then returned for a second load. The "camp"—which we were now beginning to get—consisted of a handsome large building hidden among the trees with several guest cottages connected by mossy paths. All around there were green woods. The main house had a stone fireplace almost big enough to walk inside. There was a tin-lined cedar closet for the blankets and, best of all, there were two elegant guide boats set up on the dock waiting for us to use them. The camp finally made sense of all those L.L. Bean catalog covers I'd seen for years, even though they referred to Maine and not upstate New York, canoes and not guide boats.

The shore of the lake was lined with camps, but they were invisible from the water so you felt as if you were alone in your guide boat. No motorboats were allowed, which meant there were loons. The first time Dan and I heard a loon it was just before dawn and we were swimming in the dark waters of the lake. When the bird cried we were sure that someone was being murdered in a nearby camp. (They weren't.) Soon we became accustomed to the loons' manic screams and looked forward to hearing them.

During our months at the lake Nancy wrote; I helped her with office details, massaged her stiff shoulders, and cooked. Dan worked outside doing manly things, and at the end of the day we all worked in the woods together, clearing dead trees and shaping the forest into a rock and moss garden. Come evening we had cocktails, a slow dinner in front of the fire, and hours of conversation.

It was not a happy period in Nancy's life. She missed her husband, and her daily reading of *The New York Times* told her of friends who had passed. Nonetheless, each night she dressed up in a cotton Chinese shirt and pants outfit, wrapped a cloth around her head to fashion a turban, put on bright pink lipstick and some dazzling jewelry, and came downstairs for cocktails and dinner. She did not allow herself to succumb to gloom and depression, at least in front of us. When a depressed student showed up for a visit, she told him firmly to go upstairs and take off his lead suit. One had to make the effort.

Food at the lake was much like it was on Long Island except that it now included potatoes and squash (from the gardens of town residents who were willing to sell us their vegetables) and Nancy's "barbecued" chicken. She made this dish with the help of a magical pot called a Swedish steamer. This was a great pot; someone could make a fortune developing one like it today. It looked like a short angel food cake pan from the outside, but under its lid were five metal wells that fit into a rack. You put your chicken pieces into the wells, put water in the bottom, then added the top and steamed the chicken until it was done. The steam dropped onto the meat and created a thick gelatin in the cups, which I later used to make one of Nancy's floury-creamy chicken curry soups. The cooked chicken was covered with the barbecue sauce, then grilled. You never ended up with raw chicken, and it was utterly good.

The sauce was a secret, as are all barbecue sauces, but it started with something in a jar to which Nancy added her own touch. She didn't share her tricks. This was the summer dish for all occasions—Saturday night, company, starbursts, birthdays, Tuesdays—it was good all the time. We served it with the vegetables that Dan and I found in town. There wasn't a lot of variety but when those good New York State apples arrived later in the summer we frequently turned them into crisps and Betties.

Garlic was impossible, though. It was still sold in little boxes with cellophane windows exposing the two small heads that were invariably too old to use. One could not imagine then that a trip to any farmers' market in the country would offer count-less varieties of garlic with fresh, hard cloves. No wonder cans of garlic powder were preferred then. Nancy's stove was lined with them.

As engrossing as life at Nancy's camp was there came a point in the summer when we had all grown restive with our routines. To sweeten our collective darkening mood, Nancy decided that we'd take a drive, so we set off for a small town where we spent a few hours picking around antiques stores, admiring old barns, and having lunch. We had just turned back toward the lake when we passed a table on the side of the road. A sign on the table read: STRAWBERRIES.

"Stop!" Might this be something special? The table stood under a grove of white pines, which provided shade for the berries. Some of the pines' long green needles had fallen over the fruit. There was a jar for money. I tasted a berry. It was uncommonly good. I tasted another and it too was good. I put five dollars in the jar and returned to the car with two quarts of strawberries.

These strawberries were little and dark red throughout, nothing at all like the giant white-centered and even hollow strawberries we were used to seeing from California. They didn't have that familiar pointed shape but were round and a bit lumpy. It was warm in the car and after a while a sweet scent started to rise off the berries, gradually filling the car with an immense perfume. I started thinking about what I might do with the berries and after considering this and that dessert, I would decide to make a strawberry tart with pastry cream. Then I'd get another waft of that perfume, fall back into the seat, inhale, and think, No, maybe a sorbet. Or strawberry ice cream. The scent became increasingly intoxicating as we drove onward until all at once it occurred to me that I was, just maybe, finally having a "gourmet" experience! This was definitely a big experience in the realm of the senses, one that surpassed any notion I had ever had of a strawberry. Surely this must be what people like Caroline Bates were experiencing and sharing with the readers of *Gourmet*.

It was too late to make a tart that night so we just sliced some berries, sprinkled a tiny bit of brown sugar over them, and poured on some cream. None of us had ever tasted strawberries like these. They were more like a tropical fruit than what we think of as strawberries. There were still enough left to make a tart the next night and while it too was extraordinary, the crust and the pastry cream actually detracted from the purity of the fruit. In the end, it was really enough just to put one berry at a time on my tongue, bite off the stem with my teeth, and slowly crush the fruit in my mouth.

Years later a young man from Portland, Oregon, sent me a note. "It's strawberry season here and our very special Hood variety are the sweetest, softest berries, and red all the way through. Squishing a soft berry in the mouth is like eating the best strawberry jam you've ever tasted. They are so soft that there is no way to ship them to other parts of the country. A great reason to visit Portland in the late spring sometime!"

And I have, during the season of the Mount Hood strawberries, and they are delicious in the same way those New York berries were.

. . .

Since that ride, I've had other car-filling perfume experiences, like riding around Italy with a white truffle tucked safely in the back seat, or driving in the heat of a southwest summer with a cargo of quinces, a ristra of chiles, and a branch of *tridentata* sage—all filling my car with a flurry of scents that inspired not only pure pleasure but recipes. Today I stop when I see that big silvery sage covering a plain and break off a piece. It's an *Artemesia,* not a *Salvia,* so it's too bitter to cook with. Rather, it's tied into sage bundles that are lit and then used to purify a place with fragrant smoke. It can do the same for your spirit simply sitting on the dashboard, absorbing heat and imbuing the air with miracles of sweet fragrance.

While Nancy's camp didn't involve camping as Dan and I knew it, like Tassajara, it was something *like* camping and food still tasted best whether eaten by a rushing stream or by a fire while looking out at a silent lake. As Labor Day approached, people started leaving their camps and the weather turned nippy. The woods grew more hushed and we saw the leaves on the trees turn color, then break off and glide, dipping from side to side, to the forest floor. Mist now rose off the lake in the morning and it was too cold to swim. Nature seemed to be gathering herself for winter, and we did as well. We hauled in the boats, put the woolen blankets in the cedar closet, and had a last barbecued chicken dinner with a special bottle of wine before packing up the boat, rowing across the lake, and turning to say goodbye.

ALICE, LINDSEY, AND CHEZ PANISSE

Green Gulch was a long property in Marin County that ended at Muir Beach. When I was a child, I remembered passing it on our way to Stinson Beach to escape the valley heat, but in 1972 it was acquired as another place for students in the growing Zen Center community to practice. Today its farm supplies many Bay Area homes and restaurants with beautiful produce sold at the Ferry Plaza market.

Soon after I returned from Nancy's, the same abbot of Zen Center who had sent me to live in New York invited Alice Waters and Lindsey Shere of Chez Panisse fame to take a tour of Green Gulch. Knowing that I was interested in food and cooking, he generously asked me to show them around. I really had no idea who they were, and unlike the abbot, who had eaten at their restaurant many times, I had never been to Chez Panisse, though I think I had heard the name. Maybe.

As we walked down the fields I noticed Alice's eyes traveling to the rows of lettuce. Deer Tongue. Marvel of Four Seasons. Tender butterheads. She wanted lettuces like these for her restaurant. She asked a lot of questions about the farm and what else we grew—herbs? Fingerling potatoes? Golden beets? Greens? A cow lowed, and she asked about cream. Lindsey was quieter. As a pastry chef, she would be more interested in fruit or nuts, neither of which we had. It was too foggy and cold. After a while I started asking them questions. Had they ever heard of Richard Olney? (He had just been at the restaurant that past week.) Did Lindsey make tarte tatin? (Indeed!) What about Elizabeth

David? (Yes, they knew her, too, and had, in fact, just seen her.) After a few more questions in this vein, Alice turned to me and asked, "Have you never been to the restaurant?" That, it seemed, would explain a great deal. But on a fifty-dollar-a-month stipend and with no car, I hadn't been to Chez Panisse.

"You must come!" she gushed. "Come tomorrow and bring friends!"

During our stroll Alice had made Chez Panisse sound like a funky, modest little place with picnic tables for furniture. At least that's how I imagined it, so when three of us arrived the next night in a borrowed car and pushed back the plush velvet curtain we were astonished at how beautiful the dining room was, the tables with their thick linens and little French lamps, the enormous bouquet of flowers, even printed matchbooks. Suddenly we were a bit unsure of ourselves, our strange clothes, our lack of experience, but we were welcomed warmly and put at our ease. Immediately we ate two baskets of bread and the extra butter the waiter brought us. It was just so good!

Dinner unfolded. I still recall a ragout of green-lipped mussels and other shellfish in a saffron and tomato broth, a plate of tender lamb with a creamy turnip gratin, a salad of very tiny lettuce leaves, our first taste of goat cheese, and an array of desserts, especially Lindsey's raspberry tart. The waiter kept bringing us desserts and we kept eating them, picking up every last crumb with our fingers until we had to stop. When we finally left, I experienced heartburn for the first (and only) time in my life. The food had been so astounding, so good, so beautiful, and, of course, it was nothing at all like Zen Center food. It was as if I were on another planet and I realized finally that this was the food I'd always wanted to eat and that it was right here, in the Bay Area, just across the Bay Bridge from the Zen Center, in Berkeley.

When we got back to San Francisco I noticed the abbot's light was still on and although students didn't normally do things like this—say what they wanted to do—I knocked on his door and announced that I had to work at Chez Panisse. Amazingly, he agreed. I suspect now that he was thinking about Zen Center opening a restaurant and having me involved in the kitchen somehow. In any case, Alice had invited me to work there and I started the next day.

The F bus to Berkeley stopped practically in front of Chez Panisse. I picked my way to the back door through hoses and cartons and cases of produce and started my day around nine, after zazen, service, breakfast, and the commute. It was a busy time at the restaurant. Deliveries were being wheeled to the back door and checked in. Grates and knobs were plucked from the stoves and run through the dishwasher. Stripped of their thick white tablecloths and little French lamps, the dining room tables looked dowdy, and the floor was littered with petals and branches as Carrie Wright arranged the flowers. These were the restaurant activities that customers don't see and shouldn't have to think about. The atmosphere was hopelessly chaotic for most of the morning and it never ceased to amaze me that somehow everything was tidied up and resolved by the time the first customers arrived and were led into a spotless, welcoming room that looked as if it had been waiting for them forever. Even today when being led to a table in a restaurant, I often feel as if this very table has been waiting for just our party and for no one else's. Yet as we get our coats and glance back before leaving, we see that what was *our* table has already been reset and is once again looking virginal and expectant as another party takes our place. But this is the magic of restaurants: to make every diner feel as if she has walked onto her own stage, which has been waiting just for her.

There was no set menu to work from for lunch, and Alice would show up and start going through the walk-in to figure out what to cook. A few days after I began working there, Judy Rodgers graduated from Stanford and came to work, setting Alice free. I worked with Lindsey in pastry and as she sketched out her day, I collected butter, chocolate, nuts, eggs, and tart pans. In the midst of the planning and organizing bustle, a moment would arrive when Kathleen Stewart glided into the kitchen with her cheerful good morning, a tray of café lattes, a warm baguette that had just arrived from the baker, and ramekins of butter and jam. I assumed that all restaurants had a Kathleen who happily brought trays of coffee and warm bread to the kitchen. This was something I would incorporate in the Greens kitchen.

I worked with Lindsey through lunch, then took a break and walked around North Berkeley for an hour before returning for the dinner shift. My place was on the end of the line, where I peeled onions and garlic, chopped parsley, and watched everything. I usually stood next to Mark Miller, who always had a lot of interesting things to say about anything, really. During service I put together appetizers and salads, the two courses I've always liked the most, then switched to desserts as those orders came in. Today the dessert people don't make salads or first courses—just desserts.

Lunches rolled along rather smoothly, but dinners were another matter. Nearly always chaotic, they were of course adventures. Alice frequently had to figure out how to make something she had never made before, and there were times that it didn't quite work as she had hoped and some grappling was needed to pull it off. On other occasions—many in fact—a special ingredient was too hard to find or to count on, so the words "if available" appeared quite often on the weekly menus to prepare the customers for possible disappointment. Or the ingredient showed up, but there wasn't enough of it for both sittings. Or Alice generously gave extra portions of something special to special customers during the first half, leaving the kitchen short for the second half. The half-hour break between sittings was a time to recoup losses and make menu changes. All the while music was playing—opera and Clifton Chenier's "Black Snake Blues" were favorites then—and everyone was working hard. It was fast and intense and utterly different from the Zen Center kitchens, where people worked in silence as they tried to be mindful of what they were doing, taking mindfulness to an absurd point of slowness. Here conversation, music, and enjoyment didn't get in the way of concentration and attention to detail. It was hard work that was also focused, fast, and fun.

This was the era that Alice's first book covered. It was a time when people were showing up at the back door with a bag of sorrel, a basket of *fraises de bois,* a cardboard box of wild mushrooms, some quinces. It was a time for celebrating people, their milestones and other events, with special meals and Patricia Curtan's beautifully designed letterpress menus. M. F. K. Fisher's seventieth birthday was celebrated while I was there, each course named for one of her books. One night Mikhail

Baryshnikov leapt up the stairs and I was sent out to find vodka, "the highest proof possible," I was told. Writers came over after giving a reading at Black Oak Books up the street. There were always interesting, exciting, and often famous people in the dining room. In fact Alice and the restaurant knew so many of the customers that dinner felt like a big extended dinner party rather than a meal in a restaurant.

And there were the foods themselves, the foods that had provenance at that time: Amador County lamb, Garrapata trout, Joseph Phelps's Zinfandel, Laura Chenel's goat cheese, fresh garlic, and this delicious Provençal olive oil. There was also the odd smell of mesquite charcoal catching fire. A continuous parade of tastes, smells, and flavors marched through the kitchen, all of them new to me and all of them extraordinary. Deutz and Billecart-Salmon champagnes were opened for the kitchen at the end of the night. Sometimes customers sent a glass of some exquisite Burgundy or old Bordeaux back to the kitchen to sip. There was always wine to taste. Recalling all those swirls and sips I wish I could do it over again now that I have a better grasp of wine. I'd love to know what it was exactly that I got to taste. I do know that it was nothing like the wines I grew up drinking at home, and of course there was no wine at Zen Center.

I worked with Lindsey for quite a few months making countless tart shells, trying to get that almond tart utterly smooth on top, turning out her divine chocolate cake along with crème anglaise, ice creams, sorbets, compotes, bombes for birthdays, and other Chez Panisse desserts, including the tarte tatin I had asked her about when we walked through the fields at Green Gulch. At first I was so nervous that I could be looking right at a flat of eggs and not see them when she asked me to pick them up and do something with them. It was as if I had holes in my eyes. It was nerves. But Lindsey was so patient and kind that eventually I regained my vision and learned enough to be able to take her place while she and her husband, Charles, went to Europe for six weeks. I loved the seemingly simple but often exotic, aromatic desserts that typified Lindsey's style. I always think of her as a most subtle and exquisite cook, and to be able to work with her and learn from her was one of the big blessings in my life.

That first year at Chez Panisse was a heady, dazzling experience for someone who had come to it straight from the Zen Center's vegetarian trenches. Since all I had in the way of experience were the minor skills I had accumulated on my own, I couldn't make nearly the contribution to the kitchen that the kitchen made to me. I still carry a debt of gratitude to Chez Panisse, especially to Lindsey and Chef Jean-Pierre Moullé for their patience and the kind acceptance given to a rank beginner.

Despite her many talents, it was Alice's spirit of generosity that touched me most deeply at the time. Not just that she was generous in making a place for me at Chez Panisse and seeing that I tasted everything—and got paid—but that she embodied a spirit of plenty, that there was always enough. It was the opposite of what I had grown up with, that sense of insufficiency, that there was never enough. At Chez Panisse there was never holding back. If something ran out, there was something better to take its place. There was always room for another party in the dining room, another diner at the table. Probably the hardest lesson for me was to see the world as full. Alice was the perfect person for me to meet at that time, for she saw abundance in the world, had an outpouring of confidence, gave gifts of beauty, including the possibilities we needed to imagine rearranging the world so that everyone could enjoy its plenty.

How did I go from Chez Panisse back to Zen Center each day? I don't recall a difficulty. I was still a Zen student and still sitting every morning. And I was young and had a lot of energy. It's just that I had this job across the bay. And as for my family, my parents once came to the restaurant for a Valentine's Day dinner. I had a gift certificate I could use for them so they didn't have to worry about the cost. They were very stiff and uncomfortable. But my sister, Jamie, ended up working as a waitress at Chez Panisse for a few years, and we both always eat there when we're in Berkeley together.

A TRIP TO FRANCE

After a year at Chez Panisse had passed it was summer again and Alice and others from the restaurant were planning a trip to France in October. Alice invited me to meet her there, and it was finally time for me to see France for myself. I sold my tea ceremony equipment so I could buy a ticket and one day, quite terrified, I boarded a Freddie Laker flight to London. There I met up with Peter Overton and his wife, Susan. Peter was the large, affable head baker of the Tassajara Bread Bakery and we had coordinated our trips partially with the purpose of sampling pastry and maybe getting ideas for the bakery. We took the boat to Calais, then the train to Paris. Of course it was unbelievably thrilling to be in Paris. I was there, it was Paris, and it was simply the most beautiful city I had ever seen.

We checked into our hotel, changed, then left to find dinner.

A little café not too far away looked friendly and attractive, and we went in. The menu didn't read quite like I had expected a French menu to read, but then, it was our first meal. When our dinner arrived I was surprised to find that it actually resembled the food I had cooked at Zen Center. There was some sort of vegetable quiche with a thick crust, a trustworthy vegetable soup, a ponderous dessert, but a very good salad. I was simultaneously relieved, disappointed, and confused. Shouldn't it have been a lot better than this, in spite of the fact this food tasted wholesome? All made sense when we discovered that we had wandered into a macrobiotic restaurant, "the only one in Paris," the waiter proudly told us. Counterculture food in France, it turned out, was pretty much like it was at home: healthy but clumsy. Except for our learning this, that meal seemed like a wasted opportunity.

Peter and I were interested in bakeries, while Susan was interested in textiles, so we went our separate ways during the day. Essentially Peter and I crisscrossed the streets of Paris to sample a tart in this bakery, an éclair in another. This was research and it was a dessert eater's dream. Crêpe stands offered the relief of savory tastes when the sweet ones got overwhelming. Then it was back to the bakeries.

Among the many pastries we sampled, there was one that stood out above all others, and that was the apple tart at Poilâne on Rue Cherche-Midi. We had been told about it beforehand so we were looking forward to trying it, but when we saw the tart, it looked very unpromising and every bit as unglamorous as our first dinner had been. It didn't seem to be much more than a piece of brown pastry with some shriveled-looking apples on it. No cream, no caramel, not even powdered sugar. It was extremely plain.

Not feeling too optimistic, we bought a medium-size one and took it to a nearby park, set it on a bench, untied the string, and unfolded the paper. We each broke off a piece and took a bite, then we looked at each other. Was this not the very best thing either of us had ever eaten? We ate in silence and when it was gone, we searched around the papers, our clothing, and even the bench, picking up every flake of shattered pastry with moistened fingertips until there was not a shard left. I was sure that if Peter could master nothing other than this one tart, he could do away with the lemon bars, poppy seed cakes, brownies, and all the other now common sweets back at the bakery.

It was probably too early for such a radical offering, one whose goodness was based entirely on the quality of the apples, the flour, butter, the flaky layers of pastry, and their smoldering stay in a wood-fired oven. But today it is possible. I think of Kathleen Weber, a baker in Petaluma, California, who also baked in a wood-fired hearth oven. She and her crew at Della Fattoria produced some memorable breads and pastries. She baked an awesome loaf seasoned with rough salt, Meyer lemon, and rosemary that grew just feet from the ovens. Among her own exquisite pastries were a small polenta cake and a wicked peanut butter cookie—two cookies, actually, the classic design molded not by forks but by fingers, the halves fused with an ethereal peanut butter cream. As with Poilâne's apple tart, my fingers searched for every stray crumb before calling it quits on one of Kathleen's breads, cookies, or polenta cake. And she could have made such an apple tart if she wanted to.

After we finished the tart, Peter and I went right back to Poilâne's for another, and this time we met with Lionel, the owner and baker, and his father, then a very old man. We sat with him under a chandelier made out of bread dough and looked through his vast collection of postcards from admirers and fans. Then Lionel showed us the oven, the little shriveled apples from his family's land with which the tart was made, and a handful of flour, which was not as white as ours. Lionel encouraged Peter in his baking, then we watched the balletic movements of the bakers maneuvering their long bread-laden peels around one another in and out of the fire.

In the evenings we three met up and walked around looking at the city. On one of these walks we were in the vicinity of the Sorbonne and I figured that one of the university buildings had a restroom. I went off to find it. As I entered the stall I saw a hundred-franc note floating in the toilet. The rate of the franc against the dollar at that time only added to my amazement at seeing one hundred francs. I wondered if this could be a part of a French version of *Candid Camera,* but decided that it wasn't. I picked the bill out of the toilet, washed it off, and blotted it dry. Was there someone around, who might have dropped it? There was no one. Outside, I showed it to Peter and Susan and suggested that we use it for a nonmacrobiotic dinner.

This idea coincided nicely with our visit to Chartres. The cathedral was immediately recognizable, but I hadn't expected to see it soaring in the distance above wheat fields, the way a grain elevator rises above the American prairies. After hours of touring the cathedral in the chilly autumn air we found a tiny restaurant with lace curtains on the windows and a fireplace with a small fire burning. We ate pork cooked with prunes, one of those dishes I knew from my French cookbooks and therefore had to try, a chicory salad, and for dessert goat cheese with a slice of walnut bread. The cheese was placed in a small copper pot and set beside the fire to warm. Once the waiter brought it to our table, we spread the warm cheese over the thin pieces of bread and washed it down with the last of our wine. It was a thoroughly enjoyable meal, made even better by the knowledge that it was a gift of found money. But when we went to pay, the money was gone. We looked everywhere; no one had it. It had disappeared as mysteriously as it had appeared.

After a few more pastry-intensive days in Paris, I left Peter and Susan and took the train to Marseilles, where I eventually found Alice, who was drinking a bowl of coffee in a café on the quay. There were a number of other people from Berkeley and we all went to Bandol to visit Lucien and Lulu Peyraud, bringing twelve bottles of California Zinfandel.

Bandol Tempier and Lulu Peyraud are well known today. The house has been photographed for books and magazines; the wines are now available well outside of Provence and Berkeley. The family, especially Lulu, has been immortalized in Richard Olney's book *Lulu's Provençal Table*. But in 1978, Bandol Tempier was more Alice and Kermit's discovery.

At a bakery we bought enormous fougasses that looked like giant ladders. Alice cooked dinner outdoors and we feasted at a long table under the grape arbor. I have a picture of that party. Richard Olney was there, as was Nathalie Waag, who lived in

Provence but who sometimes came to Berkeley and cooked at Chez Panisse. Later her sons did the same. The Peyraud family occupied quite a few seats. Therese Shere, one of Lindsey and Charles's daughters, was there, and there were others. We drank all those bottles of Zinfandel, then after dinner, Lucien took us into the caves and we sampled every wine back to 1961. Before we went to bed, Lulu offered everyone a bowl of garlic and herb soup to drink. Nathalie and I accepted the offer, then fell into our shared bed. The next morning we awoke feeling fresh and fine, but those who had passed on the soup were not so buoyant. I've been a big believer in *aïgo bouido* ever since, not only for hangovers but also for colds and fluish feelings. This thin broth of garlic, sage, thyme, and water is a powerful drink. It's one we served often at Greens in the winter, with the addition of pillows of dumplings or potatoes.

After a few days with Alice and friends, Therese and I took the train to Lyon to eat at Troisgros, the three-star restaurant that everyone was talking about then. Of course it was stunning food, the kind of food that's meant to awe, and I was duly impressed by it all, especially by a plate of venison with a sauce made from wild bilberries. It was a woodsy dish that had its own intrinsic logic; it tasted as if the deer had been eating the same berries that we were, and the whole dish was the flavor of the forest. Since then, I've had a similar feeling when eating bison that was raised by my friend Hugh Fitzsimons in south Texas. A bite of this noble animal and you feel that you are eating the land and sky, grass and flowers of that southwestern rangeland. It is one of the most deeply nourishing foods I've ever encountered.

After that meal I worked my way up to Normandy, sampling regional foods along the way, a hugely gratifying experience, as it always is when one finally eats the dishes one has only read about—and in their place. Even today I am surprised, no matter how good a version of Greek food I've had in the States, or how delicious a Moroccan tagine might be when cooked from an authentic recipe, that food is always different when you encounter it on its own turf. Everything is—the size of the portion, how it's served, where it comes in a meal, the smells of the place, the weather, whether it's meant to be shared or not, if it was delivered on a bicycle or served in a luxurious restaurant. Then of course there are the ingredients themselves. The taste of food in situ is always different from our interpretations.

I ended my trip with lunch of fish, fennel, and truffles in Paris at Ledoyen, a gift from Chez Panisse, then flew to London to meet up with Peter and Susan. There were problems at the airport and planes were delayed for hours. We learned that our mayor, Harvey Milk, had just been murdered by a man who blamed this horrid behavior on Twinkies. We were sad, out of money, and hungry. None of us had a credit card. We started digging through pockets to see what we could put together and one of us unearthed a bill that was neatly folded into a tiny square. It was the hundred-franc note we had intended for our meal at Chartres and we were very glad to see it. The coffee and airport sandwiches that it bought weren't exactly a French meal, but we were grateful for them. In fact, they tasted quite good. Hunger will do that.

15. Starting Greens

Ireturned from this first trip to France dazed, inspired, and laden with bottles of walnut oil for Alice. It was then that I learned about the plan for Zen Center to open a restaurant. I had heard some murmurings about this before, but that was all. Suddenly there was a possible venue and a restaurant might just be more than a vague idea. I also found out from the abbot that I would be the chef and I immediately became a bundle of nerves, a state that persisted for the next few years. Why would I be the chef? Probably because I was the one most interested in food at Zen Center. I had worked at Chez Panisse and I had been to France, with the abbot's blessing. Still, I did not feel at all qualified to do this.

San Francisco's Fort Mason had recently been turned over to the Golden Gate National Recreation Area (GGNRA), and this wartime waterfront collection of wharfs and warehouses would soon house more peaceful endeavors, such as art and theater groups.

Situated next to the marina, across from the Marina Green, in view of the Golden Gate Bridge and with acres of parking, Fort Mason was a rare property. Had it landed in private hands, it would surely have become the site of luxury apartments. Fortunately, the enormous old buildings were to remain, along with the name, and Fort Mason would come to take on a new life as one of the most animated places for theater, art, and big events in San Francisco. But then it was lacking an important element, a restaurant. And one was wanted and needed.

The challenge for restaurateurs who might have wanted to open a restaurant at Fort Mason was that they were not legitimate nonprofit organizations with a 501(c)(3). And even though many restaurants often don't make profits, they certainly hope to and when they don't that doesn't make them legitimate nonprofit organizations, only broke and out of business sooner than later. Zen Center, however, was a nonprofit organization and for years our summer visitors to Tassajara, many of whom were from the Bay Area, had been asking if we would open a restaurant in San Francisco. Zen Center's abbot certainly thought we could and he wasn't afraid to think big.

Building A, which would house Greens, ran along the westernmost edge of Fort Mason, faced the marina, and overlooked the water. The melodic twang of sailboat riggings sounded continually as the boats bobbed outside the glass wall of the building, and there was that perfect view of the Golden Gate Bridge, where the sun set each evening. Or there would be if the floor were raised a few feet. Clearly this would be the dining room.

The building had good possibilities, but the cavernous space, having housed enormous chunks of industrial machinery for the past forty years, reeked of old machine oil. A great deal of iron would have to be moved before a restaurant could be built, and that floor would have to be raised if people were to enjoy looking at the boats, the Marina Green, and the bridge while lingering over their meals. Carving a restaurant out of this old space was an enormous project for Zen Center. Not only did it take a lot of money, but it also took all the carpenters, builders, and other talented students away from whatever else they were doing in the community to convert this old warehouse to the sleek restaurant that would eventually be known as Greens.

The Marina Green was a cheerful place where people went to fly kites, sun themselves, throw Frisbees to their dogs and one another, skate, and take a break from whatever else they were doing. Given the proximity to the green, our vegetarian menu, and the name of our farm, Green Gulch, the name Greens seemed like a good one for our restaurant. It was nicely ambiguous, but if one were pressed, it could easily be explained because it made sense on a number of levels. The theme was clearly green.

The enormity of the job ahead cast a dark, anxious shadow over my life for the year leading up to the opening. This was hardly the little five-table restaurant I had imagined, hoped for, and could far more easily conceive. I was scared witless just trying to imagine what might lie ahead and trying to figure it all out in advance—a fruitless effort, in any case. I woke up most mornings feeling as if a mountain were sitting on my chest, one I had to somehow climb by the end of the day, then revisit the next. And we hadn't even opened yet.

My part in this endeavor was to design the menu and the kitchen, and then become the chef once we opened. Although I was scarcely trained to do this, even my limited experiences were greater than those of anyone else in the community. But I was very fortunate to have someone to work with who had a more practical sensibility and more experience than I, a student named Karin Gjording, who grew up in a restaurant family. She was enormously capable and had the nuts-and-bolts vision that I lacked. I never managed to cultivate Karin's perspective as my own, but I grew to appreciate it. Greens couldn't have happened without Karin as the manager.

Right away I started working on the menu. I tested recipes in the Page Street kitchen and served the results to whoever was around. "More cheese!" was the main response to my efforts. Once again, Zen students were seemingly addicted to cheese and this was the era of the more the better. Bring it on, they'd cry. But it turned out that our customers didn't want everything drowning in cheese. I worked to expand our offerings and to find a middle way between gobs of cheese and a little. Recently while reviewing recipes I made at Greens that I especially liked, I noticed cheese appeared where none was called for in the original recipe. I think that I, too, was nervous people would leave Greens feeling hungry if there wasn't at least some cheese, our main protein, in a dish then.

Since we were building out the restaurant, we didn't have to design a menu around existing stoves, counters, and other features, but we needed a menu in order to design the kitchen from scratch since the menu would drive its layout. Once I had a menu pretty much in place, the kitchen started to take shape. The lineup went like this: an old three-ring candy burner was installed because it would be useful for making huge pots of soup and boiling gallons of water for pasta. A mesquite grill—de rigueur at that time—would go next to that, then two Wolf six-tops with ovens, followed by a double stack of pizza ovens and a salamander, a narrow broiler for browning dishes. There was a cold area for salads and yards and yards of wooden counters. Vegetables took a lot of room, especially when you were breaking them down from their foliage-laden, right-off-the-farm state, so all those countertops were constantly in use and covered with produce at one stage or another, from raw to cooked.

Few American seed companies in 1979 offered seeds for the kinds of vegetables we commonly see now. Seed Savers Exchange, which played the most vital role in establishing heirloom vegetables and fruits in America by connecting people and their seeds with one another, had only just begun and was not yet as far reaching as it is today with its gorgeous catalog, organic seeds, classes, campouts, and website. Inspired by the produce I had seen on my trip to France, before leaving Paris I bought seeds from Vilmorin, a distinguished seed house, to take home. Wendy Johnson planted them and what she raised gave Greens its unique produce, frequently vegetables that had never before been seen or tasted either by our customers or by us. We had stunning varieties of lettuces, rows of sorrel, and a new green called roquette, or rocket, or arugula. Wendy grew out seven kinds of cucumbers and all kinds of new exotic potatoes, such as fingerlings, which hardly anyone knew about then. There were the first golden beets and the striped beets of Chioggia plus King Richard leeks with their tall white shanks and lengthy wands of blue-green leaves. Borage and other flowers tossed into salads weren't a tired conceit but a novel bit of flavor and colored surprise. Vegetables that were new to us filled our walk-in—slender green beans, purple-fleshed beans, wildly striped shelling beans that I cooked with pasta. And that was just the beans. In the fall there were stacks of gorgeous Cinderella pumpkins, or Rouge Vif d'Etampes, and that sweet little buttercup squash called Perfection, which made the best soups. People always asked if we put sugar in the soup, but we didn't. It was just made from that very sweet, roundly flavored squash. Among the herbs were lovage, marjoram, sorrel, and rosemary. When I drove to work, number 10 cans of herbs of all kinds filled the car with their perfume. The scent was dazzling. I planned my menu for the day by smell.

As with our cooking at Zen Center, much trial and error was involved in learning to farm. Our first carrots were stunted, twisted roots that managed to penetrate only a few inches into the hard clay soil. We grew corn, but the raccoons got it all the night before the farm crew intended to harvest it. Tomatoes utterly failed to ripen in the fog-soaked summer days of Muir Beach. Broccoli grew, but so did colonies of aphids, an alarming sight that made you forever nervous about eating broccoli that hadn't been heavily doused with chemicals, an even scarier proposition. The lettuce was gorgeous, but sometimes the deer got into the field and nibbled just the heart out of each head. (I've always found it amusing that there's a lettuce called Deer Tongue.) In addition to the deer, the rabbits and quail did their share of munching. Organic gardening seemed to be one big heartache. The exception was the Sweet 100, a variety of cherry-type tomato given to us by Alan Chadwick, which thrived even in the foggy clime of the farm. Those sweet little red spheres gave us hope.

Except for the stellar Sweet 100s, Green Gulch was too foggy to produce hot-weather crops for Greens when we finally opened. For those heftier tomatoes, peppers, eggplants, and summer squash my sous chef, Jim Phelan, and I drove up to Suisun Valley, near Fairfield, on Saturday mornings and spent a few hours at a u-pick farm, our knees digging into the scratchy soil while our hands got busy picking produce and loading it into boxes. The car loaded and bill settled, we drove back to the city, stopping at the Union Hotel in Benicia, where Judy Rodgers, having left Chez Panisse, was cooking her wonderful traditional American foods, like yeasted waffles and scrapple. After breakfast and during the rest of the drive, we got serious and planned the evening's menu based on what we had packed into the back of the car. Sweet perfumes rose up from all those vegetables and again, we were planning a menu by smell.

Eventually, we met Dorothy Coil, a farmer from Modesto, over the Coast Range and right in the Central Valley, who was willing to drive a pickup of hot-weather vegetables to Greens. She and her elderly mother pulled up to the restaurant around nine each Tuesday morning and again later in the week. We rolled back the tarp on their truck and there were the most beautiful zucchini, eggplants, tomatoes, peppers, all vegetable-fruits that loved the heat of the valley. We fed Dorothy and her mother a good breakfast for their efforts and the long drive back. With our Dorothy connection, our menu managed to stay fresh and mostly small-farm-driven nearly year-round.

At first some foods, especially fruits, had to come from the big San Francisco produce terminal, but over time it became increasingly possible to buy good fruit from small-scale organic farmers who grew enough to sell it at some of the smaller produce houses, like Greenleaf and Veritable Vegetable, both still in business today. I sometimes see the Veritable Vegetable truck delivering the best foods from the small organic farms in California to our local co-op to fill the gap created by our desert winters. I always feel the need to flash a peace sign when I see a VV truck. As for olive oil, Mr. Sciabica still delivered his five-gallon tins of Mission oil to us, and the tofu still came from Quong Hop. That's no longer the case as there is far more choice today. If you look at a menu from Greens online you'll see that there are more producers named for everything, from olive oil to tofu, grains, chiles, and cheese.

A few other people in the area were growing beautiful organic vegetables when Green Gulch began, like Warren Weber over at Star Route Farm in Bolinas. Chez Panisse now had its own salad garden in Berkeley, so we weren't the first or the only people growing vegetables. But at Greens hundreds of customers had their first encounter with the deep burgundy leaves of Marvel of Four Season lettuce, thin-sliced fans of those seven different cucumber varieties, piles of tiny green filet beans entwined with slivers of opal basil, those odd-shaped fingerling potatoes, and salads that sparkled with lavender chive flowers and bright blue borage blossoms. Chef Jeremiah Tower brought his students to lunch so that they could experience all these new vegetables.

It was a joy to be cooking with this food and a joy to be able to introduce so many people to the possibilities that unfamiliar varieties offered. I was madly in love with this produce. And except for some golden hills blocking the view, Green Gulch was pretty much right in the eye of our diners; we were literally eating from our landscape. Talk about local and seasonal eating—this was it. But those words weren't being spoken at that time. We didn't seem to need to put a name to what we were doing and I didn't do that myself for many years. Later "local and seasonal" formed the theme of my books, especially *Local Flavors* and *Seasonal Fruit Desserts: From Orchard, Farm, and Market*. But rereading *The Greens Cookbook*, I found no reference to eating local foods or foods in their season. It was just what we were doing. This was the food that tasted best and it was the food that made the most interesting dishes. Today, "local and seasonal" have been buzzwords long enough that, like that of "fresh," their true meaning has become imprecise and even tiresome. They are now common words. I liked to think of Greens as having had a farm-driven menu, rather than a local/seasonal menu, because that was what it was, and of course if the food was grown locally that always meant it was seasonal. But it wasn't all from our farm. It couldn't be. The foggy farm was new, too, and it didn't get the summer heat of the Central Valley. It was perfect for lettuce, greens, and herbs, but there were other nearby growers we could buy hot-weather produce from and we did.

16. Creating a Predictable World

The unknowns we dealt with each night at Chez Panisse—
the changing menu, dishes that had never been tried
before, the possibility that ingredients wouldn't be there—were
conditions I assumed existed in all restaurants. I didn't realize
that one could create a more predictable world where dishes
were always on the menu except for a few specials, the ingredients for them always available, and the know-how to make them
something you could count on. Having become comfortable
with the unpredictable adventures of the Chez Panisse kitchen,
which really were quite exciting, I assumed that I'd bring that
way of doing things to Greens. In addition, I had an inherent
dislike for restaurant equipment and time-saving machines. I
foresaw doing everything pretty much by hand, as we did in
the different Zen Center kitchens, a notion that Karin tried to
correct. I tended to view the kitchen as an extension of a home
kitchen, albeit a very large one, with everyone peeling garlic

and chopping parsley just as it was across the bay in Berkeley or over at the farm, or at Page Street. In the end we didn't buy a lot of kitchen gadgets—a Hobart mixer, a Robot-Coupe, and a blender were about it—but I did have to alter other parts of my vision.

Karin must have been driven up the wall by my refusal to comprehend what would be entailed in serving what we guessed would be at least a hundred lunches a day. Actually the average quickly became 250 and a few times we served 300-plus lunches. Karin knew that rolling racks were more than useful; they were essential. I fought her on those ugly racks until she just went and bought them. It wasn't until the very day we opened that I finally understood what Karin had been trying to explain all along: that this was not a large, warm kitchen responsible for calmly turning out fifty, maybe one hundred tops, lunches a day. There were about a hundred seats in the dining room and a crowd of people wanting to check us out and enjoy the view. It was bedlam from the start and we needed every piece of equipment, every rolling rack, and every stainless steel bowl, insert, and pan that we had. Plus some.

We opened on July 4, 1979, with one hundred guests who had been invited to try the food and view the fireworks bursting over the Golden Gate Bridge. That was fine—but it was a single menu with no choices, and not at all our intended menu. Plus it was dinner, not lunch, and we wouldn't be serving dinner for another six months. When we opened for real the next day, it immediately became a struggle to keep up with the numbers while basically learning to cook what our menu promised. That is not uncommon in a soft opening, but we hadn't really had one. I'd been to enough soft openings to know that even the most experienced chef might end up serving a greasy chile relleno, or the coffee might be cold, or any number of things that shouldn't happen, did, as you figured out your equipment and what it could and couldn't do. That's why there are soft openings, where friends are invited and don't have to pay for being guinea pigs. They're the only way to have a dry run. But because we hadn't really had that, we were learning by the seats of our pants.

There were lots of reasons people came to Greens besides the opportunity to eat vegetarian food, although that was one. There was the stupendous view of the bay and the Golden Gate Bridge. It was new and different. The dining room was interesting with large paintings by Edward Avedisian, and JB Blunk's redwood burl seating area, "the most uncomfortable seating in San Francisco," I once overheard a customer say. The food promised to be different from what was found in most restaurants, vegetarian or otherwise. There was some curiosity about the Zen connection and there were those who knew us from Tassajara. Along with all of this, a certain amount of buzz had been put into motion before we opened. And there were scads of free parking.

For the most part our customers weren't vegetarian, but sophisticated diners looking for a new dining experience. Regardless of what was on the menu, there were certain vegetarian clichés that I was determined to banish before they got started. There would be no grassy clumps of alfalfa sprouts bursting out of sandwiches, no cheerful snippets of parsley or orange slices decorating plates. And certainly no broccoli "trees." Appearance, as well as the taste of the food itself, mattered because an impression is formed the second a plate is slid in front of the customer. Above all, I didn't want the plates to scream "vegetarian" or "health food." "How beautiful!" would be a more desirable response, or a good hearty "Umm!" Each red-rimmed white Ginori plate should look bright, pretty, and nothing less than utterly appealing. The main challenge for me was figuring out what foods worked best for a mostly nonvegetarian dining public, and how to make them sparkle on the plate.

But the really challenging part (what wasn't challenging?) was keeping an eye on the plates as they left the kitchen and subtly deconstructing any clumps of sprouts or orange slices or broccoli "trees" that might have wandered over. I had to be really watchful as well as tactful. The staff didn't like my fussing and they complained to the abbot. I was called in and reprimanded for my behavior, but I was also reminded that the success of this huge investment essentially rested on me. It was a Catch-22. I did try to be nicer to everyone, but I was still a watchdog. I believed that these were the details that did make a difference, especially when we were trying to do vegetarian food differently than it had ever been done before. When I finally left Greens, I was happy to shrug my shoulders and say, "That's fine" or "Whatever" to someone's question about cooking. Eventually, I became accepting, and maybe a little lazy.

Originally, Zen students were simply told to work in the kitchen, whether or not they had any experience cooking. We also did all of the cleanup after the lunch service was over, including hosing down those heavy rubber mats. Fortunately that didn't last more than a few months. Today Greens is structured very differently and cooks are hires with actual kitchen experience. Now it's professional. The menus are gorgeous, printed on heavy paper rather than hand-drawn and xeroxed at the last minute. It's a completely different place. The staff today knows the word is "espresso," not "expresso."

17. The Menu

A look at the original Greens menu reads as if it's made
up of pretty standard dishes, even dated ones, but they
weren't standard or dated in 1979. Black Bean Chili, a favorite
and menu standard for years, was a very new idea. Why did we
use black beans? Because they were the most exotic beans available then. Now we have so many more varieties, more interesting ones. The Rio Zape bean makes a great version of that
chili. Still, it was a good dish—a bowl of smoky-hot black beans
sporting a dollop of crème fraîche and a single sprig of cilantro. It looked simple, but a lively group of flavors danced in the
background. What made it special was the presence of chipotle
chile, a new ingredient that Mark Miller told me about when we
were both on the line at Chez Panisse. These smoked jalapeños
have been part of our food culture for a long time now, but then
no one had heard of them outside the Mexican community and
Mark, apparently. We could find them, canned, in San Francisco's

Mission District markets. Chipotle chiles gave us a great way to introduce smokiness to a dish, but because they were hot, they had to work with dishes that were intended to be spicy. This chili was the perfect vehicle for them.

Today, Spanish smoked paprika (*pimenton de la Vera*) introduces smoke to a dish without the heat (unless you want the hot pimenton). This means that your split pea soup can taste as if a ham hock has been involved without climbing the Scoville scale scarcely a point. It's delicious with potatoes and eggs and wherever you might imagine a piece of bacon has been. Before smoked paprika appeared on the scene, I had the idea of cutting Delicata squash into rounds, seeding them, smoking them, then threading them together to make what I called Missing Links. The dried squash slices would become a vehicle for the smoke, and, again, there was no heat. They looked very odd once they were reconstituted in a dish, like a big ugly bone, but they worked, and, like a bone, they could be removed. A more successful smoke-inducing ingredient than my Missing Links were the smoked dried tomatoes from Boggy Creek Farm, in Austin, Texas. Since Larry Butler started making them in the 1990s, I've seen other smoked vegetables at farmers' markets that serve the same function, introducing smoke without heat.

Salads of spinach wilted with hot bacon fat were popular in the 1980s, but of course we didn't have the option of using bacon. For our Wilted Spinach Salad I heated olive oil and wilted the leaves with that, then tossed them with olives, feta cheese, crunchy croutons, red onions, and torn mint leaves. Sherry vinegar, another new ingredient then, provided the acidic kick. It's a good salad still.

Inspired by Chez Panisse's forays into pizza making, we

made small pizzas for lunch. Our standard pizza was covered with onions and red bell peppers cooked down to a jam and seasoned with thyme and tomato, Niçoise olives, and thin slices of fresh lemon, which provided a surprising lift for the mouth. We called it a Niçoise pizza. It was nothing like pizza I have eaten since in Nice, but it was good, especially with those bits of lemon embedded in the onions and peppers. We branched out into other toppings that were also unusual for the time—new potatoes and grilled peppers; mushrooms with Ig Vella's dry Jack cheese; escarole and walnuts; or, for the pizza Mexicana, a jalapeño and cilantro pesto, which gave it a sizzling punch.

The mesquite grill got used for grilling peppers and eggplants and other vegetables intended as ingredients in soups and salads. One of the benefits of the grill we hadn't even thought of was that its fragrant fumes spilled onto the sidewalk in front of Greens, warming the air and the appetite with the scents of rosemary and charcoal, the best invitation to come in and eat. But it was also used daily for brochettes, which involved a lineup of skewered vegetables and cubes of tofu that had been marinated in wild mushroom and red wine broth for days. (I cannot stand the sight or smell of this marinade today!) This was a colorful, pretty dish that was served with brown rice and herb butter. We did have requests for brown rice, so it was always available but we cooked with other grains as well. Quinoa, however, had not yet appeared, though it would soon.

Another popular dish was the TLT—a sandwich of the marinated and grilled tofu with lettuce and tomatoes. We also made an egg salad–like spread using tofu, but otherwise we didn't get into tofu look-alikes and meat analogs. Tofu never went into a lasagna on my watch, that's for sure. I've never cared for tofu that pretends to be cheese, but I do like tofu as tofu. For a short while a young Japanese Zen student was working with us and a few times we featured a special that included the fresh tofu she made along with small Japanese vegetable salads. Her tofu was exquisitely delicate, nothing like the durable Chinese blocks of firm tofu that we blithely tossed on the grill. I was surprised—and pleased—to see that these specials always sold out.

I wanted to go in the direction of making more of our own tofu and featuring it in traditional Japanese dishes, and there seemed to be an appetite for it. Making our own tofu would have showcased some of the possibilities that could be realized when tofu is truly fresh. But to start making tofu in earnest required the kind of dedication that we simply didn't have then. Like cheese, making tofu requires some consistency and practice in order to produce a really fine product, and at Zen Center people were always leaving for different jobs. You couldn't just turn to someone on the crew and say, "Would you make the tofu today?" as if it were mayonnaise. In fact, we could barely manage making mayonnaise. We were not a sophisticated crew with a lot of culinary experience.

Eventually fine tofu made its appearance in our culture, but not at Greens. There is Hodo Soy Beanery in Oakland making more delicate, organic tofu and *yuba,* or tofu skins. Sylvan Brackett's Izakaya, Rintaro in San Francisco, makes its own tofu. Umenohana, sadly now closed, in Beverly Hills had a menu driven entirely by handcrafted tofu. This was an elegant, expensive restaurant with a tranquil, minimalist setting. One of the dishes served at Umenohana was tofu cooked at the table. A spell in a wooden tub set on the table converted soy milk into a quivery warm custard that you scooped into your lacquer bowl then garnished with a sauce. It was exquisite and even more ephemeral than the tofu I remember eating as a teenager in little cafés in Sacramento. In the fall of 2005 *Food & Wine* magazine ran a piece called "It Takes a Tough Man to Make Tender Tofu," which elevated tofu to heights never before glimpsed in our food culture. Were I still at Greens, I would want to have a dedicated, skilled tofu maker on board, too.

Of course we made good use of all kinds of lentils and legumes, largely in soups but also in gratins that might feature grilled eggplant or pasta as well. We made a lentil salad that was brightened with grilled red peppers, capers, feta cheese, tomatoes, and herbs. The comment it produced from one customer still makes me laugh. He came into the kitchen and announced, "You've done for lentils what Kennedy did for the presidency!" More than anything this compliment probably pointed to how stodgy lentils and other legumes used to be, as well as the presidents who came before the handsome JFK.

We always had a pasta dish or two and frequently we made our own pasta, which was just as expected then as cooking over mesquite was. Everyone was making fresh pasta and people loved to eat it. Fear of carbs (and grains) hadn't been lodged in the American psyche yet and pasta could be combined endlessly with vegetables as they passed through the seasons. Pasta could also be finished in cream, which we didn't hesitate to do. This was the era of rich food and not only at Greens. It was everywhere.

Our repertoire of soups was large and they changed each day. We rotated through a number of sandwiches, salads, and entrées, and of course, everything changed week by week in response to the weather and what was available at the farm or market.

Salads were a joy and there were always plenty of beautiful lettuces from our farm. Because I was living at Green Gulch when Greens opened, it made sense to drive down to the foggy fields each morning to pick up what our gardener, Wendy, had for me to use that day, load it into the back of my dark green Honda station wagon, and drive it into town.

I usually called Wendy at the end of the day to find out what was available. The pattern of our conversations went something like this.

"Wendy, do you have any cauliflower?" I'd ask.

"Oh, we have tons of it!" she'd tell me. "I'll have it ready for you in the morning when you come down."

Reassured by her voice and enthusiasm, I'd hang up the phone and start to figure out how to use these tons of cauliflower. But the next morning there were six, or maybe seven, heads waiting for me. I think Wendy loved her vegetables so much that they grew tonnage in her mind. Eventually I learned to gently ask for specific numbers and still factor in for exaggeration, but after a while it didn't really matter how few or many heads of broccoli, cauliflower, or anything else there was. I knew there would be a collection of this and that when I drove down to the fields, and not a great deal of any one thing.

The farm was still young and not producing masses of anything yet, but I had that twenty-five-minute drive to the restaurant to figure out what to do with this miscellany of vegetables. Invariably it ended up as a Farm Salad, the dish that expressed the flavor of our farm in its purest form.

The random nature of the daily collection let me start fresh each day, something you don't get to do much except with specials. The standard menu items were meant to be reliable, unvarying from day to day, in large part for the sake of the kitchen staff. The repeated items lent a bit of sanity to already hectic days. But customers also developed their favorites, which they always ordered and grew to depend on. The Farm Salad, however, was the most dynamic, changeable, and impeccably fresh dish we served. Sometimes the vegetables fit together easily into a jumble; other days mounding discrete little salads on the same plate seemed a better way to go. Either way, fresh herbs and eggs, also from Green Gulch, their bright yellow-orange yolks just beaming at you, always found a place on these plates. Later, when we started doing dinners, the farm salads became small, jewel-like first courses. Green Gulch was able to supply some, but not all of our needs, but those dishes that revolved entirely around the farm's produce were, for me, the most inspiring ones to make. They just cooked themselves, basically, and I tried not to get in the way.

I still make farm salads today, only now they're farmers' market salads, or I call them platter salads, or even garden salads made from vegetables and herbs picked from my garden.

18. Dinner

Once we got lunch more or less figured out, we added weekend dinners at Greens. Dinner was the meal that transformed Greens from a noisy, busy lunch place to a more tranquil restaurant. Tablecloths were laid out. Chunks of Swedish crystal held candles, and the dining room atmosphere turned quietly festive, a place where diners could take time with their meals while enjoying the unfolding evening sky and the eventual end of the day.

This is where I immediately took up the Chez Panisse style of offering a set menu rather than an à la carte approach. Now Greens offers a limited choice dinner menu, which I imagine makes it much easier to accommodate today's more choosy eaters. But then we really didn't have requests to cater to the special preferences of vegans and others. I'm not sure that there were vegans then. But that's not what influenced my decision to go for a set menu. I simply felt it would work well for us because it would help introduce the concept of a somewhat formal four-course vegetarian dinner, which was still a foreign notion to a great many people.

How do you put together a menu for a meal that is meant to go on for a while, without the anchor of meat? This was the question I faced every weekend and how to answer it was a challenge for me, for us. I imagined it might be even more baffling for our customers, to have things all twisted about, to have what were usually appetizers suddenly become main courses. Some form of crêpe? A vegetable ragout with polenta? Today this is hardly as problematic as it was then. Good vegetarian food—and Greens itself—has been around long enough that the meatless menu is not as mysterious as it once was. But in 1980 such possibilities were new, and people were unaccustomed to the idea of eating this way, without meat at the center of the plate.

There was another reason for the set menu. By being able to concentrate on a single menu and a particular progression of dishes, rather than having to produce a whole range of foods, I was hoping that we might be able to undertake somewhat more challenging fare, which we did. And having an ever-changing dinner menu was a way to accommodate all the new ideas that I had been putting in my notebooks, but it made for some dicey afternoons and evenings.

Most of the dishes we made none of us had ever cooked before, or even tasted before. We put our heads together and tried to figure them out before we started cooking. Of course getting that food from an idea to the table was a group effort. I could never have done any of it without the amazing staff I had. Jane Hirshfield, the poet, was then working with me. She was the most faithful and trusting right (and left) hand one could have. I'd ask Jane to make something I had only a vague idea about, and she would pleasantly say, "Okay," and charge ahead without showing any worry or fear. I think she actually believed that things would work, and her assumption gave me the belief, or at least the hope, that they would, too. I wonder if she would have been so accepting had she known how thin the ice beneath us actually was.

Usually our untried dishes worked. But I held my breath a lot, hoped a lot, and I was continually anxious and always vaguely amazed when people let us know how much they liked the food. The best moment was when a guest would come into the kitchen and tell us, "The food was so good that we completely forgot there wasn't any meat." That was the highest compliment.

I'd never forgotten the good bread and butter that started the first meal I ate at Chez Panisse in 1977. Why not begin a meal with the best promise possible, good bread? (Remember, people ate bread then.) Those giant fougasse that Alice and I had bought in France impressed me with their bold shapes, and I thought we could make smaller ones suitable for two-tops or four-tops and just put them, still warm from the oven as they invariably were, right on the tables for people to break apart. A few slashes of the knife followed by a series of tugs, and an oval slab of rustic dough flavored with olive oil assumed the shape of a ladder or a tree. Sea salt and rosemary or sage were rolled into the surfaces and when the breads came out of the oven, they were brushed with olive oil. Their crusty perforations invited customers to pull off a rung or break off a branch. The crumbs scattering over the tablecloths said, "Relax and enjoy yourself; you don't have to worry about keeping that tablecloth pristine."

While we always had the bread, another thing I liked to do was present a table with roasted, salted almonds twisted into a package of parchment paper. This was an idea I gleaned from a few sentences in Elizabeth David's book *Spices, Salts and Aromatics in the English Kitchen,* about a Somalian cook she had in Egypt, who twisted roasted almonds in paper to stave off nibblers. We could have put the almonds in a dish, but there was something about the rustle of that paper parcel being opened that warmed up the big dining room, especially early in the evening, before it filled. And of course, everybody likes a present, even roasted almonds.

First courses and soups weren't a problem; we were pretty competent there. Salads made with the beautiful lettuce and herbs from Green Gulch were something we could count on to please. And from my time with Lindsey Shere at Chez Panisse, I was confident about making desserts to fill out the offerings from the Tassajara Bread Bakery. It was what to put in the center of the plate that I had to wrap my head around.

As I mentioned, our customers were not necessarily vegetarians. People came to Greens for the view, its growing reputation, maybe curiosity about what vegetarian food was like, but not because they were true believers. A lot of women came to lunch, then when we opened for dinner, they dragged along their husbands, who were probably looking forward to a steak, not to a meatless meal, on Friday or Saturday night. We had a good wine list, but I imagined the husbands would prefer to pair a Chalone pinot noir with a piece of beef over whatever we could offer. I tried to imagine some tired man dully anticipating a plate with a big hole in the middle where the meat would have been, should have been. He was the customer I worried about, and I thought constantly about what might fill that hole in the center of the plate. This was my big concern, what I lay awake thinking about.

I knew that it had to be something that caught the eye and proclaimed without wavering, "Here I am! I'm what's for dinner! No need to look elsewhere!"

Of course, the "it" dish also had to be sufficiently familiar that the diner felt at ease. It was the same problem I had dealt with so many years earlier in the Zen Center kitchen. But it also had to have physical stature. It couldn't be some shapeless thing like a plate of pasta or a stir-fry or a vegetable ragout. It had to have substance and form, be something you could point to, look at, focus on. As one gets used to not eating meat, this problem pretty much tapers off and finally goes away, invariably returning on special occasions when, once again, the answer to "What's for dinner?" has to be more than the name of a vegetable.

The most difficult kind of dish to present, and this was generally true whether there was meat present or not, was a stew, or ragout, which was too bad because these were dishes that I felt I had something of a gift for. Sadly, lunch favorites, like the Zuni Stew or Corn, Bean, and Pumpkin Stew, never made the dinner cut, and a dal, as appealingly as it can be made and garnished, didn't either. Not then, anyway. A mushroom ragout, I found, did work, though, if it were paired with something that had a clear shape, like triangles of grilled polenta, a square of puff pastry, or a timbale of risotto. But the stew also had to have a very good and well-crafted sauce, and wild mushrooms helped enough that they became almost mandatory.

Years later, after having left Greens, I was visiting Calgary's Blackfoot Farmers' Market, researching my book *Local Flavors*. That chilly fall evening I ate at the River Café, a rustic building that sits on an island in the middle of a river. There the chef presented me with a vegetarian stew, which worked perfectly in her fine-dining restaurant although I think she made only the one serving since it wasn't on the menu. The stew was based on winter root vegetables, but this handsome dish also contained black lentils and a potato puree and it was all circled with a rich, deeply flavored red wine sauce. The flavors were harmonious and complex. There were different textures to go to so that the dish was interesting to eat. It was also gorgeous to look at and extremely satisfying in every way. It was a perfect vegetarian entrée. In fact, I was so impressed that I came up with my own version of it in *Local Flavors*. That was the kind of stew that worked at Greens, but you can see how many elements have to be there for it to really grab the diner.

Stir-fries were out of the question. They were too pedestrian, too much like what people were cooking at home, plus they could never be as good as those that could easily be ordered in one of San Francisco's hundreds of Chinese restaurants. And besides, stir-fry was not my favorite dish, outside of those made in a good Chinese restaurant.

Mostly I looked for dishes that could be folded, stacked, layered, or otherwise given shape. Tart-based and crêpe-based dishes were shoo-ins when it came to form and they still are. Crust always helps provide definition and many things can fill a tart shell besides the classic quiche filling that had introduced the idea of a savory pie in the first place. Some possibilities were chard and saffron; roasted eggplant and tomato; artichokes, mushrooms, leeks with lemon, and goat cheese (new then); winter squash with Roquefort; goat cheese thinned with cream and seasoned with fresh thyme. A tart made into a single serving with the help of special small tart pans really stood out. It was far more special than a wedge, even if everything else about it was the same.

I came up with a far less rich but tender yeasted pastry as an occasional alternative to the buttery short crust I usually used. Eventually, years after Greens, I left behind the tart shell formed in a tart pan when I discovered that either type of pastry could be rolled into a rough circle, the edges flopped over a vegetable filling to make a more rustic pie, just the way a fruit galette was made. Because everyone likes a pie, I developed ideas for savory galettes. One of the first articles I wrote, in 1986, was for a magazine that wanted a vegetarian menu for a wedding. That was really when I came up with the idea of a savory vegetable free-form pie. It was handsome, flexible, caught the eye, and basically did everything an entrée should do. As I was not settled anywhere during that difficult transitional year of the divorce, I phoned my story in from a truck stop somewhere in Arizona. Later that year a friend showed me her Rolodex card for me with one address after another crossed out then replaced with a new one. But despite personal upheaval, I still managed to cook.

Although I didn't know about sweet or savory galettes when I was at Greens, now they're familiar foods in our culture. Sadly many people won't eat any crust at all, because of the carbs, or calories, or because they're trying to be gluten free. This is especially true today. But at the same time, good grains of all kinds, including older wheat varieties, are being grown organically—which means no glyphosates—on a smaller scale than industrial wheat, and carefully milled.

Crêpes had the dual advantage of being familiar and being endlessly versatile. Personally, I don't think crêpes ever really lose their appeal; I still make them and people always like them. Plus there are a great many things you can do with crêpes. At Greens we made them using different flours—wheat, corn, buckwheat, masa harina—and filled them with an assortment of good things, then folded, rolled, or stacked them. Today I season a crêpe batter with saffron and herbs and serve it in place of bread. I also use quinoa, spelt, and other flours that have since entered the culture in the batter. The Many-Layered Crêpe Cake, inspired by a Marcella Hazan recipe, not only was one of the most delicious entrées we served, but, when cut, its eight exposed layers told the diner that a lot of care had gone into her entrée, and surely that counted for something.

Years later, I was on a book tour with *Vegetarian Cooking for Everyone* (where those savory galette recipes ended up) when I had a memorable meal with Miss Edna Lewis and her friend and assistant, Scott Peacock, at the country home of Anne Quatrano and her husband, Cliff Harrison, of Atlanta's restaurant Bacchanalia—one of my favorite restaurants. When I arrived, Scott was just putting the final touches on a stacked cake, which consisted of a dozen thin cake layers joined with a chocolate frosting that also covered the top and drizzled down the sides. Speaking in his soft Southern drawl, Scott explained that making all those layers showed honor to someone because they took more trouble than a mere two- or three-layer cake. I was truly honored. What was also wonderful to me about that meal was that yes, there was that famous roast chicken of Miss Lewis's, but also a great many vegetable dishes. She didn't speak much at lunch, but she did point out that one could eat a lot of vegetables and a very little meat, as we did that day. At that time that was quite a forward-thinking view.

Timbales—those vegetable and herb-saturated custards paired with sauces—also made good entrées with their solid yet tender textures and attractive shapes. The basic idea came from Julia Child's *Art of French Cooking,* but we expanded on it, changing the size and shapes of our timbales so that they could transcend their original role as a small garnish to a meat dish and assume their position as a main course. Roulades, or rolled soufflés, were light and pretty to serve with their spiraled interiors showing the layers of filling. Being egg based they went especially well with spinach, chard, sorrel, and mushrooms, or sauces based on these vegetables, such as the sorrel-mushroom sauce in *The Greens Cookbook*. Filo pastries assumed the form of spanakopita but not the flavor as the fillings changed to include vegetables other than spinach (such as artichokes), plus nuts (like hazelnuts), and cheeses other than feta.

We were careful about serving pasta as a main dish. A main dish had to have some volume so that it lasted for a while, but a large portion of pasta could become tiresome to eat—*and* it could chill down before it was finished if people were eating slowly, as they generally were when enjoying dinner and conversation in a restaurant. Yet there were many intriguing pasta recipes to explore, especially filled or layered ones. If we did serve pasta as a main course, we made our own dough, formed it into crescent-shaped agnolotti, and filled them with things such as herb-flecked ricotta, butternut squash with toasted pecans and sage—not common then—or a mixture of roasted eggplant and pine nuts. We might feature wild mushrooms in a lasagna. Simpler pasta dishes appeared as smaller first courses, where they could be eaten more quickly, without being too filling.

Cheese and Nut Loaf was the kind of seventies vegetarian dish that I dreaded meeting up with. I didn't see any need to offer meat substitutes when vegetables could be so stellar on their own, but when a senior student brought in a recipe that her sister had sent her with the promise that this was a truly fantastic dish, I felt obligated to try it. We did and unfortunately people loved it. There was no big mystery as to why they liked it so much, despite the funky name. Nut Loaf was insanely rich with roasted cashew nuts, pecans, a miscellany of grated cheeses, cottage cheese, eggs, mushrooms, and finally, a little bit of brown rice to give all this fat something to cling to. It was dense, chewy, and good in an obvious sort of way, the way sausage, bacon, and meatloaf are good. Once we put it on the menu as a lunch special it was hard to get rid of. We served it just like meatloaf with tangy tomato sauce; turned it into a meatloaf sandwich, grilling it first over mesquite; and we used it to stuff peppers and cabbage. It made a few appearances on the dinner menu but I always found it embarrassing to serve. Still, people loved it.

Aside from this foray, we never made bean and lentil loaves and dishes of that ilk, but we did serve both beans and lentils as side dishes, where today they are still underutilized and underappreciated. Warm, well-cooked legumes seasoned with butter or olive oil and a smidgen (or handful) of fresh herbs are simply delicious; their modest flavors make the olive oil and butter sparkle. We could also garnish them with crisped bread crumbs, or bake them into savory crusty gratins with great success. We had no problem figuring out other side dishes, sauces, and all the other flourishes that accompany dinner. There were far more recipes jotted down in my notebooks than there were opportunities to make them.

In general, the dishes that had the best possibilities of succeeding were those usually served as first or second courses, or as (amplified) garnishes to the main dish in more classic cuisines. If I just shifted everything a notch and eliminated the meaty center, I could usually solve my main dish problem. Even a vegetable gratin worked if I made it in an individual dish and slid it onto a bed of wilted greens or perhaps a salad that benefited from being wilted by the heat. One of my favorite gratins was Richard Olney's recipe for eggplant layered with tomato, then smothered with golden custard of saffron-stained ricotta. Rice drank up the juices that ran out of the fresh tomatoes we used, and the reds, golds, and purples were handsome indeed. It was always very successful for us and I still make it today. This was one of those dishes to which I added Gruyère cheese that wasn't called for because I was nervous about our food not feeling substantial enough for our diners. (The cheese has long since left.) Also, because we had plenty of summer tomatoes from Dorothy Coil, we made a fresh sauce that happened to be on the thin side. Today, not having that luxury in New Mexico, I make a thicker sauce from canned tomatoes, another difference. But it is still a fine dish.

Another one of Richard Olney's recipes was a deceptively simple gratin of tiny cubes of winter squash dredged in flour and garlic and laced liberally with olive oil. It was one of the best dishes I knew, but it didn't have enough complexity to work as a main dish. However, we did often serve it as a side dish and it was the painstaking fine dice from that dense winter squash being grown at Green Gulch—again, Perfection—plus its very slow baking that made this gratin special. A classic *pommes dauphinoise,* which also relied on few ingredients, worked because it was familiar, rich, and an unwavering favorite. So what if there was no beef next to it? Sautéed chanterelles or wilted chicories both worked beautifully, which was just the kind of pairing that Edouard Pomiane was suggesting in his books.

At that time I had a tendency to cook richly, using plenty of butter, eggs, and cream when it made sense. I was unsure about bringing vegetarian food into a mainstream venue, and I knew that we could always make something good when we relied on cream or buttery crusts, and that customers would like them. Fat was easy to fall back on in this way. Also this was 1979 and the early 1980s, an era of cream, butter, and cheese—not just at Greens, but in restaurants everywhere. Our dinners were rich, celebratory splurges, not substitutes for home cooking. I can't tell you how many people have told me they were proposed to at Greens, or got married there.

Think of this: When we first opened we had only one vegan customer, whom we nicknamed "Non-Dairy Jerry." Jerry made a big deal about not having cheese in his meal and as he was the only one, we could easily accommodate his wishes. We could even give him a name. Today I suspect there are plenty of vegan, gluten-free, raw, grain-free, and other special eaters. But it is also true that now people find lighter dishes as appealing as the rich dishes that we offered then, even far more so than when we first got started and vegetarian food was pretty much a novelty and eating out was special, not just a way to find sustenance.

When I look at the menu of Greens today online it seems much more sophisticated, occasionally lighter, sometimes more complex, and also more familiar in the sense that you will find some of these dishes in other Bay Area restaurants as well. More farms are mentioned by name, because there are more farms growing vegetables, and the same is true of dairies and the cheeses that come from them. Also more varieties of vegetables and fruits are named, something the Bay Area food culture is sensitive to today. And I know that the kitchen has for many years been staffed by professionals rather than reluctant students recruited from the Zen Center, and that makes a big difference in terms of what's possible.

19. What Inspired the Food at Greens

Myideas for dishes came from different places. One was foods I had eaten and liked. To the extent that I had traveled, I had encountered foods that inspired me, but I was, once again, also inspired by reading. Looking at my library today I immediately recognize the books I used then by their torn covers and traces of greasy fingerprints. There's Madeleine Kamman's family memoir, *When French Women Cook;* Jane Grigson's books on fruits, vegetables, and mushrooms; all of Elizabeth David's work; Waverley Root's books on France and Italy. By the time Greens was going, Italian foods were starting to insert themselves into the culture through chefs, restaurants, and cookbooks. In addition to Ada Boni's book *Italian Regional Cooking*, there was Giuliano Bugialli's *The Fine Art of Italian Cooking*, and Marcella Hazan's classic volumes. Diana Kennedy's and Paula Wolfert's books on Mexico and Morocco respectively were terribly exciting to us. Occasionally one of us got to take a class from one of these great women, and when we did we returned to Greens with all kinds of ideas and techniques in hand to share. None of these writers were vegetarian, but again, I found that when I slowed down and looked closely at recipes, there was often an element in them that I could extract and use. For example there was a lamb tagine with fried eggplant in Paula Wolfert's book *Couscous and Other Good Food from Morocco.* That fried eggplant garnish was absolutely delicious and if you didn't mash it up but just browned the slices, it was gorgeous, too. I did it both ways and served it as an appetizer or a side dish. I'm sure Paula would have been horrified had she known.

I started visiting New Mexico the first year Greens opened. That and subsequent trips introduced me to another round of ingredients and flavors based largely on chiles, beans, blue corn, and posole, all of which I brought back to the kitchen. Slender volumes fastened with staples on the traditional Native and Hispanic foods of the Southwest inspired the recipes I developed, like Zuni Stew. (Having recently enjoyed a vegetable stew at Zuni Pueblo, I have to wonder about the one I made at Greens and what it had to do with Zuni.) Traditional American foods, such as Shaker and Amish recipes and the kinds of dishes described by James Beard in his memoir, *Delights and Prejudices,* also resonated deeply with me, but they were among the most difficult to work into our menus given their solid reliance on meat.

My old, worn notebooks listed foods to learn about, dishes to make; there was so much to discover and realize. When I read down the columns of "recipes to try" and other notes, I still get at least an echo of that surge of excitement about food that filled my life then. I can't say I often feel that way today, for, as tends to happen to people, I've figured out pretty much what I want to grow, cook, and eat, and feel less that I have to try everything I encounter, although I'm not entirely free of that impulse. Curiosity does last. When traveling, I'm still unable to order what I want as opposed to what I want to know about. Sometimes I'm jealous of my husband, who blithely orders what he wants to eat, say, in Italy, which can be the most unadventurous but mouthwatering plate of ravioli, while I'm left to face down a huge bowl of unpeeled fava beans swimming in a watery broth. On a recent trip to Turkey, I discovered a number of dishes that were made with spinach crowns, the parts usually thrown away here, and I ordered them every time I saw them. I was thrilled to taste them and to see them used, but I also wanted to try other foods. This time, I did.

Unfortunately I didn't travel to all the places that inspired my cooking today until after I left Zen Center. I have learned that it's deeply sobering to taste food in its proper setting rather than approximate it through my own efforts, an experience that makes me feel either painfully humble or like giving up. Authentic flavors are very hard to translate. Some people can do it. Writer Clifford Wright is one. I am not one. But even without the benefit of travel, the food at Greens did, in its own way, work. The strongest thing we had was the integrity of our farm ingredients. In the end, I was a chef who "made things up," not one who tried to duplicate the foods of other cultures.

One of the ways I spent my time in the kitchen was showing the other cooks, so often inexperienced, how to hold a knife and getting them to practice, to loosen their arms on the scraps of vegetables that would be returned to the farm for compost. Some students clearly did not want to be in the kitchen or anywhere else in the restaurant. It wasn't what they had come to Zen Center for and they weren't happy at the prospect of turning out hundreds of meals and missing the opportunity to sit zazen as often as they wanted to. I didn't blame them. I rather missed sitting, too, but I didn't want to get up for zazen on Sunday mornings, when I was utterly exhausted from the week. I didn't wake up with that mountain on my chest that I did before Greens opened, but I did wake up feeling as if I had been run over by a very large truck.

I was not at Greens that long. Maybe just three years. It only seemed long. Very long. Regardless of its size or menu, it's hard, hard work to get a restaurant up and running. It was a huge responsibility and it was exciting, but it wasn't necessarily fun. There was the pressure to make Greens a success along with the reminders of what it had cost Zen Center to build the restaurant and how I was supposed to be nicer to the kitchen crew. I couldn't do it all. Not only was I not very well trained but most of the staff had far less experience than I did and even less interest in cooking. The lack of interest and the lack of vision made starting Greens especially difficult. The lack of understanding from the Zen Center board about how exhausting it was meant there was little support for all of us. I never got credit for the restaurant's success, either. I was just figuring it out as I went along. The nervousness I felt was there at all hours.

I finally left Greens to go back to Tassajara for a practice period to be the head monk, or *shuso*, something every ordained student was expected to do. It was my turn. I stayed for a year. When I arrived at the monastery, I broke out in boils. It was as if all the anxiety and doubt about running a restaurant was mixed up with the hunger for a meal that wasn't leftover food warmed up but food cooked maybe just for me, or me and fifty others. The tension finally had to erupt one way or another, and nasty red boils were the way. Then they subsided and I had other worries in my new position. After all, the shuso was the one who got up extra early and ran through Tassajara ringing the wake-up bell. The shuso had to give lectures and make the compost. And at the end of the practice period, the shuso was grilled by all the students in a ceremony where they asked their most difficult questions. This position, too, was a challenge.

20. Kitchen Lessons

There were lots of lessons to be learned in running a restaurant. The experience felt a lot like, in the words of
Dogen-zenji, "one continuous mistake." I made mistakes with
the food, with the staff, with customers, with myself. They did
seem to be endless, and they were especially endless when we
started doing dinners. With the single menu everything had to
work. Of course that was always true, but it was even truer at
dinner because the customers didn't have any choice about what
was coming to them.

Some of the lessons I learned at Greens were about making
menus and about simply paying attention. Without realizing it
until the last minute, I might discover that my menu was made
up of all white foods: onions, tofu, potatoes, risotto. Or maybe
everything was soft, or all the shapes were round. Or maybe I
had made a menu that was cooked entirely on the stove or mostly
in the oven, resulting in some pretty frantic evenings. Actually,

these were the kinds of mistakes I learned from very quickly; I only had to make them once. But I did have to remember, as a matter of routine, to make sure that the serve-up was spread out over the kitchen and not cooked entirely in the pizza oven, or that there was sufficient variation in color, form, and texture to make a pleasing meal. Discovering and correcting errors like these was really about learning my craft in the kitchen. There were other kinds of lessons though, lessons that were often taught by our customers.

DON'T APOLOGIZE

One lesson that I'm still working on after all these years is not to apologize. Alice had told me that. Julia Child had written that. I guess we all have to learn it. I don't mean not to apologize for things that should be apologized for, mistaken orders and that sort of thing, but there's no need to go out into the dining room and tell everyone you're sorry for the disappointing food they're about to have, even though you may feel that the impending meal is going to be a disaster. Sometimes I wasn't so confident about a new dish, I was not sure it would work, but beyond giving it my best effort, the next best thing was to try to relax, move carefully and deliberately, and of course, not cry. At least in the kitchen.

One night we were serving a mushroom soup, the Bresse mushroom soup from Jane Grigson's vegetable book. Someone had mistakenly transferred the finished soup to a stainless steel warming pot, but the wrong one. It was a thin pot used only for pasta water. Bit by bit as the evening went on, the solids that fell to the bottom of the pot had begun to scorch. It wasn't obvious to us and no one noticed until a waiter came in and said, "So-and-so wants to know how you got that smoky flavor in the soup. He loves it! He says it's a ten!"

"What smoky flavor?" I wondered. There weren't supposed to be any smoky flavors in this soup. I rushed over to the pot, tasted the soup, discovered that it had become scorched. Not wanting to spoil things for our guest, I lied and said that we grilled the mushrooms first for that soup. Then we quietly changed out the soup and substituted another for the rest of the evening.

If he thought it was a ten, so be it. Why ruin it for him? After all, the lines between smoked, scorched, caramelized, and just plain burned are often more crooked than straight, more blurred than exact. Baba ganouj made with eggplant cooked slowly over a fire until scorched and collapsed has a rich smoky flavor, but if you're not prepared for it, it can be read "burned"—and therefore most likely wrong. Fortunately, that night, at least for one customer, it was possible to read scorched as smoked, and therefore right. But after that mishap we got jacketed pots for the evening's soup so that there would be no more scorched "tens."

BE FOREVER GRACIOUS

When people came in the kitchen beaming and then exclaimed that they had just eaten one of the best meals they'd ever had in all their lives, I had to bite my lip not to say, "You're joking!" and simply say instead, and with some enthusiasm, "I'm so glad you enjoyed it." It was the hardest thing in the world to do. I suspected they were crazy and had been eating only the most awful food available, maybe even cat food. But I finally did learn that the food I'd been looking at, smelling, and tasting for the past few hours was not the same food the guest experienced. Nor was standing on aching feet in a hot kitchen the same experience the customer had just enjoyed. To the customer everything was new and fresh and physically comfortable, even as I was hot and tired and struggling to figure out dishes and menus, then make them come to life. That Saturday night's leftovers, rewarmed the following day for lunch, tasted good always surprised me. Even though they were damaged and smushed together, they were, in fact, delicious.

TREAT EVERYONE THE SAME

Another lesson that I learned more painfully was a simple one: Always do your best for everyone. Treat everyone the same. No exceptions.

After giving me some time to figure out what I was doing at Greens, Alice came to dinner. We were having a salad with artichokes for the first course, and I had set aside the most beautiful ones for her. I made sure that someone was tracking her table, then I made her salads, spending extra time on them, using the prettiest leaves of lettuce, the best artichokes. Then, a bit more hastily, I made the salads for the next two orders. Of course they got mixed up and I was utterly humiliated on all accounts. Not that the second set was bad, but I wished it had been as nice as the one I made for Alice. It still hurts to recall this.

SALT AS YOU GO

I had a real cooking lesson when Marion Cunningham came into the kitchen after a dinner and pulled me aside. "Debbie dear," she said, which was what she always called me. "Is it against your religion to use salt?"

I found such a possibility rather amusing, though I have since learned that salt and other seasonings had, in the past, been intentionally left out of the food of some fanatic vegetarian groups. But not ours.

"Of course not!" I answered. "Why?"

"Well, your food tastes a little flat; it all needs salt." Marion was always very direct.

She then proceeded to tell me that every part of the dish should be salted as you go, a practice I quickly adhered to. Since I had traveled in both vegetarian and nonvegetarian worlds, I had noticed that meats seem to have their own salts, and that if you were really vegetarian, you tended to want or need less salt. Since my palate was pretty meat free at that time, what seemed all right to me, or to any of us in the kitchen for that matter, might well not have been up to par for most of our nonvegetarian diners. True enough. But the whole business of *when* you add salt is crucial. If you just add it at the end, you get something—whatever you've made—plus salt. If you salt each part of a dish as you go, you feel like you're reaching for the salt all the time and you are, but in the end, it should be well balanced. Maybe you want to add a few drops of lemon, other acid, and a pinch of salt to correct any lacks, but you won't need a lot. Your dish will be seasoned.

This is now such a given in my cooking that I find it very odd that Marion had to explain it to me. It was a long time ago and it was a gift that Marion was so frank; it would have been a shame to see all our hard work and effort fail due to the lack of something as simple as knowing how to salt a dish. I will always be grateful for her honesty and also her encouragement, for she seemed to really like Greens and she ate there often with her friends. And she wrote the foreword for *The Greens Cookbook*.

EAT LIKE A GUEST——IN THE DINING ROOM

One way I came to understand not only the salt level but also the overall impression of what our food was like was to eat it, not simply taste it before service or standing up at the end of the night eating at the counter like a famished little animal, or reheating leftovers on Sundays. I mean eat it sitting down, in the dining room, and experiencing a meal in its entirety, from beginning to end. It was hard to get a picture of what our food really was like, how the menu flowed, whether the portion sizes were interesting or tedious to eat, without experiencing it the same way our customers did. Also, because our dinner menus didn't read the way meat-based menus did, it was important to see how they worked or if they worked.

I was relieved to find that generally they did work, although there were flaws I hadn't noticed in the kitchen that did show up in the dining room. Once I experienced them, they were easy to correct. Of course, it was hard to eat in the dining room when I wanted to be cooking and it was hard to leave the kitchen and enjoy myself on the other side of the wall when others were working or without wanting to get up and go back every few minutes and check on things. But when I did manage to sit down and experience the food like a guest did, it always proved to be the most worthwhile experience. Although flaws and errors were revealed, it was also good to discover that the food was never as terrible as I feared; in fact, it was good. And it was an unexpected bonus to experience the niceties of the restaurant—the pretty room, the view of the Golden Gate Bridge, the flickering candles, the waitstaff doing what they did—and seeing other people eating and enjoying themselves. Yes, it was all a big experiment, but it seemed to be working.

KNOW THAT YOU WILL GET TO LEAVE ONE DAY

A very special lesson, or maybe it was more of a hint of things to come, came from another chef, who told me that the first six months would be the hardest, that I would never leave the restaurant during that period, but to have heart because the situation would change. My friend was absolutely right. It was practically six months to the day that I left the restaurant for the first time one sunny afternoon and went to North Beach to pick up our coffee at Graffeos. While out I ducked into Mario's Bohemian Cigar Store and ordered an anchovy sandwich and a beer. It was so wonderful to drink that thirst-quenching beer and bite into flavors that were entirely unlike those I had been immersed in for the past half year. I recalled my friend's promise and took a deep breath. I'd made it. We had made it. At least six months. Today Greens is forty years old!

21. My Vegetarian Problem

Somewhere in the Midwest a smiling man rushed up to me in the airport and said that he had seen me that morning on a television show.

"Your food looked great!" he said. You could even say that he gushed; he seemed so enthusiastic. But then he became a little lower key, adding in a softer voice, that unfortunately he wasn't a vegetarian.

Of course this sotto voce comment begged the question "But don't you eat vegetables, too? At least sometimes?"

This encounter was maybe the strongest reason why I didn't like the vegetarian label—and still struggle with it. It seemed to be about pushing food away, not toward embracing all these wonderful new to many but old to the world vegetables and other plant foods. Unfortunately, our man in the airport was not vegetarian, as if you had to be one to enjoy these foods.

There are no recipes for meat, fish, or fowl in any of the books I've written with the exception of *Local Flavors,* which has eleven meat-based recipes. *Local Flavors* was about farmers' markets, not about me, and meat had begun to appear there along with vegetables when I wrote that book. No one seemed to notice or care, but other than this handful of recipes, you could call the rest of them vegetarian, although I would just call them recipes for vegetables. I've always looked at my recipe offerings as the vegetable side of the plate—and many of them can take the center role if one desires. Or not. But there was the reviewer who really didn't like that I didn't describe *The Savory Way* as a vegetarian cookbook, as if it was criminal to devote a cookbook to plant foods without a warning. Again, the vegetarian spin narrowed possibilities. *The Savory Way* was suitable for a vegetarian but not, apparently, my man in the airport.

The vegetarian label has not been particularly admired in the food world at any time, and often for good reason. Say the word "vegetarian" and there's always this uncomfortable pause that suggests you are not quite a legitimate eater, much less a legitimate cook. No wonder insecure vegetarians resort to naming famous people past and present who have carried that label— Gandhi, George Bernard Shaw, Ellen DeGeneres, Paul McCartney. Of course there's always the problem with Hitler. Still, you never hear meat eaters pointing to other famous meat eaters; they don't have to. As a vegetarian you're simply on the outs, unless you happen to be a movie star of course (Natalie Portman is another vegetarian); then it's fine even to be vegan (again Ms. Portman).

There have been a number of unfortunate associations that get tacked onto vegetarians and their food, such as an earnestness that's regarded as naïve when the Bambi factor is appealed to—those who could never eat a bunny, deer, pig, or any other animal represented by Disney. There are vegetarians with political attitudes that they're happy to express any moment they can. There's the tendency of vegetarians to take high moral ground that leaves the nonvegetarian feeling judged. When I posted an event on my Facebook page for the Southwest Grassfed Livestock Alliance, where there would be an opportunity to taste a rancher's well-raised grass-fed beef, a vegetarian responded with the "Yeah, it's a dead cow" message, which was both unhelpful and unnecessary. Yes, it was that, but that cow was also why a New Mexican ranch was able to support viable grasslands and attendant wildlife in a challenging environment. The meal was also going to show the diners how a little beef could go far because the meat would be featured as small bites of flavor, not as steaks or chops. The "dead cow" response simply did not take in the larger picture, and we do live in the context of larger pictures whether or not we want to.

Because we are a nation of avid meat eaters, I have felt that it's important to explore other ways and approaches, besides eating a steak or becoming vegetarian, to raising animals and including meats in our diets: a middle way. I happen to prefer a plant-based diet, but I still think it's more important that we all understand the complexities of food. Even so, when a truck passes me on the highway loaded with cattle or hogs or sheep, I feel heartbroken, knowing that these animals are going miserably to their deaths. There must be a better way.

Regenerative ranching does point to that better way, and

maybe curbing our appetite for meat so that less is plenty is also a better way. I don't believe that not eating meat (or eating Impossible Burgers) will solve our big problems, such as climate change, but changing the nature of modern meat would help us be healthier. This would mean getting rid of the feedlots and the mentality that goes with feeding cattle foods that harm them, and getting rid of antibiotics in their diets to make them grow larger and more quickly.

When writing for food magazines, I have often been asked to write about grains and beans even though I've cooked many more foods than these two groups and have spent time as a pastry chef. There's an unending association of grains and beans with vegetarian food and "health food" when all foods might be healthful—and good. So often organic and good-for-you foods have equaled brown. Why couldn't there be color, brightness, and charm along with goodness, was a question I asked myself for years. Vegetables themselves are gorgeous, as chefs today, like José Andrés and others who are getting very "farmy" about vegetables, well know. And nutritionists know that their colors matter, too. So why were they, at least in the 1980s, left out of the picture in favor of the other plant foods that left such a stodgy impression? I suspect it was because vegetables were not yet interesting then. We forget that arugula, fingerling potatoes, endive, heirloom pumpkins and tomatoes, which can now be bought at Trader Joe's without a second thought, were new and uncommon foods when Greens was just getting started. In this respect it was not so long ago.

It has been tempting to detach myself from the vegetarian label. And although I casually threatened to write the all-meat cookbook when I moved to Flagstaff, the truth was that I really did have a thing for vegetables. Meat was harder for me to relate to, mainly because I didn't know it very well and I was not an intuitive meat cook. If I do cook meat, I use a recipe out of a cookbook. Still, I've never been able to get up on a soapbox and be preachy about vegetarianism. And I abhor the equation of vegetarian food with a better diet and improved health, although it's true that for many, a vegetarian diet might well improve health, and that's good. But there can be poor vegetarian diets, too. Coke and chips? That's a vegetarian snack, if not a meal for some. I would never star a recipe or a dish on a menu as "heart healthy," although it's good to have a healthy heart, or "cruelty free," although it's very desirable not to inflict cruelty on animals and others. And I've never accompanied a recipe with the "eating-by-number" breakdowns of fat, calories, and carbohydrates—an omission for which I've been criticized, especially by vegetarians. I believe that if we are paying attention to what we eat and how we eat, we can figure out what foods are right for us. If we live in America and read any popular magazine or use the Internet, we can't help but be informed about what's in foods and how they affect us. But to find foods in this country that don't harm us and others (field workers, wildlife, domesticated animals, waterways) takes work. A lot of work. You have to research food and farming practices. You may have to say no to GMOs, which I do as often as possible, or the like. Maybe attend a local farming conference to become informed. Good food does not come to us easily and the USDA is not always our friend.

Vegetarian dishes have been with us for a while, but what a rocky start. Until recently there were only one or two vegetarian dishes per decade available on a restaurant menu. Here's a sketch of those decadic dishes, drawn in very broad strokes, possibly a gross simplification meant to be taken with at least a few grains of salt.

In the sixties there were quiches made with broccoli but not bacon, and there were crêpes. The "it" dish for the seventies was eggplant Parmesan (very cheesy, very oily, extremely heavy). By the 1980s the vegetarian option shifted to pasta primavera, an irritating dish that never limited itself to spring and that season's vegetables. I suspect the reason was that ferns, ramps, fava beans, sweet little peas, tender amaranths, and other spring verdure are just now coming to light. Chefs who are devoted to seasonal cooking have gotten it right, but usually pasta "primavera"—even today—is rife with bell peppers and tomatoes, ripe only in months long after spring and, in some cases, even the summer months. The portobello mushroom became the vegetarian entrée of the 1990s. It has clearly been the easiest option for chefs to deal with when faced with a vegetarian customer because the mushroom is big, brown, and kind of like meat in that it isn't sweet and it does have a chewy texture. Any chef could relate to it.

In addition to these long runs on particular dishes, a vegetarian might be offered a "vegetable plate," a motley collection of all the unrelated side dishes drawn from a restaurant's menu, or a plate of grilled vegetables. One dish was too much of everything, the other not enough of anything. Eating vegetarian can be frustrating, in fact, too much to bother with for some.

Today it's not as much a vegetable or a recipe as a form: the bowl. I think of a bowl as an infantile mishmash of grains, vegetables, and probably an egg. And it's especially infantile if you eat it with a spoon. I think one of the reasons "bowls" have become so popular is that they look great photographed from above, whether you're a diner with an iPhone or a professional photographer. But food photography is a whole other subject. Don't get me started.

Even among good chefs who are discovering the charms of vegetables today there is a kind of discomfort with vegetarian food, as if they don't know what to do with the request for a meatless dish. It's not really on their register of possibilities, so they do what's easiest: a pasta, a mishmash. It can be very disappointing indeed if you care about eating well rather than just avoiding meat. A vegetarian request pushes many chefs way out of their comfort zone, so I understand why their offerings are mediocre. But it also can be infinitely better today when real cooks are cooking. Then the vegetarian items—whether they're called out as vegetarian or not—have a good chance of being enticing, interesting, and well crafted.

While I'm not one for having a portobello mushroom or a collection of mismatched side dishes every time I go out to eat, when a vegetarian dish looks promising, I order it. I'm often impressed and inspired by the meatless dishes I find today and even more delighted when they aren't labeled as vegetarian—when they're just more good-tasting, beautifully presented items on the menu.

In Ireland, where so much of the food can be really good but very meaty, the best meal I had on my most recent visit was at a vegetarian restaurant in County Cork called Café Paradiso. There was plenty of focus, complexity, and color in that meal along with a soaring deliciousness. My agent had made the reservation and I wanted to tell her that she didn't have to book a vegetarian restaurant on my behalf, but she said she wanted to eat there. She had before. Hands down, it was the best meal we ate on a trip that was filled with winsome foods and colors, and that was exactly why she had chosen it.

THE PROTEIN QUESTION

Patrick reminded me of a time when he was flying back to Arkansas to work on a bank advertising job. A Salisbury steak was served for lunch, but he didn't eat it. He noticed the man in the next seat looking askance at him so he finally turned and explained that he was a vegetarian.

"But you look all right" was his neighbor's response.

From my first book tour through almost the last tour, I've been asked if I get enough protein. It's the question that won't go away. People still ask it. Plenty of vegetarians feel that they get enough protein, some feel they don't, but either way, I decided early on that the protein question was not one I wanted to spend my life answering. I saw it as a rather personal issue and one that we all relate to differently. And one's sense of what's enough protein, or the right kind of food, can change over time. This I know from being a cooking teacher for many years. In one class a woman who had been a vegetarian for more than twenty years confessed that she found herself dreaming of eating turkey night after night. What should she do? I've met others like her. Maybe they should eat some of their forbidden foods and find out why they have entered their dreams, their obsessions. Also, those for whom we cook, or we ourselves, may change with illness or age and want more protein in the form of meat. You just don't know what will happen.

There are all kinds of reasons for the choices we make. For example, a friend who is a third-generation vegetarian from meaty Australia would be miserable if he had to eat meat. It's simply not a taste or texture he's familiar with, and he's been a robust and successful artist throughout a long life.

And here's a completely nonvegetarian issue. I have some friends who have the most wonderful organic farm where they grow the best tomatoes, which their helpers are welcome to take. An older Mexican man who works there refuses the tomatoes for which the customers pay a lot of money. Instead he prefers to go to a crummy supermarket to buy his tomatoes. Why? Because that's where they speak Spanish, it's where he mingles with his friends; it's where he's with his people, where he's comfortable. That is what gives him nourishment, not the far better tomatoes he can have from the farm. We all bring something to our personal table.

Although not a meat eater for the most part, I admit that I find a plate of falling-off-the-bone short ribs utterly irresistible. The same thing happens with fish tacos and salt cod. Something just goes off in my brain when I encounter such dishes.

What does interest me is not the slippery protein question, but the gastronomic value of food. Does a dish or a meal give pleasure? Does its appearance delight the eye? Are all the senses stimulated and does the food cause you to smile? Does it induce conversation about other meals and dishes enjoyed? Does the food have a provenance that makes good sense? Does it provoke a feeling of appreciation? Gratitude? Does it matter if there isn't any meat? And why doesn't it? Or why does it?

How food is raised and where it comes from has held my

interest for a very long time. This interest began when I heard the first line of the meal chant in the zendo of Tassajara in 1971: "Seventy-two labors brought us this rice, we should know how it comes to us." It seemed an easy step from the rice in the bowl, the grain in the bread, or the vegetable on the plate to an interest in how food was grown, the conditions of farm workers, the provenance of seeds, the life of the soil, as well as the lives of the growers, farmers, ranchers, and their animals. Such an interest was not a big topic in the 1970s or even in the eighties.

Today everything is "farm-to-table" and all the tiresome iterations of that phrase—field to fork, vine to wine, spoon to soup. (These variations are not only banal but endless.) One thing we have had to do as chefs is encourage our customers to try something unfamiliar, be it lamb's-quarters, or miner's lettuce, or moss. And that's just as true today, for our ingredients keep changing, as do our relationships with animals and plant foods.

When I was first being interviewed, those asking the questions weren't interested in changing foods and flavors; they were interested in the protein question and after that, maybe, they asked about the recipes. I tried to establish that I wasn't there to talk about vegetarianism, but about food in a bigger way and cooking that might include meat or not. But because I had been involved with a vegetarian restaurant and written cookbooks full of meatless recipes, it was understandable that interviewers wanted to talk about vegetarian issues. Of course a meat cook, who happened to serve a lot of vegetables, could talk about whatever she wanted to. And today there are chefs who have vegetable-driven menus at their restaurants, but claim that they are most definitely *not* vegetarians, and they can speak about and cook all the vegetable dishes they wish to free from the taint of vegetarianism.

MANNERS

One problem for me has to do with manners. What do you say to your host? "Sorry, I don't eat meat"? I know that many do that—and that the practice has extended to dairy, eggs, honey, grain, gluten, carbohydrates, and more. Sometimes it might be a way to encourage another into a meatless (or other) way of cooking, but to me it is generally rude. I really prefer to be flexible enough to just say thank you for whatever appears on the plate. Today with Meatless Mondays, scads of vegetarian and vegan cookbooks, and so many people not eating meat, this isn't quite the issue it was in the past, but for many years it really did put a hostess through a lot of twists and turns to figure out what on earth to serve that wasn't animal protein. I am happy to do that at home because it's easy for me, but I'm loath to ask someone else who is more comfortable cooking meat to make a vegetarian dish for me.

This reminds me of the time that I attended a Slow Food board meeting at La Posada Hotel in Winslow, Arizona, in the early 2000s. When I arrived the first person I saw was a man sitting on the steps of the hotel changing his sport shoes for a pair of cowboy boots. He had a big ice chest beside him. I said hello and he introduced himself. His name was Jim-Bill Anderson and he was from Canadian, Texas. He had a cooler of Corriente beef that he wanted us to taste.

That evening he grilled his beef. It was the first beef I had really liked and it got me very interested in the small Corriente cattle, the descendants of the first beeves the Spanish brought to America. When I got back to New Mexico I told my husband about this amazing beef and within weeks we drove to Jim-Bill's ranch so that Patrick could experience it, too. When we got there, Jim-Bill's wife, Deborah, announced that in deference to my being a vegetarian, we would have lasagna for dinner.

I was the rude one this time, protesting the vegetarian lasagna and saying that I'd hoped Patrick could taste the Corriente beef!

Jim-Bill got in his truck, drove to Canadian, nearly an hour away, and got some meat from his meat locker. It partially thawed during the drive back to the ranch, then he grilled it. The flame was too high, the meat too cold, and it was nothing like it had been for me weeks earlier. But the lasagna was delicious, and we had a good visit with the Andersons, and met the wild turkeys roosting in their trees and their herd of lively little Corriente cattle.

The downside to gamely saying to a host, "No, it's fine. I eat everything," is that when we happen to be eating out a lot, we are eating far more meat than we want to. Still, I'd rather a friend feel at ease with me at her table than not.

Another consequence of taking an open, flexible position came most clearly and sadly to me when two friends and I were staying with a family in a village in the state of Oaxaca, Mexico. They had a big turkey that waddled around the courtyard all day making soft turkey sounds and fanning his dusty tail. On our last day there the turkey was gone. When I asked where he was the woman of the house pointed to a *cazuela* holding a turkey mole, our supper. Not only did the turkey no longer have his happy days in the dusty yard, but our tom had probably been intended for the family at some point. He was a tough and bony bird and there was nothing to do but express gratitude for the kindness of those who sacrificed their own meal by eating it.

And finally, others have loved to provoke me, offering me blood sausages, lardo, lamb's necks, and the like. *Will she eat them?* Sometimes I do, but not always. It's just a strange little thing that people like to do.

I often order a vegetarian meal in a restaurant because I prefer it. But I also order it because I really don't want to participate in the Big Meat of stockyards and animal shipping. I also prefer organic foods and foods that have not been genetically modified. But I know that I have to set those concerns aside if I'm to join others at the table. If we're part of a community we're not necessarily in charge of our individual lives.

Where I live, in the Southwest, I have a neighbor a mere five miles away who raises grass-fed lamb, pastured pork, and chickens that lay the most delicious eggs. Another friend, a little farther away, raises grass-fed/grass-finished beef. Like all food people, ranchers are generous, making gifts of a roast, chops, bone broth, or eggs. I am on the board of the Southwest Grass-fed Livestock Alliance (SWGLA) because I believe that as long as people eat meat, it would be best if it were raised to benefit the health and well-being of the animal, the land, the water, and the eater. Grass takes water, which means ranchers in this dry state have to change some old ranching practices into new ones, such as rotational grazing, shaping roads, and pulling up juniper trees to put the water back on the land; these practices ultimately benefit wildlife as well as cattle. One rancher I know has gone from having one kind of native grass to more than forty native warm- and cold-season grasses due to those very changes she's made on her land. True, the beef that comes from these improved lands is costly and there's not much of it, but those lacks shift the focus from a fast and easy weeknight chop to something eaten less often but valued far more.

Meat is a true luxury. Any animal's life is. No animal willingly steps up to become our meal. All creatures want to live, and fiercely so. None are like the cartoonist Al Capp's Shmoo. Shmoos were white, bloblike creatures that multiplied generously, consumed no resources, and happily became pork, chicken, or whatever humans wanted. If you roasted a Shmoo, it was pork. If you fried it, it was chicken. How convenient! But Shmoos don't really exist; the closest we've come is tofu, which still requires land, water, and soybean farmers.

Even though I'm open to meat, I've long been puzzled about why we've felt that we have to celebrate something—Easter, Passover, Christmas—with a piece of flesh. It seems odd to me when there are other possibilities, but those other possibilities do take time to learn, to make, and to appreciate. Yet, if meat were scarce and deemed important, and you had observed all the fast days your culture required, then the feast days with their meat centerpieces would make sense—the meat had value; it was not an everyday food. But feasting and fasting days are not much observed in Western countries anymore. It seems that any day is a day for feasting, eating a chop or a steak, the tender, quick-to-cook cuts that industrial meat makes so cheap and accessible.

I don't much like to attach a name to the way I eat, or the way you eat. Names—vegan, gluten free, vegetarian, paleo, kosher—can become divisive. What has really mattered more to me than one's diet is the ability to view our differences as differences that are there for a reason and to find within us enough tolerance and understanding to overcome them—and also to know that they and we might change. I've seen my own parents and siblings change the foods they eat. My father became a vegetarian, my mother mostly. Mike is pretty much one; Jamie is not so interested in cooking but she buys mostly organic foods, and Roger does, too. Roger describes himself as a "meat eater of all types," and says that on the average he and his wife have meat once or twice a week and they're thinking of "just having eggs and no meat at all" for health reasons. I've changed also. I am thinking of small things, like the first time I bought real eggs and paid so much more for them, but never went back, or that I always buy organic butter and routinely buy almond milk because I like it.

Many of my recipes happen to be vegan, but that's just it—they happen to. And some happen to be gluten free. And I like them. But I also love the culture of cheese making and don't wish to be free of it entirely. That would be a loss to me of the tradition of humans making the effort to transform and preserve foods, including milk. I am never tempted to use fake cheese in order avoid the real thing. I have bought the fake cheeses so that I have my own experience of them, but invariably they languish in the back of the refrigerator until, covered with mold, they go out. (I do try them before that happens.) On the other hand, it's quite possible that someone will make a cheese-like substance that is really good and I'd like to be open to that. As for gluten, suffice it to say that I have a bumper sticker that reads, GRATE-FUL FOR GLUTEN. I suspect there's a lack of critical thinking when it comes to gluten.

If you're truly vegan (or fill in the blank with whatever dietary channel you swim in) you can't eat a lot of foods that others eat and probably you can't eat in a lot of places your non-vegan friends may want to eat in. You're divided. Separated. How can we cross the divides that we make if we can't break bread together? There are a few rare individuals who are able to join in simply through their warmth, friendliness, and general good spirits, and still eat what they want to eat. I admire them. Richard McCarthy, the former president of Slow Food USA, is a vegetarian, but he is able to attend Slow Food's Slow Meat conference with grace and intelligence and advocate for eating smaller portions of meat, rather than none. The last time we ate together was at a nose-to-tail meal in Denver. Although it was excellent, I envied Richard, for he was served vegetables while the rest of us hardly saw but a shred of one.

In the end, I have chosen to say I'm an omnivore—if I have to say anything—not because I have a deep, atavistic response to the dishes that my dad cooked when my mother was away each August, but because I prefer to be flexible rather than rigid. Patrick is also flexible, but because he grew up in a household where steak was served several times a week, he still occasionally enjoys one, whereas steak has little appeal for me. It's not a food I know from my deep past, except for the gray experimental university steak. I do like a real BLT at least once during a summer, though if I don't have any bacon it doesn't matter that much. The ripe tomato, however, does.

I am also an omnivore because I want to be open to those who are involved with meat, both ranchers and eaters, as a way of being able to change our culture's practices, to become less meat reliant, to enjoy it in smaller amounts or less often or even to forgo it, or to correct wrong impressions in the industry when they exist. Jim Hightower, the former agricultural commissioner of Texas, chided me about this, reminding me that the middle of the road is where you're likely to get hit. And it's true. If you're a neither-nor, like I am, you might just be squashed because you don't really belong in any camp. The middle of the road is a dangerous place and I do have to dress my wounds from time to time.

While the meat I have eaten has taught me about how to make vegetarian food work for nonvegetarians, I love the food I cook without it. I love vegetables. I like tofu a lot. I'm very happy eating vegetarian food. And sometimes I eat meat.

22. Making Books

The summer I was sixteen I acquired my first cookbook. It was French and I wish I still had it. I liked it because the pictures showed food in a more earthy way than we were accustomed to seeing then. In the 1960s food looked flawless and perfect on the pages of magazines and cookbooks. In the 1970s ribbons got added to the food. And flowers. But in my French book, the apricot tart was shown with some of the edges of the fruit burned. It was a bit shocking, but it certainly gave permission for life to be what it is: Sometimes the edges do burn. (And don't we like those best?) In 2015, food was regularly shown with all the burns and imperfections that are usually present when it's made at home. Food has also been shown partially eaten, crumbs stuck to a fork, dirty dishes on the table, a cigarette extinguished in the remains of a dish—real to the point of being off-putting. Food images in the last years of *Gourmet* were dark and the people at the table looked as if they could use a good scrubbing. I had to wonder if the photographer even liked food. But in the 1960s and on into the 1980s, it was as if home cooking could sustain no imprint of the human hand or chance of any kind, let alone a stray crumb, and that wasn't so great, either.

While at Greens I did a few photo shoots for national magazines. Cumbersome lights were hauled into the kitchen and ice cream was formed from Crisco so that it would hold up under their heat. All the food we made was garnished with inedible items like shoe polish (for grill lines) and shaving cream (for whipped cream), so we had to throw it out. When I finally was able to work with photographer Laurie Smith on my own books, she used only natural light and all the food was edible.

Since leaving Greens, I've written fourteen cookbooks. That's probably how most people know me. I've loved making books, seeing them grow from an idea to something you hold in your hand and open and, in my case, cook from. Over the years, I have found that no matter the subject and how clearly I've thought about it, a book has a way of coming into its own and saying quite firmly at some point, "This is what I am." Even " 'who' I am." Until that happens, the book is vague and amorphous, cloudlike. But there's nothing to do except to noodle away, pushing at this, pulling at that, working while knowing there has to be that moment when the breath of the book is suddenly taken. Then you become partners, you and the book. It may be an uneasy partnership, but that's okay. Finally you are working together.

The Greens Cookbook was my first book. I had already tried to sell the notion of writing it to the Zen Center Board but the board didn't think it a good idea. "Who would buy it?" they asked. I remembered all the requests we had had for recipes.

A few years later, when I was living in Rome and had just about decided to stay there, I got a call from an agent who told me that Bantam was interested in starting a cookbook program and that they want to start with *The Greens Cookbook*. Did I want to talk with them? Of course I did! Greens reflected years of my work and I knew that if I didn't write the book, someone else would. That was how Zen Center worked. So I flew back to California, had the meeting, and signed the contract. Then I moved back to the States, settled in Berkeley, and got started. I had my notebook of recipes from Greens, so even though I was no longer there, I had a lot to go on—plus I had the fairly recent memory of cooking there.

Each of the books I've written serves a very specific function, and *The Greens Cookbook* was intended to duplicate the flavors of the restaurant. As such, the recipes tended to be complicated, reflecting what a ten-person crew might pull off in a morning. When the first "fancy" vegan cookbooks came out, I remember looking at them and thinking, "This is too much work!" Then it occurred to me that's how people probably felt when they first saw *The Greens Cookbook*! And it was true—there were a lot of ingredients and a lot being done to them because that was what we did to get the flavor to go beyond something merely simple. Now vegan cookbooks, like vegetarian cookbooks, are far simpler. Sometimes too much so. But when they're complicated, they're also too much so. How to find that happy middle? That was a challenge I'd face with later books. But this one, I felt, had to accurately reflect the flavors of Greens.

I included the recipes as they were made at the restaurant because they were the taste and flavor of the food at Greens and I didn't want people to be disappointed in their results at home. Still, I have always been amazed when people tell me that they use *The Greens Cookbook* all the time. I don't necessarily believe them, but then I go to the book, look carefully, and see that in fact there are quite a few very straightforward, even simple recipes among the more complex ones. So maybe they do use it often. Even more amazing is meeting people who tell me they were raised on *The Greens Cookbook*. And I fear they are telling the truth.

It took a year to write *The Greens Cookbook* and another year to turn it into a book. There's a reason publishers tell you to read your book when you finally hold it in your hand but before you take it to the world. After a year, it's possible that you've forgotten quite a few details.

The year I moved to Berkeley was a hard one for me, as were the following few years. I was still newly separated from Dan and Zen Center. I wanted to somehow stop being "me"—the Zen student, the former chef of Greens, the vegetarian. And now I had this cookbook to underscore the vegetarian part and the Greens part. I'd say yes to all kinds of invitations, then back out at the last minute. My friends had been generous with their invites, but at some point I realized that I'd better say yes and mean it with some follow-through or there wouldn't be any more invites coming my way.

It was partly a reaction to Nancy Reagan's "Just Say No!" campaign against drugs, but to "Just Say Yes!" gave me the encouragement I needed to start following through with some action. Just Saying Yes helped me do that for quite a few months, but I did get into some trouble when I went to L.A. to meet up with a possible new boyfriend. He was interesting, to be sure, but maybe a little bit too much so that weekend. Saturday night, after dinner, we got into his big black Mercedes. He was carrying an enormous boom box and was playing Wagner. Loud. He carried it into a liquor store where he bought some vodka. He was already pretty high on cocaine but that didn't seem to matter. We started driving up the Pacific Coast Highway. Fast. At some point he showed me the gun strapped to his chest, which he said the government allowed him to wear because of his work, which was indeed dangerous. It was about then that I thought maybe just saying yes to everything wasn't such a good idea. When he turned the car around, I vowed that if I lived through the weekend, I'd apply a little more common sense to my actions, and I did. But it was a useful and good policy for a while. It definitely got me out of my expected ways. And it made me realize that maybe it was time to move.

A friend had told me if I ever had a chance to hear Sweet Honey in the Rock, I should go, no matter what. It turned out they were coming to sing in San Francisco so I called the Great American Music Hall and bought a ticket. I had never done anything like that before and it didn't occur to me to invite someone to come along. When the night of the concert arrived, I got dressed and went. I found a table and sat down. People kept coming up and asking if the other chairs were taken and when I said no, they just took them to another table. I was hoping someone might want to sit at the table, too. I felt so alone. But it didn't matter, because when the women came onstage and took their seats I felt immediately at ease, safe in an ample lap where I was at peace. When they started to sing I basked in this sense of newfound calm and safety, and I realized that now was the time to leave San Francisco. I had been fearful about moving to a new city where I knew no one, but now my fears were gone. I could calmly see what was next. My eyes were clear and I felt joyous.

The move didn't happen immediately. I was still working across the bay at Chez Panisse and I wasn't quite ready to leave that situation. But a few weeks later, on the fourth day in a row of being stuck in the stagnant crawl across the Bay Bridge on my way to work, I noticed a pickup in front of me with a dog in the back, and Arizona plates. That was it. I suddenly longed for the clear air of the Southwest. I was ready to go and within the month I left for Flagstaff, Arizona, a part of the world I had gotten to know over many summer trips to New Mexico. And I did know a few people there and my way around. It was a good place to be at that time. I felt like an adult on starter wheels buying my first house, first car, phone, and more.

I never intended to write a cookbook, but writing *The Greens Cookbook* introduced me to bookmaking and I found I liked it, a lot. I wanted to write another book, and I had a stash of more personal recipes that weren't in *The Greens Cookbook*, but I had moved to Flagstaff, where there was nothing to eat—at least nothing that I was used to finding in the Bay Area—so I was a bit stuck, at least at first.

My challenge, as I finally came to see it, was to find a way to produce all those good, lively flavors when there weren't the same resources that a coastal, urban area offered. I gave cooking classes in my home to my new friends in part to learn what they were interested in cooking and eating. My students, I learned, didn't want to spend the time to make complex dishes that layered flavors in order to end up with something that read as simple but actually was not. They had families and jobs, and not much time. But they did want to cook. *The Savory Way* was based on the limited variety of foods that were available and the limits of time, but not on the limits of flavor and appeal. Unlike *The Greens Cookbook*, *The Savory Way* was a more direct, personal, and intimate book. It also marked my beginning as a home cook and my commitment to write for home cooks who, like my students, were curious but busy and often overwhelmed.

In 1988 Flagstaff was pretty dismal as far as food went. I'd go into a Chinese restaurant and it was the smell of rancid oil that hit me. I might find fennel or celery root at the local supermarket, but I suspected that if I carved my initials into the base of these vegetables, I would find that they were all there weeks later. The checkers in the stores never knew what I was buying. "Is that an apple?" they would ask about the wayward quince I had found. But there were good things, too. I went to the county fair, noted the interesting vegetables grown by locals, and wrote down their names. When I met those people they were generous with their produce and advice. I took a gardening class and learned about sucking up grasshoppers with a Shop-Vac as part of gardening in that part of the world. I also learned that if you wanted good fruit, you contacted the Mormon ladies who went to Utah to bring back lugs of apricots, peaches, and tomatoes. I found good farmers who sold their produce. None of it was easy, but it was possible to get good food if you worked at it. After I left there was a Lebanese deli, a farmers' market, and even a chapter of Slow Food, but while I was there, northern Arizona was something of an impossibility when it came to fresh food. Still I did manage to teach and write a book. I loved living where no one had heard of Chez Panisse or Greens and where it was expected that you would go to the pancake breakfast on the Fourth of July, where you would see a man riding a bull in the rodeo parade.

I really wanted Flagstaff to work for me. I loved the landscape of northern Arizona, the cinder fields and the San Francisco Peaks. It was close enough to California that when I needed more olive oil or wine I could—and did—jump in the car and drive out there. Plus I had a wonderful job as a studio assistant to the artist James Turrell, who was Dan's cousin. But it never was a good fit. What finally did it for me was opening a bottle of Bandol rouge to let it breathe before a new friend arrived for lunch. When she called to say she couldn't make it after all, I wondered about the wine. I had a few other friends who I knew would happily drink it, but they were devotees of Gallo's Hardy Burgundy. I realized I knew no one who would enjoy this wine for what it was. And I also saw that I had to live where there was more agriculture and a farmers' market and maybe even someone to open a good bottle for. I called Dan in Santa Fe and asked if I could come over. It was just 350 miles east of Flagstaff. He said sure, though I'd have to work out the details with his other guest, Patrick McFarlin.

. . .

Some years—it felt like a century—after Dan and I separated, I met up with Patrick McFarlin in Santa Fe. He was (and
is) an artist and an old friend of Dan's. We got together after
that weekend encounter at Dan's, one in which we finally clicked
with each other after more than twenty years of being like oil
and water. When our paths had first crossed at the San Francisco
Zen Center he was a bearded hippie artist and I was an uptight
Zen student who absolutely loved all those Japanese forms that
he had no use for then, and still doesn't. It wasn't a fit for a very
long time, not until that weekend when, after giving Patrick
a hug and saying that I had heard X and hoped Y, he reached
down and grabbed my ankle. It was a weird gesture, but somehow it opened my eyes to him and all at once we were more like
vinegar and oil, and bound to make something together as fine
as a good vinaigrette.

Recently we found out that his people in Scotland used to,
centuries ago, steal cattle from my people. Maybe that explained
our initial antipathy and just maybe our marriage healed an old,
old wound. At least I like to think that it has.

As happy as I was when Patrick and I finally got together,
my heart sank when he told me that he was a vegetarian and had
been for the past twelve years. At that time I so wanted not to be
a vegetarian. I wanted to shake off that image of uptight purity
and become a full-bore lusty carnivore. Or at least I thought I
did. I knew that while I was not exactly a willing vegetarian,
meat was not that compelling to me, either. And while I was disappointed to learn of Patrick's tendencies, I was also comforted

by the thought that at least I could put my experience to use: I could cook for him, and that felt good. Eventually he discovered that pork was deeply entangled in his Southern roots. It took just one bite of Serrano ham eaten very late at night after a long day of travel from New Mexico to Spain to do the trick. He was so hungry he just ate it and suddenly he knew he wasn't a Southerner for nothing.

After that trip, the vegetarian phase came largely to an end. Not that we don't eat plenty of vegetarian meals; we both have that inclination for sure, but as I write, my freezer holds some bison from a rancher friend in Texas; elk steaks, a gift from a hunter friend; grass-fed beef raised by another rancher friend in New Mexico; and lamb raised by my neighbor down the road. There's not, but there could be, a chicken roasting in the oven. But I think we're having a chard and saffron gratin tonight. We actually do prefer vegetables to meat.

The first time I went to visit Patrick, he met me at the airport with a big sign saying, ART IN AMERICA WANTS YOU. Once we got to his studio-home in the Arkansas woods I noticed that his kitchen shelves consisted of a wooden plank with two of everything on it—two plates, two bowls, two cups, two forks, two knives. I found that I loved cooking in this minimal kitchen. So many questions were answered by the lack of choice. Back home I had several sets of dishes and would accumulate even more.

It was hot and humid in Arkansas and I didn't want to wear more than a T-shirt and shorts. But I had arrived with a *Gone with the Wind* dress in my suitcase—imagining romantic hours spent lounging on a grassy riverbank. The first thing Patrick said when we went for a walk the next morning was "Don't touch anything green!" That is, unless I wanted to be covered with ticks and chiggers. That dress was never worn. Shorts and T-shirts became like that wooden shelf—minimal, sufficient, and workable.

Patrick is not too inclined to cook but he can feed himself if he has to. A few times—very few—I have had the pleasure of coming home to the smell of brown rice steaming and Patrick cooking a vegetable, an experience that has helped me understand how wonderful it must be for anyone to come home to the smells of his or her partner cooking. It is a wild, nearly inconceivable pleasure.

When I traveled, which I did frequently the first twenty years of our marriage, I left a well-stocked refrigerator. Invariably I returned to find everything pretty much as I'd left it. Patrick hadn't eaten elsewhere; he simply hadn't eaten. Mostly he was thinking about art. Or he was painting. He could ignore hunger. In fact, Patrick is the kind of person who, when asked "Would you like some more soufflé?" can actually say, "No thanks. I'm full."

"Full?" I think. "But *now* is when a soufflé should be eaten. Not tomorrow!"

I find his response to the "more soufflé" question admirable, but hard to understand. I, of course, go for the seconds while it's hot, full or not. I have found that leftover soufflé is not too bad the next morning fried in butter—but then, what isn't? By then it's another dish altogether; heavier and somewhat sodden; no longer a puff of air. But it makes a very good breakfast.

That's how Patrick is. Of course, he is thin. He doesn't eat when he's not hungry. He stops eating when he's full. He *knows* when he's full. He eats slowly. "You don't have to sit and watch me eat" is a statement I hear often. I'm still on that rapid-fire zendo schedule.

We are not alike when it comes to the table. In addition to the fast-slow, full–not hungry continuum, Patrick has an excellent palate for both food and wine, and a good wine memory, while my palate is a bit off, I suspect, and I have a more feeble wine memory, though it has improved over the years of opening some amazing bottles and having many winemaking friends. Patrick is good with wine. Not only does he remember it, but he has designed wine labels and created a few brands.

Once, only, in thirty years of marriage have I seen Patrick consult one of my cookbooks and that was because he was supposed to bring a bowl of coleslaw to a Super Bowl party and didn't know how to make it. He said it was difficult: so much slicing! When he complained about how hard it was for him to cook pasta dishes that didn't all taste alike, I suggested that a cookbook might help and I reminded him that not only did I have a huge library of cookbooks but I had written a number of them, with Patrick himself as my chief taster. Just the other day he called a friend for her recipe for latkes, never mind that there is one in *Vegetarian Cooking for Everyone*. But it was a delight to hear him becoming truly excited about slicing an onion, grating a potato, and frying the latkes. He seemed astonished by the act of cooking, and the results were good.

While Patrick isn't generally inclined to go so far as to open a cookbook, it is because he doesn't cook (at least for the most part) that he's a pleasure to cook for. He truly appreciates my efforts and he thanks me always.

Patrick and I got married at Dan's house in Santa Fe almost

thirty years ago. Dan and David Tanis, an old friend from Chez Panisse days, cooked our wedding dinner. "Some sort of peasant food, I think" is how Patrick described Dan's little pizzas, the grilled salt cod, the roasted king salmon, the flower-graced cake. Although he insists that it is I who called it "peasant food." I can't remember if we fed each other cake at our wedding—I think we did—but we have enjoyed a sweet and mutual nourishment in our care for each other and our enjoyment of the table, despite our differences.

Although Patrick and Dan are dissimilar when it comes to the kitchen—Dan being extremely enthusiastic about food and cooking and eating in a way that Patrick isn't—in other ways they are so much alike that I have to ask, Did I marry the same man twice? Both have a low tolerance for rodent visitors, for example, whereas I don't really mind them—except for gophers.

Patrick has known Dan nearly as long as I have. Patrick, Dan, and I shared many of the same experiences over the years, as Zen students and Zen dropouts (or recovering Zen students). Because the three of us enjoy one another's company and get together often, Patrick and I refer to Dan as "our first husband." I hope he's okay with that.

I had chosen to move to Santa Fe for several reasons: it was more sophisticated than Flagstaff when it came to food, I had planned to open a restaurant, and I didn't want to go back to California. Also there was a farmers' market, which was very important to me. There were the remnants of older cultures, which, after living in Rome, was important to me as well. And Patrick and I had thought Santa Fe was a better choice than either Flagstaff or Little Rock, his home, so we decided we'd give it a try. It's been thirty years and we're still doing that.

When we moved here, the day after arriving and before I had even unpacked, I went to the farmers' market, where I overheard a man say he could use some help running the market. I tapped him on the shoulder and told him I could help. I'd come to open a restaurant, but that was now a year or more away so I was free. He was delighted and told me I could start by managing the market the following week. I asked if I could team up with him first to see how it was done. Fortunately he agreed but after that I was on my own, arriving before dawn in the chill hours, setting up barrels and tapes and trash cans, welcoming sleepy farm families as they pulled their trucks into their spaces, then later, spelling them while they walked around or bringing them hot coffee to warm their hands come late fall. I had volunteered to do this because easier access to good food was partly what brought me to Santa Fe. But it turned out that I was the one who benefited. I met so many people in the farming community who told me their stories, who were warm human beings working hard to raise our food. I became stitched into the life of northern New Mexico in a way I wouldn't have been otherwise.

The farmers' market movement was in its toddler stage at this point. There were about three thousand markets across the country, and I started wondering about the existence of these volunteer, more or less pop-up markets that unfolded every weekend around the United States. I began to tie my cooking classes out of town to market visits, from Portland to Kansas City, Phoenix to Cleveland, New York both upstate and in the city, until I finally gave up the teaching component and went on my own to visit markets—nearly one hundred markets in all. I wanted to write a book that was not so much about our market in Santa Fe but about the rise of farmers' markets on the whole. No one had really written about that and it was such an interesting phenomenon. Today, many markets have their own cookbooks, and a beautiful book has been written about our market—finally. It came out in 2016, but in 1990 it was too soon.

Originally I thought of this book as *Saturday Market, Sunday Lunch*. That title reflected what I did—shop heavily at the Saturday market then produce a lavish lunch on the following day for friends, but that was just at home, of course. If I were visiting a market in Santa Barbara, I was more likely to fly home on Sunday with a few quarts of amazing strawberries on my lap than to cook lunch where I knew no one. Besides, with time I found I was eating food from the farmers' market all week, not just on Sundays. Titles have a way of shifting around and *Saturday Market, Sunday Lunch* became *Local Flavors: Cooking and Eating from America's Farmers' Markets*.

I loved writing *Local Flavors*, visiting so many different markets and talking with farmers and managers and shoppers. I included stories about individuals, like Jake West and his melons, about weather—how a hailstorm could destroy a farmer's livelihood in a matter of minutes—about different kinds of sweet potatoes, avocados, and other foods, about a Hmong market under a California freeway with all its strange vines and beautifully bundled vegetables. No two markets were the same, and I wrote about the good ideas I came across that might be picked up by another market via a reader. Of course the book was filled with recipes inspired by the markets I visited. Among them were eleven recipes for meat because meat was just starting to appear in markets and it was of high quality. Mostly, though, it was vegetables that ruled the scene, for that's what farmers' markets were chiefly known for and they were what I liked to cook. But meat was there, too, and cheeses, and in our market, chicos and chile.

Books are like children, in a way. You spend a long time with them, nurturing them and hoping they'll get a good start in life. I shouldn't confess to this, but *Local Flavors* was one of my favorite books to write. And its theme—markets, farmers, and produce—is one I have returned to over and over even though markets themselves have changed a great deal and there are nine thousand or more farmers' markets today.

Around the time I was managing the Santa Fe Farmers' Market I went to Esalen, in California, to give a weeklong cooking class. The students were all caregivers and they needed to find some way of nurturing themselves. Learning to cook might just be one way, so over the course of a week we made everything—salads and their dressings, soups, stews, gratins, breads, cereals, desserts, breakfasts, tofu dishes—everything that we could possibly fit into a week. When the class ended and I was putting gas in my car and leaving for Santa Fe, I thought how much easier all this would be if a whole lot of recipes could be captured between two covers: something like a vegetarian *Joy of Cooking*.

At this time, soy milk was a totally strange substance that you had to buy at a health food store. I personally held it at a distance until a woman wearing a leopard skin coat came to class in

St. Louis and asked about soy milk. Why? Because her children were seriously intolerant of dairy products. She was clearly not a vegetarian, but she had a problem that soy milk might solve. Might that not be true for other people who were looking for the foods that I had learned about through some strange outsider publications? What about putting everything on a level playing field? Surely such a book existed, I thought. I went to bookstores but I didn't see it. Maybe I'd have to write it. I was quickly seized with the idea of the *Vegetarian Joy of Cooking*. By the time it came out, seven years later, its name had changed and I was vastly relieved to be finished with it.

Clearly *Vegetarian Cooking for Everyone* (*VCFE*) was a book that had its own parameters: The way I saw it, it was, again, not about me but about food in the culture. What foods were people eating that were meatless and what might vegetarians expect to find in such a volume? For example, I was not a fan of stir-fries, but they were very popular when I was writing the book, so there had to be a number of them. I hired someone who was really good at making this sort of dish to teach me and then I included stir-fries. I might skip breakfast (I don't), but the word was that we shouldn't, so there is a breakfast chapter. And so on.

I also wondered what dishes people might be thrilled to find in the book, foods that they might be able to serve their vegetarian children or nonvegetarian husbands. Would a rolled soufflé work? Or Battered and Baked Stuffed Chiles with Roasted Tomato Sauce? Or that eggplant gratin with a saffron custard? It didn't all have to be hummus and eggplant Parmesan, although they had to be there as well.

And I wanted to give attention to each vegetable, its characteristics, what it went well with, what were some simple ways of featuring the vegetable. And while I was at it, what about beans and ways to cook them? Or the nature and variety of grains, or tofu, or miso. I was thinking this should be a book that could teach one about ingredients and how to cook in general as well as a book full of recipes from the most simple to the more complicated. People often have told me that I'm in their kitchen, or they refer to *VCFE* as the Bible. When they say they have my book, I know that's the book they mean.

Getting *VCFE* out in the world was as challenging as writing it. There were issues of all kinds that didn't have to do with the theme of the book. We wanted to use a dark red for a second color, but it reminded the vegan designer of blood so he wouldn't use it.

Bantam wanted to end their cookbook program with this tome, but if that happened, who would care about it and promote it? After such a long, involved project, this mattered. Could we move to another company? We did. That took about a year. Meanwhile, *Joy of Cooking* was coming out with a new edition the same year my book was coming out, so could we change the title? We did and it became *Vegetarian Cooking for Everyone*.

When the book finally came out I was on the cover holding a lot of wooden spoons over one shoulder and looking a little strict. "The vegetarian dominatrix" was what one friend called me in that picture. Actually, I was exhausted from a day of shooting but that picture (and comment) embarrassed me for years. Occasionally I've met people (now young adults) who "knew" me from that cover. In one case the book was at a child's eye level so that this youngster in fact did spend a lot of time at least looking at my picture when he was a certain height. When

I finally met him, he acted as if I had been in his mother's house for years.

I really didn't want to put the word "vegetarian" in the title, but "Plant Foods for Everyone" lacked a certain ring. Ironically, that would probably be an acceptable title today.

After seventeen years, I felt *VCFE* needed updating. Times and foods had changed—again. Stir-fry was no longer the "it" dish for home cooks. Some recipes for stir-fries came out, but not all. Soy milk was now in any supermarket, but so were hemp, almond, rice, and other plant-based milks whose existences I had never even guessed at when writing *VCFE*. Today we have coconut oil and a coconut milk beverage as well as coconut sugar and flour. We can buy really good ghee. Olive oil is a different creature now, no longer pressed through mats, which changes the language related to it. Teff, black rice, quinoa, amaranth, frikeh, emmer, spelt, farro, and other grains are far easier to come by. Arugula, fingerling potatoes, and heritage pumpkins—even heirloom tomatoes—can now be found in supermarkets. It is a different world.

23. Book Tours

Before food TV there were book tours. A constant feature was the TV morning show that ended its day with a segment in which an author talked for a minute, two at the most, about something that had taken years to produce. Then she would make a recipe. It was usually a she. It was like the women's pages of newspapers past.

Of course it was an honor to be able to tour. It got me out of my neighborhood and into the larger world, plus tours help get an author known and tours sell books. I went on several long tours and they were grueling. And strange. Tours today, such as they are, are much better—more meals in restaurants that feature your book's food, less TV or even no TV. But they can be a little more difficult for companies to figure out.

When *The Greens Cookbook* came out I got shoved into the world unexpectedly fast. I had been, until then, living in the Zen Center, working at the American Academy in Rome, at Chez

Panisse, and otherwise dwelling in the food-obsessed Bay Area. I had never bought new clothes, had a facial, a television, a dog. Suddenly I was on a crash course, at least for clothes, facials, and TV. The dog came much later. I think I was more terrified of going on a book tour than I was opening Greens.

Book tours were opportunities for misadventures. Some of these have grown humorous with time, others less so. TV was the hardest part, the worst part, and the least satisfying part for me. But by the time I said I'm *not* doing TV anymore, it was over. The Food Network and cooking shows had taken the place of the final segment of the morning magazine. Still, before that, one did TV every day, like it or not.

I'd never owned a television as an adult nor did I grow up with one, so I had never even watched a morning show. But I started my tour in San Francisco on a morning show that featured a swarm of gorgeous women dressed in gowns for an upcoming ball. I watched from the sidelines, my stomach lurching; then, it was my turn. I walked out onstage and tried to smile and look relaxed. Yes. I was going to make a warm vegetable salad that got turned in olive oil and lemon zest and fresh herbs. This was a pretty dish and took the idea of salad away from lettuce leaves. The pot of water was boiling for the vegetables, which were cut and set out on a platter. A woman from the Midwest was called up to the stage to be my guest; it was her birthday. The vegetables easily slid into the pot, but when I went to take them out, the strainer was larger than the pot. I could only dip a corner of it in and get a few asparagus spears. I couldn't empty the pot into the sink because there was no drain. The producer was circling her hands to hurry me up, so the few bits of asparagus and shards of other vegetables I was able to fish

out got plunked in enough olive oil for the entire mass of vegetables. It was a disaster. I said to the guest, if I had known it
was her birthday I would have made a cake, then I served this
poor woman, who clearly didn't know what to make of any of it,
a few bits of asparagus swimming in olive oil. Then it was over
and I went home to my little sublet apartment in the Mission
District.

And that was just the beginning.

I learned that the sets were always fake. There was never
a drain in the sink and the situation in San Francisco was not
unusual. TV kitchens were not well equipped. It felt as if an office
worker had been given some petty cash and told to buy things
for the studio kitchen at a garage sale. In Los Angeles old diapers
were used for pot holders. In Washington, DC, the Fox set was
filthy and the plants that once gave it cheer were dead—no one
had thought to replace them. Elsewhere the counter was grimy.
The staff obviously warmed up their lunches in the TV kitchen,
but they didn't clean up. I quickly learned that it was a good idea
to arrive at a studio early enough to make things look fresh and
clean. I didn't forget to bring flowers or fresh herbs along with
a sponge and paper towels. I also learned to accept that the host
was probably just becoming acquainted with my book moments
before the camera rolled.

There was always something topical in the news. On one
tour it was surrogate motherhood. On another it was organ
transplants. It was as if the same groups of people were traveling around the country with me. On one tour I kept running
into the comedian Phyllis Diller, who slid onto the set looking
as if she hadn't gone to bed yet. She was funny and I was grateful
for her presence, her humor. During the surrogate motherhood

stage, we both watched a formidable lineup from our backstage vantage point: the hopeful mother, the nervous father, the possible surrogate, any children that were the products of the current marriage or previous marriages, a priest, a lawyer, maybe a theologian. They were all talking at once about whether or not God would permit this. We thought that he/she wouldn't simply because it was so damn complicated.

When organ transplants were in the news, I was in Michigan, again peeking from behind the curtain at an audience of beefy, jowly people listening to one member of the audience telling the rest how his beeper went off when he was shopping for groceries and how he had to just leave his cart *with all the food in it, just like that!* and go for his organ transplant. Then I came out and made a salad. I have never felt so irrelevant.

Sometimes a news story was breaking and you just got dumped—after getting up at 5:00 to be at the station, that is, having landed at an airport late the night before. A young child wanted to set a record and so she tried to fly a plane across the country. It crashed. She died. It was a sad and stupid story. And suddenly I was not interesting anymore. In fact, I was utterly dispensable, as I had suspected all along.

Escorts were hired to pick me up at the airport and take me wherever I had to be. They had done the shopping for me and maybe made my dish since I didn't have a kitchen. Usually I was so tired when I finally landed somewhere that the last thing I wanted to do was answer the one question the escorts tended to ask, "How did you get interested in cooking?" Really, I just wanted to go to sleep. But they worked hard and tried hard and I couldn't do a book tour without them. Occasionally they rescued me from situations I didn't want to be in, inviting me into their homes for a meal and maybe a bed in a quiet bedroom. A few of these hardworking escorts have become friends over the years and have gone on to their own successful careers.

Today, there are no more escorts. At least for me. Rather, a person from my publisher goes with me on a small tour, and it is fortunate that we've had a great time together. Other authors might go by themselves, hopefully to places they already know, but sometimes not. Uber and Lyft make some things possible, but they can't do it all. They can drop you off at an address, but it's hard to go inside a bookstore alone and find the person who sits with you, bored, while you sign books. The escorts usually have close and warm relationships with the booksellers, which is really important. They chat while I sign.

I did get to stay in extremely nice hotels, hotels that served Japanese breakfasts for Japanese businessmen and me, the former Zen student. They welcomed me with chocolates and handwritten notes, and prided themselves on having bathroom fixtures that were unique—like drains. Once I checked in there was nothing I wanted to do more than take that hot bath, but there were times when I couldn't figure out how to make the water stay in the tub. I wanted to cry in frustration, but I called housekeeping and waited for the man to come and show me how this particular drain worked. Until he arrived, I was stuck, waiting. And every moment was precious because I was going to have a very early wake-up call in order to be shunted to the TV station hours ahead of time to do my little dog and pony show. After that, I had a day of radio and print interviews before being dropped at the airport. It was a city a day.

. . .

I was very thin on my first tour because I was unsure about my life and frankly terrified. A woman on a radio show in Detroit took a swipe at me. "You probably don't even have children— you're too thin." I'm not sure what the one thing had to do with the other, but I noticed she was substantially overweight. I suspected she was angry and that she thought I was too vain to be suitable mom material. Or a cook, for that matter. Thin or not, I was not a happy person. I felt like a leaf about to be blown away, and she was openly hostile. I didn't enjoy this leafy feeling. But other than this particular show, I loved radio. It was immediate, warm, alive, and not nearly as silly and vain as TV tends to be.

Television hosts were often silly but they were rarely mean. In fact they generally tried to be favorable and nice, even if you were no more than that leaf in the wind to them. When I was on tour to promote California artichokes one woman started the segment by declaring she hated, absolutely *hated* artichokes. What a great opportunity to jump in and ask why or say that indeed, they do resemble hand grenades—but at the time it was a bit too startling and I was taken aback. If people hated a food, I never believed in trying to make them like it, I really didn't. But I still had to cook those artichokes. I did cook them—it was a little sauté with asparagus and scallions—and it all worked out. The hostess managed to muster some enthusiasm, and I was starving so I did, too.

On another show, I happened to have a lot of different dried heirloom beans in my pocket—maybe I was cooking a bean dish. There was a reason that I've forgotten. My hands had become coated with olive oil—yes, I must have been tossing a salad that included legumes—and at some point, when there was a lull in the conversation, I reached in my pocket and pulled out those beans to show the host. The oil on my hands made them shine. They were all different colors and patterns and sizes, beans I'd collected from markets in Mexico mostly. They were gorgeous. She gasped. "They're so beautiful!" And suddenly, seeing her pleasure, it was all worthwhile.

In New York, on the *Today* show, I was set up out-of-doors, in Rockefeller Plaza, because David Bowie was going to follow my segment and he obviously needed a sizable stage. It started to rain but most of my desserts were sheltered under an enormous canvas umbrella. Toward the end of the segment, a homeless man wandered over and asked for a piece of cake. Matt Lauer tried to shoo him away—the cameras were still rolling—but I had no idea who this person was so I said, "Sure!" I thought maybe he was one of the crew. I cut him a piece and put it on a plate for him. Time went by so fast when I was on a TV set that I couldn't register anything clearly. Guest? Homeless person? Crew? Did it matter? I had no idea.

I was exhausted when it was finally over. I had been nervously waiting since 5:00 A.M. and it was now almost 9:00. Patrick and I went to Carnegie Deli for a big breakfast.

Book tours, I concluded early on, were crazy! They were hard. I learned to think on my feet, but it took a few times. Looking back, I can't quite see why it was so difficult to have fun with it all, but I think it was just the newness of being in the world like that. To me the world that television in particular portrayed was bizarre, and it was one I didn't find easy to enter.

Book tours also tended to be bicoastal events. The middle of the country, except for Minneapolis and Chicago, was the flyover part of the United States. Those states were the ones I wanted to be in, on the ground, walking around, cooking, and talking to people. The cities may have been smaller, but they were interesting and the people often were, too. When *Local Flavors* came out I was able to revisit many of the communities, towns, and small cities I had researched for the book—Kansas City, Cleveland. Champaign-Urbana. Champaign-Urbana was great. True, I stayed in a motel that was packed with noisy, drunken fans of the Chicago Bears because their stadium was being rebuilt and the game had been moved, but when I went to sign books in a bookstore that was on the edge of a cornfield I couldn't believe how many people came and how enthusiastic they were. I was so glad that I got to be there. Plus I met some amazing farmers and writers.

I did learn one very important thing from my first book tour, and that was that the Bay Area is nothing like the rest of the country. The foods I was used to cooking and eating had not yet surfaced in Minneapolis or Washington, DC, or Phoenix. No one was eating arugula. No one was cooking with celery root or fennel. The escorts really had to work hard to find these foods and sometimes they weren't able to. Of course, over time our national pantry has changed as ingredients have spread from the West Coast to the East then started filling in the middle of the country. And they are still changing.

Another thing book tours taught me was that the only recipes that are ours are the ones we happen to be cooking—at that moment. Once they have left my kitchen, they're impossible to own. Even if I have come up with something that seems really special and unique, when someone else cooks my food, it changes, and becomes something else—and someone else's—altogether. This is inevitable and often, quite wonderful. I learned about the importance of visuals, what they say about a dish and the person who cooked it. And of course, I learned about myself. Often my response to what others had done was "Why didn't I think of that? This way is so much better!"

On my first book tour I was signing books in a supermarket where, I was told, the home economist was making a few salads from *The Greens Cookbook*. I arrived early and was chatting with her when I remembered the salads and asked her where they were.

"Well, you're looking at them!" she said and pointed to some large plastic platters. Everything on them was perfectly and symmetrically arranged—asparagus spears all radiating out from the center; eggs, hard-boiled and neatly quartered, nestled between them; olives or capers placed just so. It looked like something out of a woman's magazine circa 1986. Because I never arranged food that way—and didn't even think to—I didn't see it as "mine" at all. Of course I was embarrassed that I hadn't recognized the dish, but it had never occurred to me that asparagus, eggs, and whatever else on the plate wouldn't be tumbling over one another, loosely organized, the way I tended to do it. Years later while traveling in Tunisia I saw a lot of food set out in decorative, repeated patterns, not unlike that of the home economist, but somehow it looked right there, perhaps because it mirrored the symmetry of the tiles on the walls. Within their static design was an element of poise that I hadn't recognized before in such perfectly arranged dishes.

On another occasion a different home economist (do we even have these anymore?) made a vegetable stew from *The Savory Way*, cutting all its components into large, rough pieces. Again, I didn't recognize the dish because my tendency was to cut things smaller and more carefully. My version had a very different look and feel about it, but I was surprised and delighted with hers and the bold statement that her vegetables made. I felt a lurch of jealousy. Why didn't I do it like that?

I realize that often we do things just because it's the way we do them; we don't really think about it, it's just the way we see the world and we probably don't know why we see the world that way. I knew that I tended to cut things carefully and finely but not evenly, and here was someone who just went at it, producing big chunks of vegetables. It never occurred to me to make the dish that way—until the moment I saw hers. Clearly it had its own allure, but my own tendencies had never allowed me to imagine what that might be. Today, at least in respect to stews, I always stress the importance of making the vegetable components big and robust so that the eye has something to go to and settle on.

More recently, when I was touring *Vegetarian Suppers from Deborah Madison's Kitchen*, a chef in Seattle prepared a menu of my dishes in his restaurant. I was delighted that the food tasted so good. I knew that it helps to have a little distance from the actual cooking. But I was even more impressed with how the dishes looked. The chef made them chic, interesting, and slightly unpredictable. After changing my focus from restaurant cooking to the needs of the home cook so many years ago, I had, it seemed, gradually ceased to push my food to the same aesthetic limits a chef would in a restaurant setting. Suddenly, my own cooking seemed rather pedestrian, not so much the flavors, but the appearance. I was stuck in time and my food, at least the presentation, wasn't up-to-date at all. I'm not sure this was necessarily bad—I still had my own particular style—but when I saw the chef putting out plates I found myself asking, as I often did, "Why didn't I think of that?" The same thing happened at least three times in a restaurant just north of San Francisco. The chef there completely transformed my food, giving it sparkle and panache.

It's jolting to see what others can do to transform your food.

A few years earlier a similar thing had happened at Charlie Trotter's To Go in Chicago, where the impeccable young staff had prepared a few recipes from *Local Flavors*. I couldn't imagine a more different approach to my food than Charlie Trotter's. He was so refined and painstaking in his presentation while I tended to prefer food that fell onto the plate and arranged itself. I was a bit worried about the lack of fit here, but then, out came my dishes. I couldn't believe it was my food; it was so "Charlie Trotter" and so beautiful, these little jewel-crusted bites. The young women had made my recipes look as stylish and pretty as they were. It felt good to be nudged into a new way of seeing. Danny Kaye had it right, that yes, you're a swan, not an ugly duckling after all. Or at least you can be if you, or someone else, cares to make the effort.

Not all moments like these were so elevating, though. As spokesperson for the California Artichoke Advisory Board I did some touring on its behalf. On one trip the magazine director took me to the kitchens of a large midwestern complex where I was to demonstrate a few dishes featuring artichokes. As we toured the magazine's vast facility, I noticed a young woman off to the side cutting vegetables. She was dressed in a lab coat, not a chef's jacket, a net covered her hair, and her hands were sheathed in plastic gloves. A ruler sat on the counter. I watched her pick it up and measure a piece of carrot, a slice of artichoke, a bit of onion. When I realized that she was prepping the vegetables for one of my dishes, I rushed over to her, introduced myself as the author of the recipe, and told her that she didn't have to measure everything so precisely. She replied that my recipe called for half-inch cubes and she was making sure that's what she was cutting.

"But that was just a suggestion," I countered. "You have to say something!"

My heart sank. How do you tell someone that you don't mean for her to take your instructions literally, that measurements are only meant as ballpark figures? All her laborious cutting—the waste of time and of pieces that didn't measure up—produced a dish that looked as if it had been made from a box of frozen vegetables. It was at moments like this that I despaired of recipe writing and wished it were possible to just give a suggestion to slice something thin or thick, rather than one-eighth- or one-half-inch thick.

Even my own mother has cooked and served my recipes to her friends with scant regard for instructions. And while I have heartily believed that recipes themselves, like measurements, are essentially hints, there were points where I drew the line, such as when she blithely substituted ripe persimmons for dried plums, or refused to spend a few minutes on a crucial step or a few dollars on an important ingredient. I didn't really want to claim the dish as mine, but I had to, and with good spirit. Another well-meaning friend cooked a simple soup that pleaded for true, ripe tomatoes, shallots, and basil. That was all. But it was December and she made the soup using winter tomatoes from the supermarket. Then she announced to one and all at the table that this soup was my recipe. I knew it was a mere shadow of what it could be and I wanted to slither to the floor. But in this situation I had to smile and say "Thank you."

Sometimes I wished that people were just a little more responsive to my suggestions. But then if they were happy with what they'd made, did it matter?

I had to ask this question when I was invited to speak to an extremely nice group of vegans who had hosted my talk and made food from my books to serve to their audience. Before the program started, I asked them what they had made.

"Your Onion and Rosemary Tart with *Fromage Blanc,*" a young woman answered. She had a pretty smile, an enthusiastic smile.

"How did you do that?" I asked, knowing that the recipe called for butter, eggs, and *fromage blanc,* none of these suitable foods for vegans. She explained that they had cooked the onions with rosemary and put them on toast.

Now caramelized rosemary-scented onions on toast can be delicious, but these weren't. The copious amount of rosemary, unmitigated by cheese, was overpowering. There was too little salt. And there was nothing to contrast with the onions aside from the too strong rosemary. On top of this, the bread was thick and earnest and more bread than toast, and the whole thing was cold, brown, and dowdy looking.

The other dishes they cooked followed suit. They looked nothing like the pictures in the book, which I had hoped might serve as models. And they tasted nothing like my recipes. This was a discouraging moment. Why had I bothered trying to lift vegetarian food, vegan or otherwise, out of this pit of drabness for the past thirty-plus years when this was the result? We were right back in the 1970s. And yet, everyone but me seemed happy.

Did goodness matter? Not to them, apparently. Or maybe they found that their food was good and my standards weren't the ones to judge with. Even if you had decided to strip away all the flavors, textures, and subtle qualities that come with cheese, say, you could still make a good dish. Goodness did matter to me. I didn't feel these dishes were good and I was hoping we could do better by now. But I was grateful for the kindness and generosity of this group. In the end, this mattered more than the food. By far.

24. More About Books

After two years in Santa Fe, I was no longer managing the farmers' market but was putting together a restaurant called Café Escalera. It was the only restaurant in Santa Fe that you could get to via an escalator, hence the name. David Tanis had moved to Santa Fe from Berkeley and he would be the chef. I wanted to be pastry chef because that position was quieter, but we all worked together. The contacts I had from the farmers' market made our food vibrant and unforgettable. As the dessert cook I had the time to experiment with making simple cheeses like mascarpone, fromagina, and cream cheese, which became part of our dessert assemblages.

I loved the idea of having a job to go to after freelancing and waking up each day faced with the need to reinvent myself. But when, after two years of having a job, I was invited to be on a panel discussion in Spain, I thought that maybe freelancing wasn't so bad after all. Of course Patrick and I went, and that was the beginning of a long relationship with Oldways Preservation Trust, a group with whom we traveled the shores of the Mediterranean countries many times and were introduced to the old ways of preparing foods, from couscous in Sfax to olive oil in Liguria and ouzo in Greece. At that time food people—writers, chefs, scholars—were very interested in authenticity and the old ways of doing things, especially concerning food. Today the world of food seems to be more "anything goes." You want "sriracha hummus? No problem!" I'm too much of a purist for today's tastes.

Oldways took us to many countries. There were always well-known food people on these trips so Patrick couldn't really ask them what they did or who they might be. Everyone was also known to one another—except for Patrick, who was an artist and my spouse. To break the ice, he asked what this or that person ate when he or she was eating alone. And he took notes. I found them years later when we were moving. Entranced, I asked him what they were and he explained. I thought they were the start of an interesting book, so every time the art market died, I reminded Patrick about those notes, until finally he went into his studio and made some illustrations. They were delightful, and so we began working on *What We Eat When We Eat Alone*.

We interviewed all kinds of people—very old people, friends, family, strangers, retirees, youth, bartenders, students, writers, farmers. We had masses of material, and once the book took over, it showed us that there were natural chapters and differences among groups of folks and it readily took shape. There was meat and there were vegetables. Patrick designed the book and illustrated it, too. We both wrote it and it came out in 2008, just as the stock market crashed and the banks failed. It flopped. But it is a good book and a beautiful book to look at, too. I'm not sure how much it actually helped people who were cooking just for themselves, but I hope the humor and optimism in the book were encouraging. After all, we all cook for ourselves alone at some point in our lives.

While going through all the ups and downs with the original *Vegetarian Cooking for Everyone*, I wrote some other books. *The Vegetarian Table: America*, was part of a series that Chronicle produced, and it looked as if I had drawn the short straw: Italy would have been much easier as so many contemporary vegetarian dishes that we were eating at the time came from there. Because America didn't tend to offer the same plethora of meatless foods, I decided to take a historical approach, spending a few weeks at the Schlesinger Library at Harvard researching old books and more recent community cookbooks on American food. I found what I had suspected, that we were indeed a meat-obsessed culture for the most part, but there were some good stories and a few recipes that I unearthed and brought into the present. It turned out to be quite a wonderful experience to immerse myself in American food history. The book came out the year of the anniversary of America's first cookbook, by Amelia Simmons.

Then my editor asked me if I knew anyone who could write a book on tofu. I thought I could find someone, but I procrastinated for so long that I finally said I would do it myself. I had a history with tofu and a point of view: Basically I liked tofu as tofu, but not as pretend ricotta or other soft cheese. I liked it in its Asian context. Some of the recipes were a bit hybrid—part Asian, part Western—but every time I brought Patrick a new dish to taste he would say, "This can't be tofu!" and that became the title of the book. It's a little book that soldiers on.

A trio of books followed that I think of as soups, suppers, and desserts. The subject matter is pretty well defined for soups and desserts. It actually is for suppers as well, but for that book it is more varied. I had long wanted to write a book that answered the question What's for supper? That, I've found, is the hardest question to answer for people trying to make a menu that doesn't rely on meat. There are good wine suggestions, too, from Greg O'Byrne, a man who really knows his wines, which you'd think would help—but to no avail. The book didn't do well. My mother ripped off the cover and threw it away—"It doesn't look like you at all!" she complained. Patrick said it looked like a remaindered book, which didn't help either. It was a new low.

The soup book had a better reception. I loved making soups and I loved pottery and I used this book as an opportunity to feature a wide variety of dishes, from simple white bowls to exquisite contemporary ceramics and a few folk art pieces. As so often happens, once I began working on the book, groupings appeared that I had not initially thought of. Some were obvious, like soups based on beans, but some weren't, such as soups that used bread in some way. It was actually a fun book to write and it was fun to pair the recipes with the ceramics. There was a meal and book signing in a gallery in Aspen, Colorado, where we ate from dishes made by some of the featured artists.

Even though there was a brothy spring soup on the cover

and despite the numbers and kinds of gazpacho that appear on summer restaurant menus, readers still insisted that soup was for cold weather. That's one of those mind-sets that's impossible to change.

As with *Local Flavors, Seasonal Fruit Desserts from Farm, Orchard, and Market* was a book that I truly enjoyed crafting. I'd worked as a pastry chef, I loved fruit desserts, and I had some sense about the fruits that different areas offered. For example, we often don't have stone fruits in New Mexico if there's been a late freeze, and when we do, they're very small but very good. In California they are not only plentiful but sweet, big, and juicy, and filled with flavor and nuance—unless, of course, they've been picked green and shipped to a supermarket. Or consider the popularity of Lambert cherries in the Northwest, huckleberries in Montana, and wild blueberries back East. Or take quince, one of my favorite fruits. Quince trees actually grow in many places, but few people had heard of their fruits or knew what to do with them. My father taught me about quince when I was a kid. Foods often showed me my deeper life, not just a recipe of the moment.

After soups, suppers, and desserts, I retreated. I was old enough that I knew what I liked to eat and grow, that is, what worked for me, so I was not that interested in pursuing difference for the sake of difference. And I was repeating myself. I backed off and didn't produce anything for a few years. I turned my attention elsewhere—school gardens, Master Gardeners, Chefs Collaborative, Slow Food, the Seed Savers Exchange, local agriculture, articles, and talks. But I always kept an idea file on my desktop and occasionally I added something to it.

One such folder was labeled "VL," for "Vegetable Literacy."

It had been on my desktop for the past decade, so it was fairly large. I happened to mention it to my agent one day and she loved the idea of a book that was to explore plant families. I wrote a proposal and shortly after it went out, I got a call from Jenny Wapner at Ten Speed Press. I was so thrilled that she liked the book enough to actually pick up the phone and call me that I decided to go with Ten Speed, originally a Berkeley publisher. The West Coast was a good fit for me. It's where I'm from and where I wanted to be.

Vegetable Literacy was about just twelve plant families, those that contain our most common edibles. After the book came out, the poet Gary Snyder growled at me, "You didn't include okra!" I tried to explain that that particular family included pretty much only okra as a common edible, but apparently it was a vegetable that meant a lot to him. With writing as with cooking, you can't please everyone.

I could have gone on forever with plant families—and about people's singular feelings and attachments to them—but one had to stop at some point, draw that line in the sand that declared a family was in or out. But that's not to say I didn't have some lingering passion. I did and I do. Take the laurel family (Lauraceae). What an interesting and strange collection of plants abide here. Unlike the cabbage, carrot, and mint families, the laurel family is made up of largely warm-weather, evergreen tropical plants that don't grow in the United States except in a few places—California bay in coastal California and Oregon, sassafras in Kentucky, and avocados in Southern California. Mostly these plants prefer places like Southeast Asia, Brazil, central Chile, Madagascar, Japan, and Central America. None grow in my northern New Mexico garden; the winters are far too harsh and the air too dry, and my only experience of growing a family member was limited to a small bay tree in a pot. Yet some of these exotics are familiars in our kitchens—bay leaves, cinnamon, avocado, and if you've visited at all in Mexico, avocado leaves. Some flavors we enjoy, like sassafras, the original flavoring in root beer and the stuff of filé powder. And there are also jackfruit and breadfruit in this family, familiar in name only here, but important foods for many. Lauraceae is an amazing family that has just short of three thousand members.

I uncovered some—though not the Lauraceae—botanical family stories and histories, showed their relationships, and included a few hundred recipes that were generally pretty straightforward. Oddly, the one that was truly old school and more complicated than the rest—a classic 1980s tart with caramelized onions, cream, and eggs—was the favorite for many and the one I heard about most from readers.

Vegetable Literacy was hands down my favorite book to write. While I was working on it I read, talked to botanists, researched, and managed to grow almost every plant that got mentioned in the book. It was a wild summer in the garden and when it was too hot to be out-of-doors, it was a wild summer at my desk.

It was only when I began to garden that I started to miss California. I didn't miss it so much in Flagstaff, because while I was there it was important for me to be away from San Francisco, or when I first lived in New Mexico, because I was busy writing cookbooks and traveling. But when we moved to where we've been living for seventeen years and I finally had a real garden, I longed for my golden state. It was so hard to grow anything here, our season was so short and half the year was brown. I'd go back to the Bay Area in February and see all those star magnolias and almond orchards in bloom and ask myself, Why did I leave? I ran into my brother on his farm in Northern California walking around with what looked like long sticks. He crammed them into the earth and when I next returned, they were beautiful trees! That just doesn't happen here. But now what were the beautiful months in California, September and October, are the months of horrible fires, and what should be the welcome rains of winter produce mudslides.

In 2015, I began tweaking *Vegetarian Cooking for Everyone,* which was almost twenty years old. I wanted to take out recipes that were too rich for today, recipes that we don't make much anymore. I mentioned one as an example at a talk I was giving, and two women practically shrieked, *"No!* Please don't. That's a dish we always make each other for our birthdays!" So the Sizzling Risotto Gratin stayed in. Clearly there were celebratory foods and everyday foods. I liked that.

I added a section of easy-to-make vegetable sautés, which reflect more how and what I cook. Miso now stands with tofu and tempeh as a soy-based food. Sometimes I placed one of the new plant milks where it needed to make itself known. Recipes were labeled with a "V" when they were vegan so that those who were looking just for those dishes could easily find them. But often recipes were easy to make vegan if one was willing to use plant milk in place of dairy, or olive oil in place of butter, and so on. Still, I don't turn to fake cheeses and such in *The New Vegetarian Cooking for Everyone.* As always, if people want to use them, it's their choice. And if they want to serve the vegetables with meat, that's their choice, too. Still, I felt that a lot of the recipes seemed dated. I liked them, but they were what I grew up with, in a sense. Today's sentiments concerning food are much more lean—vegan, gluten free, free of this or that. I just couldn't fall into those camps. Perhaps it was time to stop.

After the redo of *VCFE*, I was thoroughly tired of food and recipes. I announced to all my friends "I'm done!" This is always a mistake, especially for a mutable double Gemini. I should know: I've been saying this since 1990. But when Jenny Wapner approached me about a book we had talked about in the past—a collection of recipes with much more narrative and lots of photographs—I agreed to do it. I felt this would be a nice conclusion for an entire body of work. It's called *In My Kitchen*. There is a lot of narrative, just a hundred recipes, and photographs of dishes that I didn't have to style. It's a handsome and useful book, at least for me. And now I really am done. At least, I took Patrick and Dan out to dinner, raised my glass of champagne, and toasted what had been a long and very interesting career.

Most cookbooks today seem so far away from my own sensibilities that it's a relief to no longer be involved with writing them. So many are blatantly vegan or vegetarian, or they focus on bowls, or the authors don't seem to know or care that the Arabic word for chickpea is "hummus." There are also some very interesting new books that I do look at and cook from, but it is truly time for the next generation to step in. For the moment I garden and cook often from books (including my own), something I haven't had a chance to do for years. I give cooking classes in my home for one or two people only so that they can really be tailored to their needs and wants, and I've mentored a student at a local charter school. I am involved in starting a seed library, and since attending Grain School I've been growing, threshing, milling, and cooking with ancient grains and meeting with others who are doing the same. (Talk about seventy-two labors!) It's a fascinating world that is unfolding for me right now. I give talks and write articles and cookbook reviews, but I'm also working on another book project that is not a cookbook. It's different without the guidance of a cookbook idea and for me, harder.

I still look forward to the weekends.

25. Nourishment

When I looked back to my first dinner at Chez Panisse and saw how vividly its memory remained and how it truly changed my life, I fully expected to recall all kinds of meals that were memorable for their goodness, their nourishment, meals that pointed me in some particular direction. But there were almost none. Surely I was mistaken about this. I combed over the territories of childhood and adolescence and beyond. Indeed, I came up with only a small list of meals that struck me as significant, even life changing.

- My dad's midwestern winter feasts eaten at the peak of a California summer
- My first time eating in a restaurant
- Eating in a foreign language: Japanese restaurants on the Sacramento River

· My college graduation lunch, a truly beautiful meal that
  came, seemingly, out of nowhere
· My first sesshin lunch of white rice and pickles
· Strawberries and the mystery of gourmet
· That first meal at Chez Panisse
· Eating a custard cup full of butter from our Guernsey cows

I don't actually recall eating that dish of butter. I wasn't even
two. My dad gave it to me, thinking it was custard. He was distracted. But I included it because I thought the good milk and
cream from our cows somehow shaped me into a butter eater
and later, a cheese eater. My first spoken sentence was, I've been
told, "I like cows." And I still do.

But as I sat at my desk I asked myself, Wasn't there more?
How could I have passed through so much of my life with so
little to remember of the table? The years of Zen Center meals
were memorable as a whole, but apart from that sesshin lunch,
the specifics were vague. There was the adventure of it all, but
there wasn't any dish or meal that compelled my memory to fly
into action and announce, "*This* changed my life."

I find the paucity of such memorable foods surprising and
also a little troubling. I fear that it points to a lack of joy and
enthusiasm about meals, or a poor memory. What I wanted on
my list of favorite meals were dishes and dinners that had power
and punch, meals where food became the lens that would bring
a larger view of the world into focus. I had enjoyed many stellar meals in three-star restaurants, but I wasn't looking at those.

While I was asking this for my own life, I wondered about all our lives: What were the encounters with food that lodged in our memories because they had the power to change how we saw the world and how we walked in it? Of course the details of what we would each see might differ widely.

I didn't originally think deep nourishment was what I was looking for, but it is what came up in the end: food that nourished with kindness, thoughtfulness, care, simplicity, and generosity. And it had nothing to do with the food itself, whether it was vegetarian or not.

Here are some of those nourishing meals.

A SIGNIFICANT LUNCH

I did get to go to Europe with Nancy Wilson Ross. It was my first trip abroad. Tears seared my eyes when our taxi went under London's Marble Arch; I hadn't known about old things, really. We stayed at the Ritz and ate at the Savoy Hotel, where even the carrots and peas were amazing. Then we went on to Scotland and toured about in a tiny, borrowed car. It was November and it was cold.

In the midst of a seriously chilly drive across a barren heath, Nancy and I had a case of the hungers. Not the peckish "I could go for a little something, could you?" type of hunger, but that ravenous appetite that made us antsy and on edge. We were crossing a vast section of land, a heath that was far from any town, and it was well after one in the afternoon when our hopes for lunch, which had been dismal, were buoyed: We rounded a curve and saw a weak thread of smoke rising from the chimney of a low, whitewashed stone building. We parked, unbent our chilled limbs, stumbled to the door, and slowly pushed it open. Immediately the low murmur of men talking came to a halt and we walked in silence to the bar. We were the only women in the room. The barkeep came up to us and suggested—kindly—that we would perhaps be happier if we would drive just a few hundred yards down the road. There, *surely,* he promised, we could have a drink and perhaps food, too. We thought we'd be happier as well, so leaving the men to resume their chatter, we did as he suggested and drove on to a small inn just, as promised, a short distance away.

We opened the door and this time stepped into a silent, chilly foyer. No one was in sight, but we could hear the clanking of pots and pans, doors opening and closing, the bangs and thuds that were all familiar kitchen sounds. I gently pushed open the kitchen door, and there stood the cook.

"Hello!" I called to her. "Would it be possible to have lunch?"

"Oh no, dearies," the cook replied. "I haven't any soup!"

While soup would have been as welcome as a hot bath, its lack hardly mattered to us. It was possible that the cook mentioned the soup to discourage our stay, but then she graciously agreed to feed us after all.

"You'll have to wait a bit, though, if that's all right," she warned as she led us to a small parlor.

Waiting was fine now that we knew lunch was coming. We sat on wooden chairs, fed coins to the heater, and sipped from a flask of whiskey (now those flasks made sense!) until the cook reappeared, opened the doors of the dining room, and invited us to enter.

The dining room was a comfortable space, neither too big

nor too small. We sat near the windows and looked around. The pale yellow walls were entirely covered with large blue and white china platters. The tables and chairs were simple and wooden, worn perhaps, but not shabby. There was a fireplace, but no fire was burning. Though it was cold and empty just then, it was easy to imagine this room filled with people, the warm babble of conversation, the snap of the fire. But lacking that, we gazed outside at the remains of the summer's garden. Most of the leaves were withered and brown. Orb spiders had joined various branches and stalks of plants together with their gossamer threads, now decorated with baubles of mist. At first glance it didn't seem that there were many prospects for food in this garden, but as we continued to look we gradually detected cabbages, their heads protected from frost by their ample leaves, some hardy Brussels sprouts, a row of potatoes that was just partially dug, and some tall leeks, their blue-green flags somewhat wilted with cold. Beyond the garden a ways was a small lake and behind the lake, mountains, whose flanks were covered with a plaid of dark pine squares edged with golden larch.

At last the dining room doors swung open and the cook walked in, nestling one of those big platters in her sturdy arms. She smiled, set it down in front of us, then apologized once again for the lack of soup, and retreated. On the platter were two fish from the lake perched on a soft bed of mashed potatoes, cabbage, and leeks, surrounded with a necklace of Brussels sprouts. Our lunch was the mirror image of our view. Given its innate goodness and startling simplicity, seasoned so well with our hunger and the kindness of strangers, this meal tasted better than any I could recall eating. Its close relationship to the garden and the lake established for me what became the template of the good meal that has lasted my entire life: eating food in its place and its season. It is simple, but hard to find. This rare meal gave me my one true constant, my north star.

The year was 1976, the day before Jimmy Carter was elected president and decades before words like "local" and "seasonal" were used in connection with food.

LOUD BANANAS

My father's father worked for United Fruit Company—I know, that is not at all cool—and when he came to visit he brought us bananas and a little red record of the Chiquita banana song, which I can still sing. My grandfather's job was to make people aware of bananas so that they would start buying them. I couldn't imagine that was a problem. From eating the bananas he brought us, I concluded that a banana was like nothing else we knew: You could practically unzip that skin. A question like "Would you pick up some bananas?" probably didn't exist yet, and having bananas in our house as a matter of course was inconceivable, let alone having enough of them to make banana bread. You had to be rich to do that. Today at my local market there are entire bags of bananas selling for a dollar because they've gotten spotty and need to be used within a few days.

Bananas were exotic, but people were starting to buy them. I knew this because for one blissful week when I was about six, I got to go to a free Mormon day camp in Ithaca. We kids would arrive in the morning and put our lunch sacks in a wooden shed until lunchtime. The shed got so hot that for a few hours all those smells issuing forth from the white bread and baloney sandwiches, the mayonnaise, the peanut butter and grape jelly, and the bananas became richly entwined and aromatic. "Loud" is how my Southern husband would say it. When you walked into that shed to get your lunch, there was this huge banana-dominated smell, and it left a big impression on me. It wasn't disgust or revulsion; it was the smell of plenty. It was wonderful and promising, hinting at things to come, though what, I had no idea. Just the smell of that food was exciting. It smelled, somehow, right.

THE MEAL JANE MADE FOR ME

It was a hard year, the year I wrote *The Greens Cookbook*. Newly divorced and feeling raw, I really wanted to go to bed and get up when it was over, when the pain was gone, in a year or however long it would take. That's when Nancy Wilson Ross's words about being game came into play for me. I did get up, I took off my lead suit, got dressed in something lighter, and got to work. But I never really enjoyed the recipes I was working on, partly because I had no appetite. Fortunately I did have a hungry roommate and a neighbor with small children so there was a place for the food to go once it was cooked and tasted and notes made.

I was terrified of the upcoming book tour. I couldn't imagine how it would work. The chef Ken Hom invited me to dinner and gave me lots of advice while he cooked Shrimp Billy Crystal. (Who was Billy Crystal? I wondered but didn't dare ask.) Other chefs pitched in with helpful words and horror stories about the traps one could fall into. Soon I would have my own stories to tell, but then I was just wide-eyed and full of dread.

The poet Jane Hirshfield, who had been my main assistant for dinner at Greens, gave a dinner party for me. That much-needed reassuring gesture was already a generous thing for her to do. But what made it even more special was that everything she cooked came from the new book. Of course I had tested all these recipes and eaten them many times, but after laboring over a dish for an hour or two, plus not having any appetite, it didn't have the same impact that it did if I had just come onto it. This I remembered from Greens—that was why it was important to sit down and eat in the dining room on occasion. So when I sat down to Jane's dinner and took a bite of the first course, a surprise awaited me: My appetite suddenly returned. There was a reassuring familiarity about the dishes. I knew this food and I liked it. When I told Jane how wonderful every dish tasted, she laughed and said, "They should be good; they're your recipes."

"Are you sure?" I couldn't believe this was true. "Are they really from the book? You didn't change them?"

And Jane assured me that everything was from the book and that she hadn't changed a thing. Having cooked with Jane, I believed her. She wasn't the type to improvise; Jane loved the form of the recipe and was exceptionally faithful to it. But I was still taken aback. I never could have experienced my recipes this way, with such a fresh palate, without someone else cooking them for me just as Jane had.

I ate with gusto for the first time in months. The gloom of the last year lifted, and even if I had never been on TV before, or on the radio or done any of that which I was about to do, maybe I could give it a try after all. The food was good. It worked better than I had imagined and I felt a first small glimmer of confidence. This meal was the most extraordinary gift, for it nourished hope and confidence.

HOT ROLLS AND COFFEE

There was so much to do just to get the farm at Green Gulch going that for a while there was a special morning work period right after zazen and service. This was when it was just getting light out and the fog was dripping like rain from the trees onto the roof of the zendo. The zendo had originally been a barn and there were still a few horse stalls in front, which had been converted into student housing. I lived in one of the horse stalls. Later, when Greens began, Dan and I lived in an old bull pen, made into a charming but fairly dysfunctional Japanese-style cabin. This was also at Green Gulch.

Once we changed into work clothes, we gathered in the meeting area where the kitchen crew had set out trays of Vienna rolls, just pulled from the oven, plates of cheese, bowls of jam, and big pots of strong coffee. These soft, white rolls had crisp, golden crusts with poppy seeds glued to their tops with a wash of beaten egg. As I pulled one apart, a fragrant yeasty steam rose to my face and the heat of the rolls warmed my cold hands. This was the most delicious food I could imagine. Butter melting or a slab of cheese softening into the warm bread, a spoonful of jam bringing its sweet flavor forward to be followed by the bitter taste of strong coffee, conspired to make this predawn meal one I recall with acute affection. As much as I didn't enjoy being cold and hunched over planting potatoes in the mist for the next two hours, I always remembered that moment when I walked from my little horse-stall room into the drafty meeting area of the barn, where I met up with those warm rolls and coffee.

Somehow, that made it all worthwhile. I, for one, was easily bought off.

Once Greens opened, though, there was a gardening crew to do all this and I never had that experience again.

THE SMELL OF THE SEASON: A PLUM IN JANUARY

My first summer jobs were all vaguely food related. I worked at Hunt's cannery in the chemistry lab assaying samples of tomatoes as they rolled in from the California fields. The next year I worked in the enology department at UC Davis. Another summer I was in poultry, and finally I was in a food science lab where the colors and flavors of ice cream were mismatched and given out to students to taste and assess. The students had to write down what they thought they were tasting so that the scientist could see whether color and flavor enjoyed a tight relationship—or not. I spent that summer snacking on tiny cups of pink banana and yellow blueberry ice creams.

Years later, when I was working at Chez Panisse, Alice came into the kitchen, told me to close my eyes, then thrust something under my nose to smell. "What is it?" she demanded.

The object in question was a ripe plum that someone had brought her from Chile.

It was a cold January day and the damp air, as well as the smell of wet wool coats stashed in the wine room mingling with the braising meats and simmering stocks, made the summery perfume of a plum inconceivable and ultimately unrecognizable. It was all wool and winter in that kitchen and I couldn't sift the fruit's scent from the rest of the smells.

A plum? Of course! I could see that once I opened my eyes. So yes, it turned out that the habitual arrangements of color and flavor—sight, taste, and smell—were essential for something to be recognized as seasonal.

BIRTHDAY CAKES

My grandmother always made the same cake for family birthdays, a white cake flavored with mace and served on a plate touched with gold and swaths of pink blowsy flowers. In my mother's house, however, none of our birthday cakes were the same. I don't even know if each of us four kids had a favorite. Probably we yearned to have something that was store-bought. Even a cake made from a mix would have been terrific.

On my fifteenth birthday, my mother made a cake from scratch, most likely the standard cake we always had from *Joy of Cooking*. Our oven tilted a bit so the cakes were higher on one side than the other. For this three-layered birthday creation the layers had been stacked so that the cake was maximally cockeyed, fat bits against fat. The too-wet frosting failed to cement the layers together well enough to overcome their tendency to go with gravity into a slide. To stabilize the cake my mother secured the layers with some metal shashlik skewers. Then, to make them festive, she tied ribbons through the skewers' ornate handles, after first paving the surface of the cake with bright pink icing and covering it with sprinkles. Candles were added, of course.

It was pretty and festive looking, but when the candles were lit and the cake was presented I became a mortified fifteen-year-old. I so much wanted a cake that wasn't homemade, wasn't crooked and shored up with skewers and festooned with ribbons. I was not particularly sensitive to my mother's efforts at that time, nor was I grateful for them. I am now. But little appreciation came into play at that age when social pressures, real or imagined, were strong. The ribbons could catch fire. The layers were crazy. The cake was simply wrong.

Years later I was traveling in southern Mexico with two friends. We stopped for gas on a dust road. Next to the pumps was a little café, and there, on the counter, was a cake that looked very much like the one that had embarrassed me so many years earlier, minus the skewers and ribbons. It wasn't as crooked, but it did have a bit of a tilt and it also had pink icing and sprinkles. I paid for a piece. A woman placed a slice on a plate and handed it to me. The layers were joined with more pink frosting, and I saw that the crumb was not particularly fine. Clearly it had been made with regular flour, not cake flour, an ingredient my mother didn't have, either. It was homemade. I took a bite and it swept me back to that birthday. It was my mother's cake. I brought pieces out to my friends and we stood on a road in Mexico eating cake that was the taste of home and my childhood. It felt like my birthday that day, and it was good. And finally, I deeply appreciated my mother and her crazy, festive cake.

Although I was embarrassed at the time by my mother's cake and all its imperfections, I can't claim to always turn out a perfect cake myself. On turning sixty and in want of some cheering up from my friends, I planned a festive afternoon, a cake and champagne party. I imagined the table covered with different cakes, all of them favorites and most of them layer cakes because I adore layer cakes. Of course I assumed that, just as my mother had, I would bake them myself. It was summer and we were in the midst of a heat wave. Patrick and I were also recovering from a long flight home from Greece two days earlier that had left us jet-lagged and confused. Against Patrick's doubts and cautions, I was determined to make my own birthday cakes.

Every one of them failed. Each cake had something wrong with it. Something big. The butter cakes fell—not uncommon at high altitudes but then I should have known how to correct for that. I had been a pastry chef, after all. My olive oil cake remained stuck to its pan and wouldn't come out regardless of how patiently I teased it. A big chocolate cake broke in two because I didn't let it cool long enough before moving it from pan to platter. Nothing was salvageable unless pieces were to be cemented together with whipped cream, and somehow I couldn't bring myself to do that. Instead, everything went to the compost—all that organic butter, all those expensive eggs, the good chocolate. Food for the worms and the raccoons, if they'd have it.

Fortunately, Patrick, uncannily able to anticipate these very results, had ordered a cake from a bakery, an iced cake with my name on it and clusters of flowers sculpted in butter cream. It arrived with a friend and it was perfect. It was pretty, it was sweet, and it was good to eat. Even in the heat, it didn't melt, or slip, or slide, and everyone enjoyed it, especially me.

SLITHERY OKRA FOR BREAKFAST

When Patrick and I first got together, I ended a book tour in Arkansas so that I could spend some time with him. He met me at the airport with a pizza in his van in case I was hungry. It smelled so enticing, and I admitted to Patrick that it was my first "take-out" pizza, and that's in quotes, because it came from a family's small pie shop and not a chain. This gesture showed me a caring man and I much appreciated it.

The morning I was to leave I woke up to a very different smell: Patrick was frying okra. It was slithery, and greasy, and I can't say I loved it, but the way I saw it was that he was sharing some of his food culture with me, and that I appreciated as much as the (very good) pizza.

ERNIE'S LUNCH

When I moved to Flagstaff I had a few goals. One was to start life afresh, to be out of the Bay Area and away from everything that kept defining me as I had been known, mainly as a Zen student and the chef of Greens. Another goal was to learn a sport, so I bought a mountain bike and took up that perilous form of riding. A third was to learn to barrel race and my mentor was Ernie Macy, a former cowboy then in his eighties who dreamed of moving to Colorado, "where the water was." He had two quarter horse stallions, Pride and Cochise, and we rode them in the cinder fields that spread out east of Flagstaff. I always carried a canteen on our rides, and Ernie always looked at it, then stared into space and drawled, "Water just makes you thirsty." I can only imagine what he would make of our hydration-obsessed culture today.

One day Ernie invited me to lunch. It was summer, I wasn't at all hungry, and I had company coming that evening to cook for. I didn't really want to go, but it was a kind gesture and without thinking much about it, I accepted the invitation. The menu consisted of a large steak from Smith's fried in salad oil, two foods I would never buy or eat on my own. There was also sliced zucchini cooked for about forty minutes in an entire stick of margarine, another food I didn't eat. The margarine, that is. Surprisingly, it was a delicious meal. That soggy, overcooked zucchini really tasted like squash, and though I wasn't much of a steak eater, the steak was good, too. Really good. I recall nothing else about the menu, but I have a sweet memory of Ernie cooking at his little stove in two cast-iron skillets and his big smile when I said, "This is so good!" and meant it.

And all those reasons I hadn't wanted to come to lunch disappeared completely. Everything got done: I went to the airport, I cooked for my friends and ate dinner with them. I may have been too full but, decades later, I still recall Ernie's lunch with pleasure.

A HOPI HAMBURGER

Sometimes disappointment and confusion arise over food and people. When living in Flagstaff I had time to do things spontaneously, like drive an astrophysicist to a conference in

Chaco Canyon. At the end of the conference, the governor of one of the Hopi villages asked if I might drive him home, which I did, through snow and over muddy roads. We pulled up to his little house, and out front were heaps of corn—blue corn, white, red, yellow, each in its own pile. He invited me to lunch. My hopes soared—perhaps I was finally going to experience some "real" Native American food!

We went inside and he quickly pulled together a meal of thin hamburgers, liters of Pepsi, and chips. It was so disappointing. No posole? No beans? What about those piles of corn outside? Maybe they were ceremonial. But I was hungry and had hours of hard driving ahead of me, so I appreciated the sustenance of the hamburger and I was grateful to be in the warm house having lunch. My host, in turn, was grateful for the ride and he made sure that I went home with a handsome pot, made by one of the women in the village, who, it turned out, is an aunt of a man who lives in the village where I live today in New Mexico.

I was glad that I hadn't refused his hospitality, not because of the pot but because it was, after all, genuine hospitality, something possibly more rare than whatever else might have been served. I still have that pot, and it brings the whole meal back to life when I look at it.

MEALS WITH ANN AND ARNOLD

Frequently in Flagstaff I enjoyed meals with two friends I had made there, Ann and Arnold Johnson. Ann was a potter; Arnold taught at the university and was also a Zen practitioner. Both are now retired. They lived in a tract home and had for many years.

Ann and Arnold actually succeeded in growing an abundance of food in that difficult climate and in not much space. They put food up, Arnold made wines, and I was impressed that so much goodness came out of a place as ordinary as a ranch home in a development in Flagstaff.

I ate there often. Maybe there was a stew for dinner, a salad from the garden, thick slices of bread made by Ann and served with good, soft butter. Coffee was carefully ground and brewed. There might be a cookie for dessert, or a rhubarb pie come summer, or a fruit crisp. It was simple food, but cooked and served so deliberately and calmly that I always came away from their table with a sense of having been truly nourished. I still see Ann and Arnold when I drive to California, and when I can, I stop and have a meal with them before heading onward to the Central Valley and the long fast drive up Highway 99 to Davis. The feeling of nourishment is still there.

Where did it come from, this feeling of being well fed? Nourished? I suspect from calmness, intention, maybe not having tons of foodstuffs in the house given the limits of Flagstaff. Instead there was the bounty from the garden. Ann and Arnold were not foodies, but simply people who cooked their meals whether busy or stressed, sad or happy. In no way was this modern food, or stylish food, and it completely didn't matter. What did matter was the feeling of calmness that imbued their kitchen.

When I look for a standard to hold myself to, theirs are the meals I think of. Not that I make the same food—I don't. What speaks to me is a more elusive quality—of attention to detail, and of quiet intention—that made these meals so deeply nourishing. That's what I strive for.

A MEAL AT THE GOVERNOR'S HOUSE

One cold, clear day shortly before Christmas I was invited to a meal held in the house of the governor of Pojoaque Pueblo, after the December dances. My friend Kate and I went together. First we attended the dances, which unfolded over many bone-chilling hours and were mesmerizing enough to cancel the cold, at least temporarily. Then we were invited to walk up to the governor's house. The sister of a farmer friend of ours was married to the governor and she had described the feast day meal to me in detail beforehand. There would be bison from a nearby pueblo. There would be chile and posole and enchiladas, all made with foods my farmer friend had grown. It was a New Mexican menu, for sure, and that we were now numb made it sound especially appealing.

When we arrived people were already eating. We were beckoned to a nearby room to wait our turn and thaw out by a fire. We spoke quietly with those we met there until, after a half hour or so, the governor held up two fingers and pointed to us, thus calling us to the table. The food was steaming in pots in the kitchen, where dishes were also being washed, dried, filled with food, scraped clean after eating, then washed again. The kitchen space was large enough that a number of round tables had been set up for the guests. We were seated at a table with the assistants of one of our state's senators. They were well into their meals when we joined them.

Soon, small pottery bowls of red chile stew with bison were brought to us. After that we were served, one dish at a time, green chile enchiladas, red chile enchiladas, bowls of chili, posole, beans. All the portions were small, just a bite or two. The bowls were also small and handmade. We talked quietly with the others at the table while we ate. Eventually a beverage was served and an enormous buffet of desserts was pointed out. The women who were bringing us food were gracious, but we sensed that we shouldn't linger too long, for others were waiting to eat. So we got up, thanked the cooks in the kitchen and the governor, then walked out into the afternoon.

The air was clear, the sky that full New Mexican blue, and our eyes watered in the wind and cold. We didn't speak until we reached the car. For me, time slowed down so much that it seemed to be nearly stopped. The taillights on the cars crawling along the highway in the distance below formed a beautiful red ribbon of light.

That meal was not a dinner party. It wasn't a restaurant meal either, although we didn't cook. Nor was it like a zendo meal, where one can't talk. We did talk, albeit quietly. There was a randomness about the whole thing—the order, the mix of people at the table—but the kindness with which we were served transformed cold into warmth, the mundane into the beautiful. Body and soul were deeply nourished.

We were grateful.

A FAMILY BIRTHDAY

During the years I was at Zen Center, then in Flagstaff and Santa Fe, I didn't see my family much. My father had left my mother and moved to the coast; my mother was still in Davis as were my siblings, who were busy raising their kids. There wasn't a lot of room for me in their lives, and besides, I was busy with my own life. But I always made a point of visiting my mother and drove out to California at least once a year to do that. Patrick and I attended a few Thanksgiving dinners as well, which was generous of him as he was not so interested in families, either his or mine.

It was after my siblings' kids grew up that I became much closer to the family. I visited my brother Roger in Costa Rica and attended a family wedding in Turkey, and Jamie and I speak frequently and visit with each other. Mike I've always been close to even though he can be a bit prickly. From a distance, I always imagined that Mike, Jamie, and Roger were all close to one another since they were close physically. Apparently they weren't until I came home for a visit. I was the border collie who brought everyone together.

Recently Jamie and I gave the best party ever. Ostensibly it was a family event to celebrate Mike's seventieth birthday, but we knew that it would be a lot more fun if some other people came. So we invited another Mike, who was having his sixtieth birthday, and our now mutual friend Michele from Ten Speed and her partner, Cris. We made an enormous table out of a number of smaller ones, covered it with red and gold tablecloths, flowers, and candles, and cooked a big Moroccan dinner. For dessert we had a birthday cake that was inscribed with the words "130 Years of Mikes." The bakery actually called to make sure we meant to say "130 Years."

The three guests, because they were not Madisons, had a way of breaking up our habitual family responses to things. For the first time we could all just be people together instead of older brother or sister or such. Family. The conversation was good.

New friendships were made. The feeling was warm. There were presents for the two Mikes. And no one got up and left just after eating because they had to be somewhere else. It was an entirely new experience of family.

MY FATHER'S LAST MEAL

It wasn't really his last meal, but it was one of the last times my father tasted real food. It hadn't really occurred to me that I might cook a meal for my father, his caretakers, and their fifteen-year-old son until I found myself in an Iowa woodland hunting for morels the day before flying on to upstate New York. I had gone to Des Moines to give a talk to the garden club on farmers' markets, and part of the lure of leaving my own spring garden was the promise of morel hunting. Our luck was good and we found many.

Standing in those beautiful glades with my hosts, I thought of my father not as an old man at the end of his life, but as a young boy. He was from Iowa, from nearby, actually, and he might have looked for morels on a hillside like this one. Even this one.

The earth was soft, spongy, and damp, and it smelled of both decay and new growth. Overhead the trees—shagbark hickories, black locusts, and others whose identities I learned that day from my friends—were just leafing out. Occasionally we came across a circle of mayapples, their broad leaves hiding their single, waxy blooms, which resembled apple blossoms. Woodland violets poked up through the leaves of the past winter, and there were, albeit more rarely, the exotic jack-in-the-pulpits, their stately, modest, upright flowers sheltered by their curved leaves. Of course, there were the morels, which were at first so hard to see, but which gradually revealed their odd shapes.

The goat cheese and leek tarts I brought for dinner were left over from the brunch that followed my Saturday morning talk in Iowa. At a fledgling public market, also in Iowa, a woman stood behind a table covered with asparagus from her garden. Each stalk was a different length and thickness. Curving this way and that, they looked like a handsome bunch of green snakes. I bought what she had. And of course, we had lots of morels. A menu was starting to take shape. Wine would be part of dinner, too. My father loved wine. I thought a Viognier would be floral and sweet enough for my hosts, who I knew hadn't much, if any, experience with wine. Or with asparagus, as it turned out.

"Are these artichokes?" they asked, while fondling the asparagus snakes.

The tarts in their box needed to be reheated and crisped, so I set them aside on the dining room table. Then I showed my father the morels. He looked in the bag; his thick, white eyebrows shot up, but his face was blank. He sat back. His eyes moved away from the bag. It wasn't quite the reaction I had hoped for; it was a little tepid. But several minutes later he returned to the bag and peered intently into it. Then he picked up a morel, held it to his nose, and his face opened into a smile. "Oh my, oh my!" he exclaimed. His voice quavered with excitement. He sputtered something unintelligible and went back to fetch another mushroom to look at. Then suddenly he was done with the morels.

His watery gaze shifted and his hand crept toward the box of tarts. He started fingering them. "Would you like one of these?"

his caretaker Penny asked. She put one in his hand. He nibbled at it, savored it, and then the hand crept out for another, which he also savored.

"Let me heat those up," I offered. "They'll be much better." But it was too late. Everyone was sampling the tarts. Not even a plate was put out to set them on. Goat cheese was a new food for this household, but they liked it. I cooked the asparagus— another new food—and the morels, yet another. I opened the wine. It was new, too. They cooked a steak, which was practically new to me. For dessert there were handfuls of M&M's because one of their kids had access to them. It was all a bit helter-skelter but we did share this meal together and my father was visibly delighted. I think we all were.

LUNCH IN THE MARBLE MINES

When I was living in Rome, some friends and I drove up to Carrara to see the marble mines. It was a cold day in early winter. The air was foggy and white, the marble was pale, we were cold and, eventually, famished. There was a restaurant in the village, but no lights were on. We pressed our faces to the window and saw that people were eating, so we went in. There was a sudden flurry of welcomes, and the lights were turned on. We were seated and soon eating bowls of hearty bean soup. Its warmth relaxed us, made us smile and look around at our setting. We thought that the other diners were probably men who work in the mines. We saw the green olive oil that was brought to the table; we noticed the blue scarf on the head of the woman who was serving us. We didn't need the lights, but we did need that soup. It brought us back to life. We were so happy and so grateful.

DINNER IN THE MOTEL 6

In the first few years of the new century, Alice Waters sent me off from a Berkeley visit with a lunch to eat on my drive back to New Mexico. I finally ate it at the end of the day, in Needles, in a Motel 6, on a little wooden table set in front of the air conditioner. It was about 106 degrees outside and nearly sunset. The salad leaves were flat and limp by this time, but the Bandol rosé was still cool from the ice it was packed in. I don't remember the rest of the food she had packed, really, but I loved that meal. I felt so well taken care of and it made me happy and content. My little table held just what was needed: the dinner, the wine, a linen napkin, a nestled bamboo knife, fork, and spoon. Now I always stay at that motel and come prepared to set my dinner on the little wooden table.

A POTLUCK I DIDN'T ATTEND BUT WOULD HAVE LIKED TO

A woman wrote to me to find out if she could freeze the lasagna she was planning to make for her daughter's Bat Mitzvah. The party following the ceremony was not going to be catered, she explained. It was to be a potluck. She sounded nearly breathless, even in print, and determined. This was not the way things usually were done in her Los Angeles temple and there had been some pressure to have the event catered. She was not going for it.

Yes, she could freeze the lasagna. She was going to be busy. She mentioned that she had also been planning to make her own pasta but added, "That's all well and good, but there's a certain point where you have a little sense, *please!*" I couldn't have agreed more. But I was wondering: How had this woman come up with the idea of doing a potluck for an occasion that is so commonly and predictably catered?

"I had a friend in an underground band and when she got married she had a potluck wedding. It was one of the best weddings I've been to. She rented a room at a beach club and everyone brought food. It was so much fun. Of course, given that it was a rock 'n' roll wedding, it had a fun feeling to it anyway, but it was special because it was a tattooed crowd of potlucked people. Everyone came knowing that there wasn't any judging going on about the food, or talk about how good the caterer was or wasn't and that sort of thing. And everyone knew that they were all part of it. Everyone was bringing a piece of themselves to this wedding."

This woman told me that she couldn't afford to go the catered route for her daughter, but that she was determined for her to have her Bat Mitzvah party and have it be special. Even if, as her own mother warned her, people would judge her for not using a caterer. She had decided that she didn't care.

"I thought it was impossible at first, but then I remembered my friend's wedding and thought a potluck was the way to go. I mentioned the idea to another friend and she said, Why not?" The woman who oversaw the temple kitchen was doubtful, though, and she shook her head, saying this had never been done before.

She sent invitations and in some of them was a slip of paper saying, "If you want to help, call us!" In the end there were more than thirty dishes at the party for ninety people.

One friend who was Indian made rice and lentils. Another poached a salmon, and a third made an egg dish. A fourth friend offered tuna fish because there were kids coming and kids eat a lot of tuna fish. The daughter's swim coach brought fried rice balls because she liked making them. People just cooked what they wanted to cook. And as for friends who didn't cook, they brought crudités, cheese, bread, and crackers. The party was a huge success and no one missed the catered food.

"People have been very positive about the potluck idea," my correspondent said when I called her to find out how it went. "One of my friends said that this was the way a Bat Mitzvah should be because it's about community and she appreciated that she was included. Even my daughter's friends were saying, 'Why didn't my mom think of that?' "

I loved hearing this story, and the notion of the potluck as a community event. But I especially appreciated the conclusion that my acquaintance offered at the end of our conversation.

"What was interesting about a potluck," she said, "was that I had to give up control and stop thinking that everything had to go perfectly. I had to tell myself to shut up and say thank you. Now I tell myself to shut up and say 'Great!' "

I recently heard from this woman, who caught me up on that thirteen-year-old daughter. She is now in medical school at Harvard and the second generation of her family to cook from *The Savory Way* and now, *The New Vegetarian Cooking for Everyone*.

DYING AND LIVING AND EATING

My first mother-in-law, Mary Welch, was a deeply generous soul, a kind person, a woman who was helpful and loving to all who crossed her path. Her family of friends was wide and warm. At the end of her long life Mary decided to stop eating and drinking. Her exit from this world was to be quiet, intentional, and dignified.

Dan didn't hear about his mother's not eating until she was three weeks into her fast. Her heartbeat was faint, her blood pressure nearly undetectable, and she spoke only in a faint whisper. He flew to Washington State to join her and his two sisters.

Dan has always been an exuberant cook. You couldn't keep him out of the kitchen and it was truly his joy to cook for others. So while he was there, it was only natural that he cooked for his sisters—soups for those cool and cloudy days on the northwest coast, a comforting roast chicken for dinner. After listening to the chopping and searing, and smelling his kitchen endeavors from her nearby bedroom, Mary called Dan to her and whispered to him in her faint voice, "This dying stuff is overrated and your food smells so good! What I'd really like most of all is some of your soup."

Dan used the chicken carcass from the previous night's dinner to make a little broth. Mary sipped a few spoonfuls. It agreed with her body. She took more. It infiltrated her blood and muscles and made her heart beat more strongly. It raised her blood pressure to a detectable level, and raised her spirits, too. The strength that had left her voice started to come back and bit by bit she returned to the world of the living, to the pleasure of food and the enjoyment she had in being with her children. She died not long after that, but in a much more robust and happier state.

THE NEXT GENERATION COOKS DINNER

Patrick and I were invited to a dinner party given by Kate, aged seventeen, who was leaving for college the next day. Of course we would come. After all, we had known Kate since she was born and her two brothers since they were little kids. Aside from her brothers, her boyfriend, and a brother's girlfriend, we and the other guests were her parents' friends. And neither Kate's mom nor her dad was going to be there—a sick parent needed attending for one and a truck had broken down for the other—which gave us the improbable giddy feeling that there weren't any adults around. Besides, Kate had it all under control. Here is the menu she made:

Margaritas from scratch

Homemade guacamole

Grilled asparagus and grilled steak
with a (homemade) tomatillo salsa

Polenta with fried onions

A big Caesar salad

A plum galette *and* lime mousse tarts for dessert

Nothing was out of a package *and* our offers to help were met with a cheerful "No thanks! Got it!" So we adults sat around the kitchen table with our margaritas and basked in the situation: watching the kids cook dinner. It was a terrifically fun party.

I had no idea Kate liked to cook or knew how. When I asked her older brothers about this, they replied that kids in Santa Fe generally know how to cook. They acted as if it wasn't a big deal, just a natural consequence of growing up here, which I found odd and surprising. Why would that be?

One reason, her older brother Andrew said, was the program called Cooking with Kids, which, for the past twenty years, had worked in Santa Fe schools to give children a hands-on experience of cooking and eating foods they might not be familiar with. (I actually taught Kate's brother Will through this program when he was in the third grade. After that class, I went home and had a big belt of whiskey for lunch. I was not a drinker, nor was I a born third-grade teacher.) Then both brothers added that when, years later, they finally realized how much it costs to eat out all the time, they figured that they had to learn how to cook. That seemed like a more realistic reason to me.

But they didn't mention something that had been going on right under their noses, and it had to do with their parents. Their dad, a furniture designer, was a good baker, which meant that there was always fresh bread around or the smell of bread baking. When it was pizza night at their house, it wasn't delivered but made at home. Kate's parents weren't foodies, but baking bread and cooking from scratch were just things they did. As a naturally social person, Kate's mom often entertained, and both parents made time for friends and included their kids (and those of their friends) at their parties. They also gave parties in honor of their children—one graduating high school, another getting that master's degree, a third visiting home from college—and they did so with natural ease and graciousness. So was it surprising that Kate would be able to pull off a dinner for fourteen with the grace and skill of a practiced hostess—and all this the night before heading east for college? Not really.

Not to take one single thing away from this young woman whom we love and admire, but perhaps it's true that what your parents do makes a difference and does count for something. In Kate's case, a natural ease in the kitchen and equal ease with guests, plus a certain tolerance for chaos, were already fully functioning qualities in her young life, and these skills will only deepen as she gets older.

It's been many years now, but I still bask in the joy of that evening as the guest of a seventeen-year-old whose parents weren't there, who proved herself a competent cook, a gracious host, and a lovely person. It's good to think that the next generation can cook dinner.

Nourishment and sustenance come in many forms. For many they're found in their homes and expressed in homespun memories of, say, spouse or child cooking dinner, but they can also be found in the most dreadful of industrial meats, as it was with Ernie and later, Kate, or in a humble stew with homemade bread, as with Ann and Arnold. Nourishment can lie in the food itself—a corn tortilla fresh from a *comal* in Mexico or New Mexico, for that matter (I have experienced both)—the shock of the goodness of that first meal at Chez Panisse, or the surprising pleasure of good food eaten in a place as humble as a

Motel 6. Nourishment might come from the person—again I think of Ann and her simple, thoughtful cooking and her calm table, or Dan cooking for his sisters and his mother. An extra-large table and friends attending a family event might well make a meal memorable, diffusing the usual family tensions. Or nourishment might come from the way food is offered. I think of the way utensils and napkins were set down on the wooden tables at Camino restaurant in Oakland, or the oryoki meals in the Tassajara zendo. It might come from the contrast of taking food that isn't given, like that stolen sesshin cookie, but then, maybe not. Nourishment might also issue from when and where you eat—being cold and hungry and finding that café and that hot soup in foggy Carrara. It always comes from the kindness of strangers, like the cook in Scotland who paused in her day to feed two very hungry women, or the generosity of the family at the pueblo's feast day dinner. There's the potluck, that American meal for harried folks, often short of cash, and how it has the power to express the vibrancy of community. All kinds of circumstances surround nourishment and it exists on so many levels, almost none of them dependent on the food itself. Even sounds in the kitchen can become nourishment—the tap of a wooden spoon on the edge of a pot, the sounds of chopping or of onions sizzling in a pan.

For me, beauty is also a kind of sustenance. The colors of vegetables are most vibrant when they're first being transformed by heat. And the dishes I use are important too—their colors, their stories, the impressions of the working hand when they're there, and the way their shapes set off food. Some are white, a-buck-apiece plates and others are very old French, handmade, kiln-stacked ocher plates, and there are many in between, including many hand-painted folk art dishes from countries I've visited, and that means that they are always part of a story. But I was also once startled by the pristine beauty of a taco loosely wrapped in white paper and set in a red plastic basket at the Jalisco Café in Coachella. You never know where the sustenance of beauty—or its lack—might come from. I distinctly recall the ugliest meal I ate, ever, in a Mexican bus stop in Pueblo, Colorado, where all the food on the plate was the same feral animal shade of gray-brown.

Food as nourishment is often food that is healing. Many people have told me their stories about foods that healed them or their friends after some trauma because of their familiarity or personal meaning, not because the food was replete with various compounds, or vegetarian, or gluten free. It was subtler, more personal than that.

I have a story, too.

A lovely man, a Tibetan scholar, the friend who had married Patrick and me, a man who was a beautiful light in our community, was tragically killed. The service for him was enormous. Hundreds of people felt a similar closeness and deep affection for this man, and because he had played a part in the world of Buddhism and in the life of the Dalai Lama, there were many Tibetan Buddhists present who had traveled far to be there, all of whom spoke, lengthily. A phalanx of monks played those long horns with their droning, funereal tones.

As I sat through this long service, my throat grew increasingly tight, my face dry and hot. I was exhausted and sad. I was about to get up for some water when I noticed some Tibetan women walking down each row of mourners with large baskets of strawberries.

The strawberries were not the little lumpy but stellar kind that I found in New York under the pines. Nor were they the intensely aromatic ones I'd carried home on my lap from California so that Patrick could finally taste a real strawberry. They were, in fact, the big, hollow commercial fruits that people like me love to hate. Still, as I learned shortly, even these fruits had managed to retain some of their divinity and magic despite all the devilish breeding programs they had been subjected to.

One of the Tibetan women came to our row and paused in front of me with her offering. I took a strawberry from the basket and she moved on to the next person. When I bit into it, the juice was sweet; it flooded my throat, which softened. My flushed face became cool. Now I could take a deep breath. I could also cry. And I could also smile. Sweetness prevailed over sadness, but the sadness didn't diminish. The two existed side by side. The nourishment was complete.

Postscript

I worked on this food memoir for a long time, certainly long before the novel coronavirus became the issue that it has become. But once the book was done and the virus turned virulent, I became painfully aware of how much my life experience is from another time, the time before words like "pandemic" and "COVID-19" were spoken daily. I don't think that changes the main thrust of the book, which is about the food that deeply nourishes us—even if we might not be able to share it in the way we were so recently accustomed to doing, joining with others at the table. Of course I hope we can do that again. And sooner rather than later.

I also hope that everyone who wishes to be well and strong is exactly that.

—Deborah Madison
June 2020

Acknowledgments

When writing about your life, even just a slice of it, there are a great many people to thank—for their help, inspiration, and their very being. I'm sure I've missed at least a few, but if you don't see your name here, please know that I thank you, too.

To begin with, I am especially grateful to my editor, Lexy Bloom, for her belief in this book, support, wisdom, and excellent and helpful suggestions. Thank you so much, Lexy, for taking me on. And my thanks to the entire team at Knopf, including Tom Pold, and John Gall, Kathleen Fridella, and Anna Knighton, for making a handsome book.

Over time, I've had editors and agents who have been enormously helpful: Fran McCullough, Harriet Bell, Doe Coover, and Jenny Wapner. Thank you for all you have taught me. And a big thank-you to Sharon Bowers, for taking that rainy drive through Ireland and so, so much more. Designer Toni Tajima and photographers Laurie Smith, Erin Scott, Christopher Hirscheimer, and Laurie Smith have been invaluable in book making. And thanks also to Barbara Haber, formerly of the Schlesinger Library at Harvard, for making me welcome there.

I wish to thank everyone I knew, worked, cooked, and studied with at the San Francisco Zen Center and Greens, especially Elaine Maisner, Richard Jaffe, Jane Hirschfield, Ulysses Lowry, Jim Phalen, Edward Espe Brown, Renee des Tombes, Dana Velden, David Chadwick, and those from so long ago. Thank you so much. And thank you, Richard Jaffe, for reminding me that it was you who left the William Carlos Williams poem on the reach-in door. You rascal!

Elissa Altman, your encouragement over these many years has meant so much. You have been a good friend. And Susan Turner, you're one special and swell person and I thank you for those boxes of books that I might not otherwise have read. To Gary Paul Nabhan, thank you for your wisdom and long friendship.

In the food world, there are many I'd like to thank for their inspiration and generosity, among them Lindsey Shere, Alice Waters, Amaryl Schwertner, Peggy Knickerbocker, Paula Wolfert, Yotam Ottolenghi, Renee Erickson, Cathy Whims, Marcus Samuelson, Anya Fernald, Russell Moore and Alison Hopelain, Sylvia Thompson, Steve Sando, Edna Lewis, Scott Peacock, Charlene Badman, and Chris Bianco. You have all been important to me.

In Santa Fe, I wish to thank my fellow grainiacs—Christine Salem, Alessandra Haines, Jody Pugh, Ron Boyd, and Diane Pratt for working so hard to grow the heirloom grains we want to mill and bake with—and the seed team for our fledgling seed library, including many of the same plus so many more.

Many people have touched my life in different ways—ranchers Nancy Ranney, Tim Willms and Jim Bill and Deborah Anderson; New Mexican writers Courtney White, Stanley Crawford, William deBuys and Jack Loeffler; Don Bixby of the ALBC (Amercian Livestock Breeds Conservancy); Jannine Cabossel (the Tomato Lady); Richard McCarthy of Slow Food USA; Robert and Ellen Brittan of

Brittan Vineyards; David Millman of Domaine Drouhin; California farmer Rich Collins; Celia Sack of Omnivore Books; excellent farmers and writers, Anthony and Carol Boutard of Ayers' Creek Farm in Oregon; amazing balsamic vinegar makers Steve and Jane Darland; Diane Karp for her many meals and constant love; Patrick and Andy Lannan for holding political standards so high and for so generously sharing their "Irish wine"; miller David Kaisel; farmers everywhere; our family historian (on my mother's side), Bob Golden; and many, many more. My gratitude to you all.

I also wish to thank those who are my readers, who have taken the time to follow this journey with me.

And lastly, my heartfelt gratitude to Patrick McFarlin and Dan Welch for your very different points of view in the kitchen and for your longtime friendship and support. You are both my teachers and dear friends.

A NOTE ABOUT THE AUTHOR

The founding chef of Greens restaurant in San Francisco and a student at the San Francisco Zen Center for twenty years, Deborah Madison is also the author of fourteen cookbooks. Her books have won many awards, among them the IACP Julia Child Cookbook of the Year award for *The Savory Way* and *Vegetarian Cooking for Everyone*, as well as other awards from the IACP, including a Trailblazer award in 2019. She has also been the recipient of the Les Dames d'Escoffier award, and five James Beard awards.

Deborah has served on several boards, among them the Seed Savers Exchange, the Southwest Grassfed Livestock Alliance (SWGLA), and the Friends of the Santa Fe Farmers' Market. She also started a Slow Food chapter in Santa Fe and has worn many hats in the national and international organization for several years.

Today Deborah is most interested in grain production in the Southwest and in regenerative agriculture. She has grown and milled ancient wheats at her home in Galisteo, New Mexico, where she lives with her husband, artist Patrick McFarlin, and their little dog, Dante.

A NOTE ON THE TYPE

This book was set in Fournier, a typeface named for Pierre Simon Fournier *le jeune* (1712–1768), a celebrated French type designer.

Composed by North Market Street Graphics, Lancaster, Pennsylvania
Printed and bound by Berryville Graphics, Berryville, Virginia
Designed by Anna B. Knighton